116:4 · October 2017

October! The Soviet Centenary
Michael Hardt and Sandro Mezzadra, Special Issue Editors

AGAINST the DAY

No More Deaths: Direct Aid in the US-Mexico Border Zone
Sophie Smith, Editor

Michael Hardt and Sandro Mezzadra

October! To Commemorate the Future

The best way to commemorate October 1917 is by looking forward, not back—to remember the future. We have no desire to continue drawing up balance sheets of the Soviet experience, assessing its successes and failures, identifying when the revolution went wrong, defending it from detractors, denouncing those who betrayed it, or debating theories of "totalitarianism." The time for all that has passed. The ideological clashes of the Cold War—which for decades both elevated and obscured all of those issues—and even the post–Cold War are now, thankfully, behind us.

What remains important, instead, is to appreciate how the rupture opened by the October Revolution revealed new horizons for political thought and practice, making what was previously unthinkable the order of the day. It was the source of great theoretical and political innovation, and, indeed, vast territories of that unknown universe illuminated by the October Revolution still remain to be explored and experimented. But the revolution primarily serves us today as a testament to the continuing potential of political rupture. It is a testament to the fact that a lightning bolt can shatter the continuum of historical time, not only shifting the course of history but also

The South Atlantic Quarterly 116:4, October 2017
DOI 10.1215/00382876-4234939 © 2017 Duke University Press

instituting a new calendar, a new temporality (Benjamin 2003: 395). That same lightning bolt can also scramble established geographies from the bottom up, instituting a new world map that no longer has Europe at its center, bringing together regions of the world that had previously seemed distant, as if great tectonic plates had shifted over the course of days rather than millennia. It is a globalizing event or, rather, a remaking of the globe.

Most important are the effects of the revolutionary lightning bolt on the political imagination. It is realistic to demand the impossible because such events transform what used to be thought impossible into entirely realistic and even necessary demands. And, furthermore, the transformative powers of the event carry beyond the impossible to the unthinkable, opening new and vast horizons for the political imagination, allowing us to desire what we previously could not even imagine. That is where the highest power of the event lies.

We are not advocating, of course, to replay the political strategies or resurrect the political forms of 1917—for instance, to create a vanguard communist party to play the part of the Bolsheviks like those historical reenactors who dress up on weekends in Union and Confederate uniforms to replay US Civil War battles. We take the centenary as a reminder, instead, that such a radical political rupture remains possible, even when, as today, conditions do not seem propitious. That does not mean that we should sit back and wait for its second coming (or third or fourth). Revolutionary events do not arrive from the outside. We need to explore what it would mean today for an event the magnitude of the October Revolution to open new potential for liberation and understand, moreover, what are the conditions necessary to bring it about.

Against the Day

It may seem imprudent to talk about revolution today when right-wing movements and governments are on the rise and even the specter of fascism is materializing in countries throughout the world. Keep in mind, though, that in the years prior to the October Revolution the forces struggling for liberation in Europe were at a low point. Europe was swept by war, the *belle époque* had ended up in "storms of steel" and mass slaughter in the trenches. Nationalism was the political religion of the day. While in Germany intellectuals were praising the "ideas of 1914" in contrast to those of 1789, in France major figures such as Émile Durkheim stigmatized the German "mentality" as responsible for the war. Powerful processes to reorganize capitalist society, under way since the 1890s, were accelerated by the "total mobiliza-tion" for war. Nation, state, and capital seemed destined to dominate the future. At the same time, the labor movement and the forces of internation-alism, which had shone prominently at different moments through the sec-ond half of the nineteenth century throughout the continent, descended into darkness. The vote of the German Social Democratic Party on August 4, 1914, to approve war credits, which paved the way for Germany to go to war, symbolized the end of internationalism and a deep crisis of the labor movement.

Meanwhile, something unprecedented—and completely against the day—was emerging in the East. Through the course of 1917, from the first demonstrations in January on the anniversary of the "bloody Sunday" of 1905 to the February Revolution and the fall of the czar, from the uprising in Petrograd in July to the Bolshevik October, the rhythm of an uncontainable revolutionary movement was driven by mass mobilizations and very simple slogans, such as "Bread, peace, and freedom" and "All power to the soviets." The movement spoke a new internationalist language, and the October Rev-olution was widely perceived (by friends and enemies alike) as the historic success of a project of collective liberation led by workers and soldiers, peas-ants and commoners. "For the first time in human history," Lenin (1951a: 452) wrote in early 1918, "a socialist party has managed to complete in the main the conquest of power and the suppression of the exploiters, and has managed to *approach directly* the task of *administration*." This radical novelty opened up a completely new political horizon.

A New Geographical Imaginary

The Bolsheviks, of course, were primarily facing west, looking to the Paris Commune as a precedent for a victorious workers' insurrection and to Ger-many, the historical stronghold of the labor movement in Europe, as the main source for the propagation of revolutionary theory and activity. And, more generally, as Susan Buck-Morss (2000: 68) argues, the mentality of the Bolsheviks was deeply embedded in the modernizing project dictated by the dominant line of Western European thought. And yet, despite the fact that many Russian revolutionaries imagined Petrograd as residing on a line ema-nating from Berlin and Paris, the revolution completely rearranged the coor-dinates of political geography.

Antonio Gramsci (1977) could see from the relatively peripheral position in Italy that the October Revolution was not so much a realization of Marx's vision but a revolution against *Das Kapital* and, specifically, against all assumptions of linear historical development whereby the dominant countries will lead and the others follow in their tracks. The fact that October took place in what was considered a backward country on the border between West and East had momentous implications for the geographical imagination of the day. While from across the Atlantic, especially in the course of the Great War, the rise of the United States dramatically shifted the distribution of power in the capitalist world system, the October Revolution signaled the emergence of a completely different world, one oriented primarily outside of Europe, one in which imperialism became a central object of Marxist theory and in which combating colonialism became an ineluctable and even central task for socialist struggles, as Enzo Traverso's essay in this issue demonstrates.

The Congress of the Peoples of the East, held in September 1920 in Baku (present-day Azerbaijan), was one symptom that a new geographical imagination had emerged.[1] Grigory Zinovyev presided over the encounter together with other well-known communist figures such as Karl Radek and Béla Kun. And the participants formed, as Zinovyev remarked, a heterogeneous, multicolored composition: the major part were intellectuals and activists from former Russian colonies, Turkey, Armenia, and Persia, and there were representatives, too, from India, China, and Japan. Together they sought to orient the potential opened by the October Revolution toward a global revolution against colonial and imperialist rule. In Baku the circuits of internationalism were being rewritten outside the European sphere in an anticolonial key. In his closing remarks Zinovyev recognized that "the peoples of the East" had good reason from decades of experience to distrust European and especially Russian promises, and indeed Soviet policies in later decades certainly did distort international cooperation into another kind of imperialist rule and sought to "Russify" populations under its control. But that does not negate the fact that a door to a new internationalist terrain had already been opened. The writings and activities of Manabendra Nath Roy and Mirsaid Sultan-Galiev, for instance, are testaments to how the October Revolution echoed across Asia and the Middle East. Wang Hui's essay in this volume explores the extent to which the Russian events opened revolutionary possibilities in China. And Martín Bergel's illuminates how, on the other side of the globe, José Carlos Mariátegui, through continuous journalistic and theoretical interventions, explored the reverberations of the October Revolution in Peru and Latin America more generally.

Although the Russian Revolution had a profound impact on the politics of anticolonial and popular movements in many parts of the world, this impact was far from linear: the politics of the Comintern often created and exacerbated divisions and, particularly in the age of Stalin, the national Soviet interest under the aegis of "socialism in one country" more often than not prevailed over internationalist solidarity. The Soviet actions during the Spanish Civil War, as Kathy Ferguson's essay in this issue notes, demonstrated some of the criminal outcomes to which this led. When we speak of a new "geographical imagination" spurred by the October events in Russia, however, we have something else in mind: the scrambling of the global geographies of the time and the widening of the space of politics that for the first time made peoples and movements outside Europe and the West crucial protagonists of proletarian internationalism. Even such a specific history as the one of the encounter between African Americans and communism in the 1920s and 1930s (see, e.g., Baldwin 2002), which made an important contribution to the radicalization of the black movement in the United States and to the spread of an internationalist look within it, is part of the scrambling of geographical coordinates produced by the October Revolution.

The Revolutionary Event

Although we recognize the October Revolution, as we said, as an unprecedented event, a rupture in the continuity of historical development that opened up a new field for political experimentation, challenging the boundaries of the political imaginary and of what was considered politically possible even in revolutionary theories, we are wary of contemporary theories of the event that tend to obscure the conditions that underlie the production of such historical ruptures. Political events seem to come from the outside, like miracles, but they only do so to those who are not working inside to bring them about. "Miracles," Lenin (1951b: 583) writes, just before his arrival in Russia in April 1917, "do not happen in nature and history." Like Spinoza, he attributes belief in miracles to an ignorance of causes. "Every abrupt turn in history," he continues, "and this applies to every revolution, presents such wealth of content, unfolds such unexpected and specific combinations of the forms of struggle and the alignment of forces of the contestants, that to the lay mind there is much that must appear miraculous" (583). Revolutionary events rest instead on a vast accumulation of political activity, which has become deposited layer upon layer like geological sediment, putting heavy pressure on the current order and creating a solid foundation of a new political terrain. This is not to say that political history is linear and, even less, that it is predictable. No event results merely from the accumulation of past struggle, and there are no guarantees. Every event is a leap into the unknown, full of risk, but in order to leap you need solid footing. Genuine breaks with the past are only possible because of the previous accumulation.

Gramsci, for one, understood the October Revolution as being the result of the "collective will" that had built up among the Russian proletariat and the "Machiavellian" will exercised by the Bolshevik party to seize the occasion to organize the insurrection. The writings of Lenin (1951d: 14) during the course of 1917 similarly are dominated by the attempt to grasp and further this dialectic—starting from his emphasis on the need for the Bolsheviks to forge "an ability to adapt [themselves] to the *special* conditions of Party work among unprecedentedly large masses of proletarians who have just awakened to political life." Leon Trotsky (1957: 3:167–99), too, understood the "art of insurrection" in these same terms, grasping the existing social and political conditions to make possible the spark.

Once the event is conceived in its materiality, it is easy to understand in which sense an event like the October Revolution could open up a new continent of what was considered politically possible. It challenged, as we noted earlier, the Eurocentric development of Marxism since the dispute surrounding "revisionism" in the 1890s, putting into question the linear and progressive image both of capitalist development and of the struggle for socialism that had dominated previous debates. And above all, we repeat, it contradicted the main trends of the age, concretely demonstrating through the sheer fact of the victory of the revolution that it was possible to break the rule of capital and to construct a future beyond it. This victory, which even Victor Serge (2012: 430), a victim of Stalinism, claimed as the main legacy of October in his memoir, opened up radically new spaces for a political imagination that was far from being contained by the Bolshevik party in Russia and broke free from traditional restraints elsewhere in the world.

One task today, then, is to grasp how a broad range of struggles—from those against racism, patriarchy, homophobia, and transphobia to struggles for democracy, from the struggles of migrants to the movements of the poor as well as old and new forms of labor struggle—can point beyond mere protests and form a kind of mosaic or constellation oriented toward a future transformation. Indeed, viewing events as miraculous—and, hence, waiting for them to arrive, in a kind of rehearsal of what Lenin (1951f: 257–58) called "tail-ism"—makes it all the more difficult to struggle in the myriad ways necessary to create their conditions. When the moment comes, though, suddenly all varieties of partial and micropolitical struggles, which had seemed disparate and unrelated, click together to form a powerful assemblage. That is when the conditions of the event are in place.

The Conditions of Rupture Today

Parallels between the current conjuncture and the one that led to World War I abound. Our present is similarly characterized by processes of global transition that are far from smooth, with catastrophic dangers looming at every turn. Rising nationalist sentiments (often accompanied by racism) create frictions across the globe that continually risk catching flame in mass military conflict. The financial crisis that started in the United States in 2007–8 continues to course through the bloodstream of the capitalist world system, periodically wreaking havoc in different regions. Neoliberalism seems to have abandoned altogether its seductive promises of global prosperity, presenting instead naked austerity policies combined with nationalist, authoritarian, and even protectionist ideologies. From India to Turkey, from the Philippines to Egypt, from Argentina and Hungary to the United Kingdom and the United States, an aggressive Right seems to be hegemonic in the management of the global political cycle that was opened up by the crisis. This does not mean the end of capitalist globalization, as some claim, but it does indicate that a momentous reorganization of its spaces and direction is under way. The implications of this shift in terms of a dramatic restriction of freedom and equality are apparent today, and migrants experience them in the most acute way, in the United States and Europe most visibly but also in many other countries, including Argentina and South Africa.

Is it possible to imagine today such a radical event as the October Revolution? The world has dramatically changed, and so too has the capitalist mode of production. This is something like a truism. No Winter Palace is in sight. Moreover, a century of struggles across the world has made it impossible for anything like the Bolshevik model of party organization to articulate and express the multiple processes of subjectivation that make up the contemporary working class—let alone the whole range of social struggles. And yet we still need ruptures and events in order to open up new frontiers of our political imaginary. There is no need to go back to the Paris Commune or to the global uprisings of the 1960s to grasp the relevance of this articulation between historical rupture and theoretical innovation. Theory can locate the conditions for a rupture, it can foreshadow its direction and its subjective composition, but in the experience of rupture there is always an excess that challenges theory and often points beyond its blind spots and impasses. We have witnessed such scenes of theoretical innovation repeatedly in recent years. The experiences between Seattle in 1999 and Genoa in 2001, when the birth of a new "global" movement opened up new continents for the critical investigation of globalization, were one such laboratory of innovation. Another emerged with the uprisings in Mexico, Ecuador, Argentina, and Bolivia between the 1990s and the early 2000s, which laid the basis for the emergence of new "progressive" governments in Latin America—an extraordinary, albeit contradictory, field of experimentation for social transformation well beyond the region. Similarly, the cycle of occupations and encampments at the beginning of the 2010s from Tahrir to Taksim, passing through the Indignados in Spain, Syntagma Square in Athens, Occupy in the United States, and many other points, opened a new field of theoretical innovation, particularly with regard to what democracy could be.

Such experiences do not share much with the October Revolution, one might object. Fair enough. We are nevertheless convinced that some of its aspects retain a profound actuality and have been renewed, transformed, and revived by struggles and popular politics in many parts of the world over the past decades. They are going to play crucial roles in the production of any historical rupture conceivable today. And, indeed, we are living in a global context that makes such an event all the more urgent.

What would be the conditions for an event that runs counter to the mainstream of our age, as the October Revolution did a century ago? There is no shortage of struggles and movements in the world today, some of which continue, in part, the projects of those of recent years that we just mentioned. Migrants mobilize against nationalist backlash, people of color protest against white supremacy in its various forms, women's movements are sweeping many countries and regions, movements of the poor nurture solidarity economies, environmental activists often in alliance with or under the leadership of indigenous groups confront climate change, labor struggles abound, and the list could go on. Each of these alone, especially when isolated in only one country or region, seems powerless against the dominant forces. But these heterogeneous and powerful struggles could, if woven together internationally, compose the material fabric that allows imagining an event powerful enough to once again open new frontiers of our political imaginary.

With the October Revolution in mind, then, we explore three domains that resonate with its legacy and maintain for us today a profound relevance.

State and Party as a Problem

With regard to the political role of the state and the party, the centenary first forces us to measure our distance from 1917. Lenin (1951c: 20) takes for granted that "the basic question in any revolution is that of state power." For us today, the issue of the party and the taking of state power is a real question—

sometimes even a problem—rather than the solution. This does not imply any blanket refusal of the party form or even a reluctance to take state power. Indeed, a variety of important experiments in recent years have tested these waters: from the experiences of progressive governments in Latin America that we just mentioned to Podemos and Syriza in Europe, and from the Bernie Sanders campaign in the United States to municipal governments in Spain. These are experiments that, in one way or another, emerged out of powerful social movements and have attempted, sometimes in limited ways, to maintain a space or role for the movements.

This is not the place to evaluate these experiences. Before doing that, moreover, one would have to understand the dramatic transformations that have reshaped the state over the past decades and across diverse geographical scales. Those transformations are highlighted, in fact, if we take as a point of reference the state that Lenin had in mind. The recurrence of mechanical metaphors in Lenin's writings on the state demonstrates that he was not only working in the wake of Marx's (1963: 122) well-known dictum that "all revolutions perfected this state machine instead of smashing it" but also following the mainstream of political and legal sciences of his time, typified by the work of Max Weber. Lenin placed great emphasis on administration. His notion of "state-monopoly capitalism," with which he intended to grasp the new figure of capitalist development emerging out of the age of the Great War, was intended to shed light on the ability of the state to organize capitalism. The resulting process of the "merging" of the state "with the all-powerful capitalist associations" had for Lenin (1951d: 19) "monstrous" implications for the "oppression of the working people by the state." For Lenin, it was absolutely necessary to "take" the power of *this* state, a sovereign political body, smashing the machine of its repressive apparatuses and developing in their stead the administrative capacities crucial for the transition to communism. The fact that the Russian Revolution ended up building a state that was extremely oppressive and repressive should not obscure Lenin's original project. And it was entirely calibrated upon a specific historical form of the state.

The state has not withered away with contemporary processes of globalization. It continues to perform important tasks in the organization of capitalist society at the national and global levels, but its role and position are completely different than the ones envisaged by Lenin with his notion of "state-monopoly capitalism," or, for that matter, by Social Democrats with their conception of "organized capitalism," or even by the *operaisti* (workerists) who analyzed the "planner state." The nature of the sovereignty of the state has been transformed as the state has been displaced from the center of capitalist rule, which has developed powerful devices of governmentality that work at the level of daily life well beyond the point of production. At the same time, some of the most important operations of contemporary capital (most notably its financial operations) structurally exceed the scale of the nation-state and deploy powerful constraints on each government. Under these conditions, taking state power can definitely be one step in a political strategy of transformation, be it reformist or revolutionary, but it is by no means a sufficient condition for success.

The same is true for the Bolshevik party, which was conceived by its founders as confronting a form of capitalist rule and a state completely different from the ones we face today. Antonio Negri (2014) argued along these lines in the 1970s that the genius of the Leninist party was to discover a kind of resonance between the existing organization of the proletariat in production and the structures of political organization. In other words, the centralized vanguard party was so powerful at the time because it corresponded to the centralized organization of the skilled industrial workers in the factory. The schemes of productive cooperation that workers already know pose the adequate structures of political organization. This does not mean that the Leninist solution can be translated to a different historical context—on the contrary. To take up Lenin's procedure, one has to study how productive cooperation is organized in contemporary society and then invent a political form that corresponds to its structures. And today, of course, one would have to take into consideration the terms of social production and reproduction well beyond the proletariat as traditionally conceived, well beyond the factory walls, and even outside the paid labor force. That would be the challenge of taking up and reimagining a Leninist organizational spirit that is adequate to contemporary conditions.

We thus disagree, on the one hand, with those contemporary authors who, understandably frustrated by the inability of social movements like Occupy to generate lasting social transformation, conceive of forming a party and taking state power (often even in terms reminiscent of Lenin's time) as the solution to our current political impasse or the weakness of the Left. And we also disagree, on the other hand, with those who maintain that the state and the party can have no role in liberation politics today. Our view, instead, is that state and party are problems that contemporary liberation politics have to address. What is urgently needed is to discover the means to guarantee the continuity of autonomous movements and struggles that confront capitalist rule at the daily level and in all aspects of its operation. We certainly need to take stock of the long history of communist, socialist, and anticolonial politics in which state and party have been conceived and practically constructed as the main actors of social transformation. Movements and struggles of the past decades seem to have come to terms with this history and claim a different politics, in which the state and the party can play a role but are far from having a monopoly on political transformation.

Dual Power

Rather than focusing immediately on taking state power or on the party as the adequate vehicle for doing so, it is more useful to explore critically the Bolshevik idea of a dualism of power.[2] As soon as he returned to Russia, in early April, Lenin wrote that "the highly remarkable feature of our revolution is that it brought about a *dual power.*" And he went on to ask: "What is this dual power? Alongside the Provisional Government, the government of the *bourgeoisie, another government* has arisen, so far weak and incipient, but undoubtedly a government that actually exists and is growing—the Soviets of Workers' and Soldiers' Deputies" (Lenin 1951c: 20). Today the goal of creating a relatively stable second power composed of a series of autonomous counterpowers provides a framework for organizing the current varied set of antagonistic social struggles into a lasting and transformative political strategy.[3]

In the Russian experience, the soviets, as institutions of self-organization and self-government of workers, soldiers, and peasants, were the foundation of dual power. What characterizes the form and the action of the soviet, as Negri's essay in this issue explains, is the combination of the economic emancipation of the working class and the political composition of self-government and democratic decision making. The soviets aimed to organize workers' and peasants' knowledge to serve as the basis for the development of the revolutionary process in the realm of production.

The global history of social and political struggles in the twentieth century and up to the present provides a rich and heterogeneous archive of experiences analogous to the organization of soviets, most often without any reference to the October Revolution. From communal forms of peasant and indigenous organization to workers' councils, from neighborhood assemblies in Argentina in the wake of the 2001 uprising to the exercise of territorial counterpower by the Black Panthers in the United States or by the autonomous movement in Italy, we can see how the "spirit of the soviet" has remained alive and traveled across the globe in various mutations. Furthermore, the movements that seized and occupied the squares of major cities in several countries from 2011 to 2013 presented powerful although "incipient" instantiations of the soviet under contemporary conditions. It now takes the form of metropolitan assemblies in which a widely heterogeneous set of social subjects gather to deliberate and to forge institutions of self-government on the basis of social cooperation and struggle against dispossession and exploitation. These assemblies thus far have not risen to the level of dual power, as both their critics and the participants will quickly affirm. Key, however, is the fact that each of these experiences has gone beyond the level of protest and resistance against the dominant power structure to create, even if only briefly, an autonomous counterpower. The potential articulation of counterpowers alludes to the promise of a strategy of dual power.

It is important to note that dual power as conceived by the Bolsheviks was a temporary and unstable arrangement, a kind of anomaly that had to be superseded as quickly as possible. Trotsky (1957: 1:207), for instance, maintained that dual power "does not presuppose—generally speaking, indeed it excludes—the possibility of . . . [an] equilibrium of forces." Lenin's understanding of the concept, likewise, is based entirely on the political wager that the occasion will soon arrive to overthrow the provisional government and establish a "dictatorship" of the soviets. "Two powers *cannot exist* in a state," he wrote in September 1917. "One of them is bound to disappear" (Lenin 1951e: 28). The dualism of power in the Russian Revolution, "unparalleled in history in such a form" (28) was for him a limit condition and a limit concept for political theory. A similar emphasis on the need to overcome the dualism of power is a defining feature of the concept throughout the dominant line of twentieth-century revolutionary Marxism. Positive instances of that can be found in Gramsci's writings in 1919–20 on workers' councils as an emerging second power and a potential basis for a new, "socialist state" or the many experiences of guerrilla warfare (starting with Mao Tse-tung) where the institution of "Red bases" was thought of as a provisional step toward seizing power (see Guastini 1978; Zavaleta Mercado 1974).

Today, in contrast, we need to reformulate the strategy of dual power as a relatively stable political framework. As we said, one weakness of even the most inspiring political and social movements of recent years is that they are short-lived. The movements need to discover the means both to become lasting and to form dynamic coalitions across different social domains and internationally. It is not necessary, and in fact would be destructive, to try to unify the various axes of social struggle today based on gender, class, race, sexuality, ethnicity, ecological concerns, and more. Instead, a relatively stable political framework that articulates together the diverse political dynamics of struggle, transformation, and governance, establishing a lasting assemblage of counterpowers, is the most effective means of strengthening the existing movements. This is how best, it seems to us, to address the state and the party as problems, as we outlined in the previous section.

A strategy of dual power today has to be conceived in terms of an assemblage of counterpowers, moreover, because the unity of state power and sovereignty, which was taken for granted in Lenin's conception, has been transformed by global neoliberal processes creating plural structures of law, governance, and governmentality. This pluralization of governmental structures and policies responds, in some respects, to the need to govern a deeply heterogeneous and often unruly set of cooperating and productive social subjectivities. A strategy to contest these emerging forms of governance and their enmeshment with operations of capital must necessarily search for processes of political organization and articulation that valorize the diverse composition of contemporary social struggles.

Such a renewed theory of the dualism of power could provide a political formula for rethinking the question of transition, which has proved so intractable in the communist tradition. In particular, it allows thinking of transition, which means the opening up of horizons of social life beyond capital, as a nonlinear process, where specific victories and achievements result in the establishment and entrenchment not simply of rights but first of all of material structures of power and forms of life that, in turn, make further advances in the field of social struggle possible. The dualism of power that we have in mind thus requires a notion of governance that is rooted within a fabric of counterpowers from which it draws its force without putting into question their autonomy. It aims at politicizing social cooperation, through institutions that are capable of both organizing struggles, to enable their confluence and mutual empowerment, and foreshadowing different forms of life—to combine social and economic emancipation with political liberation, as we saw for the form of the soviet.

It should be obvious that when we say dual power, the two powers in question are not and cannot be homologous. In this sense it remains true today that a dualism of power, to refer back to Trotsky, does not express an equilibrium of forces, either in social or in constitutional terms. Even when state power is seized by political forces engaged in a project of radical transformation, the wide array of political forms and institutions composing the "second" power must retain their autonomy and continue to work according to logics different from the ones permeating the ruling institutions—from representation to bureaucracy. It is, as Lenin (1951c: 20) says, "a power entirely different from that generally existing in the parliamentary bourgeois-democratic republics of the usual type still prevailing in the advanced countries of Europe and America." This difference is key to the political productivity of the dualism of power, which allows it to be considered "a thoroughly expansive political form," to quote Marx's (1988: 60) description of the Paris Commune, which in his assessment was basically different from "all the previous forms of government" that "had been emphatically repressive." We think of the development, rooting, and entrenchment of a "second" power, instituted through struggles and social mobilization, as the crucial political element that can make a political form "expansive," holding in check the "repressive" aspects that pertain to the working of established state institutions. But far from being limited to this control function, the "second" power plays a leading role in developing the strategy as well as in prompting and deepening the process of social transformation.

From Private Property to the Common

A third aspect of the legacy of the October Revolution that we need to revisit is the critique of private property. Today neoliberal practices of privatization and commodification are erecting ever higher barriers of exclusion and forms of violence. We have to find ways to escape from under the increasing weight of the rule of private property. This does not mean, however, resurrecting the twentieth-century forms of "socialist property" mediated by the state, in which the state claims to represent the "whole socialist society" and hence becomes proprietor in terms that mirror classical bourgeois theories of property (see Venediktov 1953). As Giso Amendola's essay in this issue demonstrates, the Soviet legal scholar Evgeny Pashukanis preemptively criticized the notion of state property already in the 1920s. Fortunately, private property and public property (i.e., property controlled by the state) are not our only options. Increasingly today are emerging social spaces and practices of the common: social wealth that is shared openly and managed democratically. In fact, the creation of counterpowers and a framework of dual power that we sketched above opens spaces for alternative forms of use and sharing wealth.

Any critique of private property today first has to take stock of the unprecedented ways in which property relations have insinuated into every crevice of contemporary society. Even sharing seems to have been turned into new kinds of property by the various platforms of the "sharing economy." In some respects, private property has gained prominence by becoming increasingly anonymous and immaterial, particularly due to the ascendance and ever more significant roles of the corporate personality as the owner of property rights. These are interwoven with the financialization of capital, and the volatility of global financial markets prompts even more a delinking of property rights from the reference to an individual, embodied subject, which was key to the legitimization of private property as a societal norm in early bourgeois theories of "possessive individualism" (see Macpherson 1962).

Even more significant transformations of property emerge across the new frontiers of capitalist development, in fields like finance itself, "data mining," and biocapital. In such fields, private property (e.g., of genomic information or of data produced through social or digital interaction) operates as a governmentality device, directing the conducts of subjects through heterogeneous platforms, disassembling individual identity and reassembling it through the creation of multiple profiles, or reframing the meaning of the very notions of health and well-being. In the circuits of finance, the meaning of notions previously key to the definition of private property, such as commodity and money, is profoundly altered by technical innovations such as derivatives and by the emergence of so-called shadow banking (see, e.g., Martin 2013; Cooper 2015). Finance continues, of course, to be dominated by private property. The rule of private property is reproduced and entrenched every day by the operations of financial markets, which can be considered as a gigantic accumulation of property titles and "drawing rights" on the wealth to be produced in the future (Durand 2015), from which finance capital preemptively *extracts* value. The mediation of property relationships allows finance to perform this extraction, which has deep implications for the life and labor of a multitude of indebted subjects across the world, whose present and future actions are violently dominated by the financialized form of private property.

Private property also configures human and social relations well beyond the economic sphere in ways that profoundly intersect with gender and racial hierarchies. Alexandra Kollontai, for example, understood the rule of private property and, especially, the way the logic of property relations defines our most intimate bonds to each other as an element of the oppression of women. "Bourgeois morality," she wrote in 1921, "with its introverted individualistic family based entirely on private property, has carefully cultivated the idea that one partner should completely 'possess' the other" (Kollontai 1977: 242). For Kollontai, the critique and abolition of property was a central feminist issue that went hand in hand with efforts to legalize divorce and abortion and promote the rights of working women (see Hardt, in this issue), whose role had been prominent in 1917 at least since the women's demonstration in Petrograd on February 23 (March 8) that spurred the February Revolution. The rule of private property also intersects with and amplifies racial hierarchies. Cheryl I. Harris, for instance, argues that in the

United States whiteness not only affords various economic advantages but is itself a form of property. The law accords "holders" of whiteness, she explains, the same kind of privileges and benefits that it grants holders of other types of property (Harris 1993). This is not to claim, of course, that gender or racial hierarchy can be reduced to a matter of property but, instead, to indicate how deeply property relations have insinuated into all corners of our social existence.

Critiques of private property and attempts to defend spaces of social life from its violence cannot but go hand in hand with experimentations with and prefigurations of forms of use, access, and cooperation predicated on the constitutive power of the common.[4] This constitutes an essential foundation for reformulating the dualism of power and of the problematic of transition in ways we sketched above. Creating the common requires not only freeing forms of material and social wealth from the control of property owners but also inventing the means to democratically share and use that wealth. It also implies a profound anthropological mutation, transforming our sense of ourselves and the bases of our intimate and social bonds to others.

Some of the most powerful contemporary social movements are oriented toward such a transformation, even when property and property relations are not explicitly named.[5] Consider as just one example the 2016 protests against the construction of the Dakota Access Pipeline at the Standing Rock Sioux Reservation. This struggle was important not only for the unprecedented gathering of North American tribes and not only for the fact that environmental groups followed the lead of Native Americans. In addition, the logic of the protest ran counter to the rule of property. The objection to the pipeline was not based on the assertion of property rights by the tribe but instead demanded a fundamentally different relation to the earth, not as property but as a form of wealth that we all must share and care for. Indeed, the only way to confront the challenges of climate change is to begin to regard the earth as common. This is just one small window on what is required to struggle for the common.

A New Century Waiting to Begin

One of the most important effects of the October Revolution, as we said at the outset, was to stimulate and liberate the political imagination. The artistic, scientific, intellectual, urban, architectural, social, and legal experimentations in the wake of the revolution involved the participation of wide masses of common people and contributed to an unprecedented mobilization of Russian society. Utopian desires and dreams, writes Bini Adamczak (2016: 136, our translation), no longer relegated to a distant horizon, became inscribed in the here and now: "The revolution made the future part of the present." The October Revolution not only tested the limits of what was considered politically possible but also expanded what was thinkable and redrew the geographical coordinates for understanding and organizing the struggle for liberation.

Today, although we are witnessing a wide spectrum of liberation struggles, forms of mass mobilization, and insurgency in many parts of the world, the possibility of a revolutionary transformation seems remote. The prospects for revolution in Russia at the beginning of 1917 did not appear promising either. Even large segments of the "old Bolsheviks" doubted it was possible and were prepared to endure a long period of reaction. This is, of course, no guarantee regarding the possibility of such a revolutionary event today. It is simply a reminder about the open and unforeseeable nature of political history. In difficult political times, as today, with repressive and authoritarian political forces on the rise across the globe, many will say we have no choice but to dig in to defend what little we have and embark, at best, at modest reforms. We are convinced, on the contrary, that now is a time to think big. There are moments when reforming the existing system is utterly impossible, whereas transforming it entirely is the only realistic course.

The twentieth century began, in many respects, in October 1917, and the revolution cast its light over the entire century.[6] The sheer fact of the Bolshevik victory and the political establishment of working-class power profoundly shifted the political terrain. It served as an example that nurtured the political passion of generations of militants and common people—both inside the established communist movement and within the many heretical experiences that blossomed outside and against it. The global history of freedom and equality across the century cannot be written without taking this communist passion into consideration. The October Revolution also made possible and necessary a series of reformist policies, such as in Germany the creation of the system of councils and the recognition of social and economic rights in the Weimar constitution and in the United States the democratic experiment of the New Deal as well as, later, the establishment of welfare states in Western Europe. The defeat of fascism and the long processes of decolonization would have been unimaginable without the October Revolution.

Acknowledging these facts does not mean ignoring or relativizing the tragic history of communism in the twentieth century. Indeed, any attempt to reinvent a communist politics today must come to terms with those horrors and the lessons of that history. But we also need to recognize that the century that began in 1917 has come to an end, long before the calendars would have it. This is not only because the Soviet Union met its demise (and the other socialist state experiments, including those in China and Cuba, have been completely transformed), but also because the political strategies of the October Revolution such as those we explored above have to be profoundly rethought for today's world.

We are once again in need of an event that opens a new century, transforming what is possible and thinkable, opening new horizons of our political imagination. The twentieth century has long been over, but the twenty-first is yet to begin.

Notes

1 On the Baku congress, see the transcriptions of the major speeches in Riddell 1993. For Zinovyev's concluding remarks, see 213–20.

2 Max Eastman, in his translation of Trotsky's *The History of the Russian Revolution* (1957: 1:206n1), notes that *dvoevlastie*, which is conventionally rendered in English as "dual power," could be more accurately translated as "double sovereignty" or "two-power regime."

3 For some recent propositions of dual power along these lines, see Jameson 2016; Hardt and Negri 2017; and Mezzadra and Neilson, forthcoming.

4 Several contemporary authors critique private property and advocate for the common. See, among others, Hardt and Negri 2009; Mattei 2011; and Dardot and Laval 2014.

5 One could investigate, for instance, the significance of property relations and property rights in the new women's movements struggling against sexual violence and for reproductive rights in many parts of the world—from Argentina to Poland, from the United States to Italy—where the mobilization for International Women's Day 2017 took the form of an innovative social strike, weaving together production and reproduction, formal and informal forms of labor, including care. It would be useful to explore, too, how in antiracist struggles, such as Black Lives Matter, which highlight the enduring legacies of slavery, property is implicated in the ways that the black body continues to be the object of violence and control.

6 As Eric Hobsbawm (1994: 55) writes in *Age of Extremes*: "Indeed, it is not an accident that the history of the Short Twentieth Century, as defined in this book, virtually coincides with the lifetime of the state born of the October revolution."

References

Adamczak, Bini. 2016. "Die Versammlung: Kommunismen 1917, 1968, 2017" ("The Assembly: Communism 1917, 1968, 2017"). In *Das Kommunistische; Oder: Ein Gespenst kommt nicht zur Ruhe (The Communist; or, A Ghost Does Not Come to Rest)*, edited by Lutz Brangsch and Michael Brie, 129–48. Hamburg: VSA.

Baldwin, Kate A. 2002. *Beyond the Color Line and the Iron Curtain: Reading Encounters between Black and Red, 1922–1963*. Durham, NC: Duke University Press.

Benjamin, Walter. 2003. "On the Concept of History." In *Selected Writings*, vol. 4, edited by Howard Eiland and Michael W. Jennings, translated by Edmund Jephcott et al. 389–400. Cambridge, MA: Belknap Press of Harvard University Press.

Buck-Morss, Susan. 2000. *Dreamworld and Catastrophe: The Passing of Mass Utopia in East and West*. Cambridge, MA: MIT Press.

Cooper, Melinda. 2015. "Shadow Money and the Shadow Workforce: Rethinking Labor and Liquidity." *South Atlantic Quarterly* 114, no. 2: 395–423.

Dardot, Pierre, and Christian Laval. 2014. *Commun: Essai sur la révolution au XXIe siècle* (*Common: An Essay on Revolution in the Twenty-First Century*). Paris: La Découverte.

Durand, Cédric. 2015. *Le capital fictif: Comment la finance s'approprie notre avenir* (*Fictitious Capital: How Finance Is Appropriating Our Future*). Paris: Les Prairies Ordinaires.

Gramsci, Antonio. 1977. "The Revolution against 'Capital.'" In *Antonio Gramsci: Selections from Political Writings, 1910–1920*, edited by Quintin Hoare, translated by John Mathews, 34–37. New York: International Publishers.

Guastini, Riccardo. 1978. *I due poteri: Stato borghese e Stato operaio nell'analisi marxista* (*The Two Powers: The Bourgeois State and the Workers' State according to Marxist Analysis*). Bologna: Il Mulino.

Hardt, Michael, and Antonio Negri. 2017. *Assembly*. New York: Oxford University Press.

Hardt, Michael, and Antonio Negri. 2009. *Commonwealth*. Cambridge, MA: Harvard University Press.

Harris, Cheryl I. 1993. "Whiteness as Property." *Harvard Law Review* 106, no. 8: 1707–91.

Hobsbawm, Eric. 1994. *Age of Extremes: The Short Twentieth Century, 1914–1991*. New York: Penguin.

Jameson, Fredric. 2016. *American Utopia: Dual Power and the Universal Army*. London: Verso.

Kollontai, Alexandra. 1977. "Sexual Relations and the Class Struggle." In *Selected Writings*, edited and translated by Alix Holt, 237–92. London: Allison and Busby.

Lenin, Vladimir. 1951a. "The Immediate Tasks of the Soviet Government." In *Selected Works*, vol. 2, pt. 1: 448–92. Moscow: Foreign Languages Publishing House.

Lenin, Vladimir. 1951b. "Letters from Afar." In Lenin, *Selected Works*, vol. 1, pt. 2: 583–96.

Lenin, Vladimir. 1951c. "On the Dual Power." In Lenin, *Selected Works*, vol. 2, pt. 1: 20–23.

Lenin, Vladimir. 1951d. "On the Tasks of the Proletariat in the Present Revolution." In Lenin, *Selected Works*, vol. 2, pt. 1: 13-19. Also known as "The April Theses."

Lenin, Vladimir. 1951e. "The Tasks of the Proletariat in Our Revolution." In Lenin, *Selected Works*, vol. 2, pt. 1: 24–61.

Lenin, Vladimir. 1951f. *What Is to Be Done? Burning Questions of Our Movement*. In Lenin, *Selected Works*, vol. 1, pt. 1: 203–409.

Macpherson, C. B. 1962. *The Political Theory of Possessive Individualism: Hobbes to Locke*. Oxford: Clarendon Press.

Martin, Randy. 2013. "After Economy? Social Logics of the Derivative." *Social Text* 31, no. 1: 83–106.

Marx, Karl. 1963. *The Eighteenth Brumaire of Louis Bonaparte*. New York: International Publishers.

Marx, Karl. 1988. *Civil War in France*. 2nd ed. New York: International Publishers.

Mattei, Ugo. 2011. *Beni comuni: Un manifesto* (*Common Goods: A Manifesto*). Bari, Italy: Laterza.

Mezzadra, Sandro, and Brett Neilson. Forthcoming. *The Politics of Operations: Excavating Contemporary Capitalism*. Durham, NC: Duke University Press.

Negri, Antonio. 2014. *Factory of Strategy: Thirty-Three Lessons on Lenin.* Translated by Arianna Bove. New York: Columbia University Press.

Riddell, John, ed. 1993. *To See the Dawn: Baku, 1920—First Congress of the Peoples of the East.* New York: Pathfinder.

Serge, Victor. 2012. *Memoirs of a Revolutionary.* Translated by Peter Sedgwick. New York: New York Review of Books.

Trotsky, Leon. 1957. *The History of the Russian Revolution.* Translated by Max Eastman. 3 vols. Ann Arbor: University of Michigan Press.

Venediktov, Anatolii Vasilevich. 1953. *La proprietà socialista dello Stato (Socialist Property of the State).* Turin: Einaudi.

Zavaleta Mercado, René. 1974. *El poder dual en América Latina (Dual Power in Latin America).* Mexico City: Siglo Veintiuno.

Wang Hui

The Prophecy and Crisis of October:
How to Think about Revolution
after the Revolution

If the nineteenth century was defined by England's Industrial Revolution and the French Revolution, then it follows that the twentieth century was determined by the Russian and Chinese revolutions. It was a "short century," and transformations of its scope and intensity had never been seen before. Wide-ranging controversies encompass the period's institutions, events, and personae, all the way down to its varied minutiae. This was a period of the transvaluation of all values, such that the reevaluation of this period could not fail but to provoke disputes arising from different value systems. It was a period that sought to differentiate itself from all other historical periods; as such, evaluating it also means making an assessment of all historical periods—not only of those past but also of those underway and yet to come.

From 1917 to 2017, in the birthplaces of two grand revolutions, the visage of revolution has already grown obscure. In the 1990s, following the disintegration of the Soviet bloc, the Chinese intellectual field popularized the slogan "farewell to the revolution," articulating the Asian version of America's proposed "end of history."[1] In Russian and Western intellectual spheres, the "October Revolution" is often seen as the original sin of

The South Atlantic Quarterly 116:4, October 2017
DOI 10.1215/00382876-4234950   © 2017 Duke University Press

the Soviet bloc's dissolution, and all talk of socialism and communism has already transformed into discussions of why the former failed and the latter is impossible. As early as November 5, 1994, Russia's Chief of Presidential Administration Sergei Aleksandrov Filatov asserted:

> Strictly speaking, Russia experienced a coup d'etat in October, 1917; consequently, state power was usurped by a small but tightly knit party on the radical left. . . . For Russia's socialist progressives, October 1917 was a most severe blow, the start of the revolution's ruin. . . . It broke with the gradual process of Russia's transformation from the nineteenth century's grand reforms to an industrialized, democratic society. February 1917 became the endpoint of the country's democratic development, and eight months after the February revolution Russia established a repressive system of collectivism. (Filatov and Volobuev 1997: 305, 307)[2]

Long before the dissolution of the Soviet Union, all manner of oppositional and revisionist views had already resurged. In the subsequent post–Cold War atmosphere, even revisionist positions became outmoded, "declassified files" having experienced a momentary surge of popularity. These fabrications presented new versions of long since refuted stories (i.e., the claim that Lenin was a German spy), which spread like wildfire throughout the media in the West (e.g., Germany's weekly news magazine, *Der Spiegel*) and in Russia.

Amid this massive wave of antirevolutionary sentiment, there are some views on current revisions of the orthodox narrative that warrant discussion. For example, Alexander Rabinowitch, a senior scholar of the October Revolution, acknowledges the revolution's inevitability while affirming that there were alternatives; namely, "establishing a multi-party system, a democratic, socialist political system, a system founded on the soviet, which certainly could have implemented urgently needed, profound changes while striving to realize peace" (Bushuyev and Rabinowitch 1997: 25).[3] Investigating other possible outcomes to 1917, in fact, raises two related problems: One is concrete historical judgment, specifically about the problem of the relationship between the February and October revolutions. For example, Anatolii Ivanovich Fomin undertook an interpretation of Lenin's *April Theses*, reaffirming Constitutional Democrat Party member Pavel Milyakov's view that the October Revolution was a continuation of the February Revolution. That said, Fomin (1997: 367) did not assume an antagonistic position vis-a-vis the Bolsheviks; rather, he sought to salvage a revolutionary tradition, believing that "the October revolution was not the first socialist revolution stemming from Communism in human history, but there is reason to believe that the October Revolution was this century's last great revolution. It consolidated the triumph of industrialized society, helping establish the foundation of civilization for a post-industrialized society."[4] From a political perspective, the October Revolution was a bourgeois-democratic revolution in the hands of the proletariat and peasantry; in other words, it was distinct from a dictatorship of the proletariat or dictatorship of the proletariat and poor peasantry (351). From an economic perspective, this dictatorship was what Lenin (quoted in Fomin 1997: 351) already described as "the state monopolizing capitalism within a truly democratic, revolutionary country."[5]

The other problem, directly related to this judgment, is a reevaluation of the revolution's character: Was the October Revolution a socialist one or an "Asiatic social revolution"? Was the Soviet nation it founded state capitalism or a socialist state? Such questions were already concealed within discussions of the relation between the February and October revolutions:

> The goal of Russia's 1917 revolution was to oppose Asia's wholly decrepit feudalism; at the same time it also opposed the development of private ownership capitalism. Its mission was to fundamentally divorce the peasantry from its means of production and build the conditions for socialized production on the basis of a system of state ownership. If we do not understand this exceptional quality of revolution, then we cannot understand the revolution's process and consequences and are thus unable to grasp why, objectively, it is capable of and in fact already has ushered in a program of state capitalism. (Borodin 1997: 137–38)

By permitting the reconciliation between various revisionist positions, the epoch of Putin has proven to be a turning point. The October Revolution rescued Russia from the war, and the imposition of the Treaty of Brest-Litovsk, which had been continuously maligned by the Bolsheviks' enemies, was also declared to have been abolished by the Soviet government in the wake of Germany's military defeat.[6] After the October Revolution, debates about it broke out within even the drifting fragments of the White Army. This was due to the belief among a portion of the White Russian Eurasianists that the October Revolution was a detour taken by Russia in the face of intense pressure from the West. The revolution, they thought, was a means for Russia to preserve its own agency and, for this reason, could not be outright negated. The national self-determination promoted by the October Revolution was ultimately presented as a form of alliance, preserving to the greatest extent and even expanding upon czarist Russia's territory, population, and authority. In sum, for modernists, the October Revolution used industrialization to clear out feudal impediments; for nationalists and patriots, the Soviet war of self-defense to resist and defeat Nazi Germany's assault amounted to a historic achievement. The October Revolution could not be altogether negated. The true challenge faced by this revolution has been the negation of its establishment of the first proletarian state, or the first state governed by a proletarian dictatorship. This is not only inadmissible within the epistemology of Western liberalism, but it is also leagues apart, as a political form, from the road taken by the contemporary Russian state. And it is precisely within this complex and contradictory atmosphere that we see an ambiguous form of commemoration: President Putin has ordered a commemoration of the 1917 revolution, but at the same time indicating that the events would not be limited to the October Revolution, but would also include the February Revolution. In order to assuage concerns about commemorating the 1917 revolution among those in Russia and abroad, he subsequently decided to establish a victims' memorial in Red Square. The political implications of this memorial are crystal clear: commemorating the 1917 revolution is by no means a reevaluation of Russia's future direction (the message expressed to the Russian people); it also cannot go against universal "human rights" (the message expressed to Western countries, as well as to Russian liberals). Perhaps it was in order to resolve the contradiction between these two orders that, throughout the entire text of the latter order, it never indicates whose victims would be commemorated by the victims' memorial. This is an ambiguous form of commemoration, but the strategy behind the ambiguity is quite clear: it allows a harmonious relationship between various sides of the historical conflicts in modern Russian society.

When it comes to upholding leftist revolutionary principles, there are different ways of interpreting the general events and thinking of the Russian and Chinese revolutions, given their distinct historical periods. The first way comes from the revolutions themselves, which had distinct views and strategies, yet shared a common objective of struggle. This objective did not belong to a single country but was recognized as part of a common movement. Within the process of carrying out revolution they sought the correct revolutionary path and strategic tactics. In the moment when the 1917 revolution burst forth, debates and divisions were especially intense within the Bolshevik party. For example, when it came to their views on the February revolution and the government currently in place, Kamenev and Stalin were fundamentally opposed to Lenin. Plekhanov scoffed that Lenin's *April Theses* were "dream talk." Amid this intellectual debate, even *Pravda* had taken a stance diametrically opposed to Lenin. On the eve of the October Revolution, no matter if it was a question of whether to attend the All-Russian Congress Pre-Parliament (this directly related to whether one should halt or promote a democratic revolution of the capitalist class in view of it transforming into socialism) or the question of whether one should promote armed insurrection, the Bolshevik party central committee and its leaders (not only Kamenev and Zinoviev, but also Trotsky) all had voiced their opposition to insurrection; furthermore, fierce conflicts erupted with Lenin.

These strategic and tactical divergences, as well as the critique of revolution in contemporary intellectual life, have many points in common, but they are not fundamentally the same. These earlier debates were a series of strategic divergences arising from within the same camp. In 1922, while Rosa Luxemburg's ([1961] 1972: 79–80) posthumous words sharply criticized Lenin, Trotsky, other leaders of the October Revolution, and the policy of the Bolsheviks, she mounted a defense of the revolution in the following terms: "criticism is not an expectation of miracles, because achieving a model and faultless proletarian revolution in an isolated land, exhausted by world war, strangled by imperialism, betrayed by the international proletariat, would be a miracle. What is in order is to distinguish the essential from the non-essential, the kernel from the accidental excrescences in the politics of the Bolsheviks." On the one hand, she criticized the serious deficits and even the mistakes in the October Revolution, but on the other hand, she praised "the capacity for action of the proletariat, the strength to act, the will to power of socialism as such. In this, Lenin and Trotsky and their friends were the *first*, those who went ahead as an example to the proletariat of the world; they are still the *only ones* up to now who can cry with Hutten: 'I have dared!'" (80; original emphasis). In the eyes of Luxemburg, the October Revolution had erupted without having gone through meticulous preparations, and so, like a seed, contained the essential fact of belonging to the future. The criticism that Luxemburg posed of the October Revolution is, as I would term it, posed from the perspective of the essential futurity that is contained in an immature revolution. In each revolutionary process, it is only with a sense of the futurity that is contained within an actual revolution that one might produce a correct critique and evaluation of the trials of that revolution, together with the strategic flaws of the revolutionaries, and thereby avoid lapsing into a negation and betrayal of the revolution itself. The criticism of Luxemburg toward the Bolshevik Revolution opened, from the perspective of a participant in the revolutionary project, the possibility of reexamining this revolution itself. For Luxemburg, the strategy and tactics of the revolution had moments that deserved critique, and it should be possible to rupture the narrative of necessity that had been woven together by the revolutionaries themselves for reasons of imminent necessity, in order that we might examine other possibilities. Precisely for this reason, she devoted yet more space to the critique of the Bolsheviks, believing that they had made a virtue of necessity, by falsely presenting those "actions they had been forced to take" under specific conditions (that is, the conditions of the era, the balance of the forces, theoretical preparation and discussions of tactics and strategy having not yet come to maturity) as universal truths to be adopted by the whole of the socialist movement as a model of revolution.

If one were to say that the divergence of revolutionary strategy in the twentieth century had as its precondition the existence of a process of revolution, the existence of a revolutionary subject in continuous formation, then the restatement of the contemporary Left toward the Russian and Chinese Revolutions and their principles is one that takes failure as its point of departure. This so-called failure is not a kind of strategic defeat. Neither is it a kind of strategic setback. The most external pattern of this "failure" is the dissolution of the socialist system that was formed through the revolutions of the twentieth century—the fact that the Soviet Union and the socialist states of Eastern Europe no longer exist, the process by which China, Vietnam, and other states are transitioning from being states under the rule of Communist Parties toward integration with global capitalism. The deeper level of meaning of this failure is the end of this revolutionary process and the decline of the revolutionary subject that both furthered and was formed through this revolutionary process. The division into classes continues to deepen, and yet there is no means of forming the kind of political class that served as the motive force for revolution in the twentieth and nineteenth centuries. The revolutionary vanguard that facilitated the birth of a political class in the revolutionary processes of the twentieth century may exist in name but has ceased to have any actuality. According to Alain Badiou (2008: 35), a philosopher who has never renounced his relationship with the revolutionary tradition, the "essential" of revolution of which Luxemburg spoke no longer exists within an analysis of the Bolshevik policy or within the disagreements of the revolutionaries that opened up around questions of tactics and strategy and can only exist in the form of a "communist hypothesis":

> A communist hypothesis means first, that the logic of class—the fundamental subordination of labour to a dominant class, the arrangement that has persisted since Antiquity—is not inevitable; it can be overcome. The

communist hypothesis is that a different collective organization is practicable, one that will eliminate the inequality of wealth and even the division of labour. The private appropriation of massive fortunes and their transmission by inheritance will disappear. The existence of a coercive state, separate from civil society, will no longer appear a necessity: a long process of reorganization based on a free association of producers will see it withering away."

The reason why communism can only exist in the form of a hypothesis is exactly because the practical attempts of the twentieth century to achieve this hypothesis have come to failure. "The party proved," Badiou continues, "ill-adapted for the construction of the 'dictatorship of the proletariat' in the sense that Marx had intended—that is, a temporary state, organizing the transition to the non-state: its dialectical 'withering away'. Instead, the party-state developed into a new form of authoritarianism" (36). As a result, reposing the "communist hypothesis" operates from a recognition of failure and recognizes that the primary content that constituted the second sequence of revolutions (Marxism, the working-class movement, mass democracy, Leninism, the proletarian party, the socialist state) has already ceased to have any effectivity. "The second sequence is over," Badiou concludes, "and it is pointless to try to restore it" (37).

Luxemburg's thought takes the living existing of a revolutionary subject as its objective premise, it is one that has, as its subjective condition, the feeling of "I can say 'our', for I was part of it, and in a certain sense," to quote Rimbaud, "I am still there, I am still there" (Badiou 2010: 101–2). If the governing party that functions as the proletariat in its capacity of the ruling class, and which functions as the revolutionary vanguard, comes close to undergoing a change in character, or to dissolution and destruction, then any discussion over tactics or strategy or any attempt from an internal perspective to expand values is no longer possible. The majority of contemporary discussions surrounding the Russian Revolution and the Chinese Revolution—regardless of the name under which they take place, and regardless of their content or form—are taking place under conditions of the displacement of the subject. Every kind of criticism and mockery directed toward the October Revolution sounds a great deal like a repetition of the partial perspective of the debates that broke out among the revolutionaries themselves during the epoch of revolution. This mockery and criticism, however, has the aforementioned "displacement of the subject" as its premise, and for this reason, the criticism of the contemporary intellectual scene is not posed from the perspective of "that which is essential and which endures" articulated by

Luxemburg, and is also never that mode of debate that operates from within the revolution in order to expand questions of strategy and tactics. I understand these historical narratives of revolution as a "historiography of regret." They are a symptom of the arrival of the postrevolutionary epoch, a form of accusation against revolution brought about by the new subject that operates under the name of posterity. As with the large majority of countries that went through socialism in the twentieth century, China is currently witnessing the same condition. "Regret" here is not only the prelude to a thoroughgoing renunciation, but it is also a means by which the contemporary world gives confirmation to itself. In this respect, a restatement of the "communist hypothesis" is a matter of fundamental necessity.

There are none among us who would deny the flaws, setbacks, and tragedies of the practice of socialism and revolution in the twentieth century. But is this indeed a failure? If this is not a failure, or at least not a straightforward failure, how are we to assess its achievements? From a historical perspective, there is a great discrepancy between the historical trajectories and contemporary destinies of, on the one hand, China and, on the other, Russia and those other socialist countries, and so we cannot simply group all of these experiences within the single category of failure. Those revolutions that were inspired or influenced by the Russian Revolution took place under different historical conditions, and each of them also comprised distinct social objectives, with their revolutionaries and revolutionary detachments also exhibiting radically different degrees of maturity. Even if one were to summarize these revolutions as so many failures, it is still impossible to depart from an analysis of their concrete processes. The question of the governing party is decisive but cannot account for the whole. What, ultimately, did the revolutions of the twentieth century, especially socialist revolutions, bring to human history? As compared to the world that existed before the revolution, in what respects did these surging and tumultuous revolutions alter the lives of human beings? Apart from the necessity of restating the "communist hypothesis," could we, perhaps, in the real practice of revolution, amid that history that is full of success and failure, triumph and folly, necessity and contingency, still search for the seeds of the future, or that which Luxemburg called the "essential" of revolution?

The Right to National Self-Determination and the Chinese Revolution

In many discussions surrounding the October Revolution, there were three fundamental questions: the question of war and peace, especially Lenin's advocacy for withdrawing from the war, which involved the problem of locating a strategy for revolution in Russia; the question of national self-determination, especially the right of national minorities to "secede," including the problem, deriving from this, of the relationship between a national revolution and a class revolution; and, finally, the question of proletarian dictatorship, or the problem of the relationship between democracy and the transitional state. As posed by Luxemburg ([1961] 1972: 79) in her formulation of "all the tactics forced upon" the Bolsheviks under specific conditions (these actions having then been presented as a general truth to be given to the international communist movement), there were the following points of crucial importance: In order to secure the support of the peasantry for the revolution, it was necessary to allow the peasants to take occupation of the land rather than pursuing the nationalization of the land. And in order to gain the support of the national minorities, the policy of opposing the war strategy of Milyukov and Kerensky and proposing "national self-determination" (especially the slogan concerning the right of each national minority to independently decide their own destinies, up to and including the right "to secede from the Russian state") was made into a key state policy after the revolution. Before the October Revolution, the Bolsheviks had demanded the formation of the Constituent Assembly and strongly attacked the continued existence of the Kerensky Provisional Government; and yet, after the revolution, Lenin and his comrades dissolved the old Constituent Assembly and had no intention of carrying out elections for the formation of a new Constituent Assembly. Luxemburg ([1961] 1972: 48) writes:

> While they showed a quite cool contempt for the Constituent Assembly, universal suffrage, freedom of press and assemblage, in short, for the whole apparatus of the basic democratic liberties of the people which, taken all together, constituted the 'right of self-determination' inside Russia, they treated the right of self-determination of peoples as a jewel of democratic policy for the sake of which all practical considerations of real criticism had to be stilled."

For Luxemburg, the right to self-determination was an unforgivable crime that the Russian revolutionaries had committed toward the international movement of the working class.

Following the eruption of the October Revolution, China and other Asian countries knew little about the political struggle that had erupted in Russia or the policies of the Bolshevik party. The first reaction toward the revolution was concentrated in the position of the Russian revolutionaries concerning the Eastern Question and Oppressed Peoples, which differed radically from that of the West. As a result, the revolutionaries of colonized societies had a different approach toward the question of national self-determination, compared to that of Western European socialists. In actual fact, the position of the Russian Revolution concerning the question of nationality had a close link with the progression of the "awakening of Asia." With respect to self-determination, Luxemburg posed her criticism from the viewpoint of the working-class movement of Europe. She emphasized the unity, solidarity, and common struggle of the working class, whereas Lenin's understanding of revolution took as its premise the search for the revolutionary moment in the epoch of imperialism. The revolutionary moment lay in the weakest links of the imperialist chain. The weakest links of capitalism would most likely be located beyond Europe. From the 1905 Russian Revolution, the 1907 Iranian Revolution, the 1909 Turkish Revolution, and, above all, the 1911 Chinese Revolution, Lenin had already discovered the potential for socialist revolution contained within the "awakening of Asia." Not only Western European revolutionaries such as Luxemburg, but also those who belonged to the Bolsheviks themselves, such as Trotsky, in the epoch of the outbreak of the Russian Revolution, had not yet begun to think deeply about the question of a possible Asian revolution. Within the discourse of "failure" among the contemporary Western Left, within the criticisms concerning class revolution, the political power of the governing party, and state capitalism, the right to self-determination together with the larger category of nationalism have all been taken as the side of innate "compromise" of the revolutions of the twentieth century and displaced to that one side. As a result, within the reflections of the Western Left concerning the Russian Revolution, we can quite clearly see a tactical and strategic divergence that derives from the working-class movements and social-democratic parties of Europe. Yet another lineage of this revolution is almost invisible: the lineage of Asian revolutions. The Russian Revolution has been seen as derivative of the revolutions of Europe. Yet, if we place this revolution at the same time within the ranks of the "awakening of Asia," could we not trace some rather different trajectories?

The October Revolution erupted in the final years of the First World War. When the revolution was won in 1918, the countries of Asia and other oppressed nations had not yet grasped the extent to which the then popular current of Wilsonian liberalism sought, with its advocacy of self-determination, to grant concessions and protection to European colonialism. The bankruptcy of Wilsonian liberalism at the Paris Peace Conference made manifest the ways in which the Russian Revolution was radically different. As people suddenly discovered after the October Revolution, the Bolsheviks immediately announced the "Decree on Peace," in which, at the same time as critiquing the war of the imperial powers and proposing immediate peace talks and an end to hostilities, they also announced the cancellation of all the secret treaties that had been signed by the czarist state and Provisional Government. Beginning on November 9, 1917, within a month, the Bolsheviks released more than one hundred secret diplomatic documents. On December 3, 1917, the Soviet government issued the text "To all the Muslim workers of Russia and the East," drafted by Lenin and Stalin, in which, at the same time as they announced the cancellation of the secret treaties that had aimed at the carving up of Persia and Turkey and the Russian occupation of Constantinople, they also restated the principle of self-determination and support for the national liberation movements of all oppressed peoples. On January 25, 1918, the third All-Russia Congress of Soviets announced the "Declaration of Rights of the Working and Exploited People," drafted by Lenin, Stalin, and Bukharin, in which they restated the right to self-determination and the cancellation of all secret treaties and announced a "complete break with the barbarous policy of bourgeois civilization" (Lenin [1960] 1977c: 26:424). All of these decisions do not merely demonstrate the birth of a socialist theory and practice of diplomacy, but they also symbolize the extent to which the Russian revolutionaries had drawn the oppressed peoples into the scope of the "revolutionary classes"—the revolutions of the twentieth century are not only revolutions of the working classes, they are also revolutions of oppressed peoples. This conception of class revolution differed from the working-class movements of the West, and its significance for China and the Third World can scarcely be overestimated.

The process of drawing oppressed people into the scope of the revolutionary classes was determined by the imperialist epoch and the transformation of the world system under the aegis of that epoch. Simultaneously, it was also determined by the historical connection between the Russian Revolution and the Asian revolution (this is something that even a revolutionary of the stature of Trotsky could understand only after a prolonged period of time). Shortly after the outbreak of the Chinese Revolution of 1911 and the formation of the Provisional Government of the Republic of China in the following year, Lenin published his articles "Democracy and Narodism in China" (1912), "The Awakening of Asia" (1913), and "Backward Europe and Advanced Asia" (1913) in which he praised China as "a land of seething political activity, the scene of a virile social movement and of a democratic upsurge" and condemned "civilised and advanced Europe, with its highly developed machine industry, its rich, multiform culture," which had, under the leadership of the bourgeoisie, come to the "support of everything backward, moribund and medieval" (Lenin (1960) 1977b: 19:99). Lenin's evaluation was an important organizational component of his theory of imperialism and proletarian revolution. According to his perspectives, as capitalism entered into its imperialist stage, the social struggles of the oppressed peoples of every part of the globe come to be organized within the scope of the world proletarian revolution. This analytical means of linking the European revolution together with the revolutions of Asia can be traced to Marx's "Revolution in China and Europe," published in the *New York Tribune* in 1853. Lenin regarded Russia as an Asiatic state, yet this perspective was not derived from the perspective of geography but, rather, with regard to the process of capitalist development; that is, Lenin came to demarcate Russia with reference to the course of its historical development. In his text "Democracy and Narodism in China," he noted that "in very many and very essential respects, Russia is undoubtedly an Asian country and, what is more, one of the most benighted, medieval and shamefully backward of Asian countries" (Lenin [1960] 1977d: 18:163). Lenin had great sympathy toward the Chinese Revolution, yet, as the problem transitioned from the Asian revolution toward the international transformations of Russian society, his position was that of a "Westernizer." From the nineteenth through the twentieth century, Russian intellectuals regarded the Russian spirit as caught up in a struggle between the forces of East and West, Asia and Europe. In "Democracy and Narodism in China," Asia is associated with barbarism, medievalism, backwardness, and other such concepts, and it was exactly because of this point that the Russian Revolution possessed a great Asiatic character (this revolution was in fact directed against all those "barbaric," "medieval," and "backwards" social relations that Russia possessed as an Asiatic society) and at the same time carried global significance.

The specific position that Asia occupied within the rhetoric of world history determined the understanding of socialists concerning the tasks and direction of modern Asian revolutions. Having read Sun Yat-sen's "The Significance of China's Revolution," Lenin criticized the socialist and democratic program put forward by Sun, according to which the Chinese Revolution would be able to transcend capitalism, as Lenin argued that this perspective was a utopian and populist one. In his view, "the chief representative, or the chief social bulwark, of this Asian bourgeoisie that is still capable of supporting a historically progressive cause is the peasant" (Lenin

[1960] 1977d: 18:165). As a result, the Chinese Revolution would first have to complete the revolutionary tasks of the European bourgeoisie, and only then would it become possible to think the problem of socialism. Lenin skillfully used historical dialectics to argue that, on the one hand, the program of agrarian revolution put forward by Sun was a "counter-revolutionary" program because it ignored or sought to transcend the demands of historical development. And yet, on the other hand, Lenin pointed out that, owing to the "Asiatic" character of the Chinese Revolution, this "counter-revolutionary program" would in actual fact complete the mission of capitalism: "the irony of history is that Narodism, under the guise of "combating capitalism" in agriculture, champions an agrarian programme that, if fully carried out, would mean the *most* rapid development of capitalism in agriculture" (Lenin [1960] 1977d: 18:168).

Lenin's understanding of the Chinese Revolution had its origins in his long-term theorization concerning the reforms implemented in Russia in 1861, and the failure of the 1905 Revolution. In 1861, following the defeat of Russia at the hands of Britain and France in the Crimean War, in which Russia had sought to gain control of the Balkans and the Black Sea, Alexander II initiated reforms to abolish serfdom. Summing up the key points of this reform in the simplest terms, there are two points that cannot be ignored: First, this reform did not arise from within Russian society itself but was, rather, the result of external pressure. Second, the Emancipation Decree released on February 19, 1861, was implemented under the premise of protecting the interests of the landlord and ensured that the peasants would pay a heavy cost for a top-down process of Russian industrialization. It was for this reason that Lenin asserted that 1861 ultimately led to 1905.[7] From the reform of 1861 to the revolution of 1905, the phenomenon of land concentration did not lead to a capitalist agrarian economy; it, instead, gave rise to strong demands from the peasants of the communes for the expropriation and redistribution of lands held by landlords.[8] Against this historical background, Lenin's summation and theorization of the 1905 revolution was closely bound up with the question of how to solve the problem of land in Russia. In 1907, Lenin wrote "The Agrarian Program of Social-Democracy in the First Russian Revolution, 1905–1907," where, taking the Russian land problem as his focus, he posed two models of capitalist agriculture, namely, the "Prussian Road" and the "American Road."[9] The so-called Prussian Road would proceed through the unification of the state and the landlord class, using violence to expropriate the peasants, eliminate village society and the village system of land ownership, and transform the serf-landlord economy into a Junker-capitalist economy. The American road, on the other hand, was one that "may be carried out in the interests of the peasant masses and not of the landlord gang" (Lenin [1960] 1977a: 13:423), those interests being "the nationalization of the land, the abolition of its private ownership, and the transfer of all land to the state, which will mark a complete break with feudal relations in the countryside. It is this economic necessity that has turned the mass of Russian peasants into supporters of land nationalization" (Lenin [1960] 1977a: 13:424–25). Through his summation of the reasons regarding the failure of land reform in Russia and the failure of the 1905 revolution, Lenin posed a fundamental position: under Russian social conditions, "nationalization of the land is not only the sole means for completely eliminating medievalism in agriculture, but also the best form of agrarian relationships conceivable under capitalism" (Lenin [1960] 1977a: 13:426).

Lenin believed that the land program of the Narodniks in Russia would lead Russia to return to a small peasant economy based on the parcelization of village lands, and that this kind of economic system would not be able to provide the motive force for the development of capitalism. He approved of the American road, on the one hand, because it would be possible, by means of nationalizing the land, to abolish medieval land relations and provide the possibility of developing a capitalist, agrarian economy and, on the other hand, because Russia possessed vast expanses of uncultivated land and, therefore, the conditions to follow the American road rather than that of other Western countries. The development of a capitalist agriculture would necessarily require the enforced reshaping of old social relations:

> In England this reshaping proceeded in a revolutionary, violent way; but the violence was practiced for the benefit of the landlords, it was practiced on the masses of the peasants, who were taxed to exhaustion, driven from the villages, evicted, and who died out, or emigrated. In America this reshaping went on in a violent way as regards the slave farms in the Southern States. There violence was applied against the slaveowning landlords. Their estates were broken up, and the large feudal estates were transformed into small bourgeois farms. As regards the mass of "unappropriated" American lands, this role of creating the new agrarian relationships to suit the new mode of production (i.e., capitalism) was played by the "American General Redistribution," by the Anti-Rent movement (*Anti-Rent Bewegung*) of the forties, the Homestead Act, etc." (Lenin [1960] 1977a: 13:275–76)

As such, "the Narodnik thinks that repudiation of private landownership is repudiation of capitalism. That is wrong. The repudiation of private landownership expresses the demands for the purist capitalist development"

(Lenin [1960] 1977a: 13:314). From this perspective, Lenin recognized the genuine, revolutionary potential within Sun Yat-sen's program. He marveled at this "advanced Chinese democrat" who understood nothing about Russia and yet resembled a Russian in his arguments, having posed "purely Russian questions": "land nationalization makes it possible to abolish absolute rent, leaving only differential rent. According to Marx's theory, land nationalization means a maximum elimination of medieval monopolies and medieval relations in agriculture, maximum freedom in buying and selling land, and maximum facilities for agriculture to adapt itself to the market" (Lenin [1960] 1977d: 18:168). In contrast, "our vulgar Marxists, however, in criticizing 'equalized redistribution,' 'socialization of the land', and 'equal right to the land,' confine themselves to repudiating the doctrine, and thus reveal their own obtuse doctrinairism, which prevents them from seeing the vital life of the peasant revolution beneath the lifeless doctrine of Narodnik theory" (Lenin [1960] 1977a: 13:282). Through examining Sun's revolutionary program against the background of Russia's specific history, Lenin was able to decide that "the Russian revolution has conclusively proved that it can be victorious only as a peasant agrarian revolution, and that the latter cannot completely fulfil its historical mission unless the land is nationalised" (Lenin [1960] 1977a: 13:425–26). If one were to say that the feature demarcating the American road from the Prussian road and English road consisted in land nationalization, then, the Chinese road represented a "peasant agrarian revolution" from below.

The transformation of Russia opened up against the background of the Crimean War, the 1905 Russo-Japanese War, and the First World War. Lenin's understanding of the Russian road of transformation must be linked together with the international relationships produced by European imperialism. If the Russian land problem could only be resolved through nationalization, then, what kind of state would be able to assume the heavy task of this kind of transformation? Lenin wrote:

> the national state is the rule and "norm" of capitalism; the multi-national state represents backwardness, or is an exception . . . this does not mean, of course, that such a state, which is based on bourgeois relations, can eliminate the exploitation and oppression of nations. It only means that Marxists cannot lose sight of the powerful *economic* factors that give rise to the urge to create national states. It means that "self-determination of nations" in the Marxists' Program *cannot*, from a historico-economic point of view, have any other meaning than political self-determination, state independence, and the formation of a national state. (Lenin [1960] 1977f: 20:400)

Therefore, when Lenin discussed the "awakening of Asia," he was concerned not with socialism but rather with the problem of how one might create the political premises for capitalist development, that is, the question of national self-determination. There are two points worth taking note of here. First, "the nation-state" and "multi-national state" (that is, "empire") form a contrast, the former being the "norm" of capitalism, and the latter, its opposite. Second, national self-determination is "political self-determination," and in the conditions of Russia and China, the necessary form of "political self-determination" was to use the means of socialism in order to create the political conditions for capitalist development, that is, the political structure of the political nation or the nation-state. "Capitalism, having awakened Asia, has called forth national movements everywhere in the continent, too . . . the tendency of these movements is towards the creation of national states in Asia; it is such states that ensure the best conditions for the development of capitalism" (Lenin [1960] 1977f: 20:399).[10] In the specific conditions of Asia, only by means of a peasant agrarian revolution and socialist state building would it be possible to create the premises for capitalist development, and so it was necessary to reject all reform programs that opposed peasant liberation and land redistribution.

There is no need to exaggerate the influence of the first Chinese Revolution on the Russian Revolution. In actual fact, whereas we cannot determine any direct influence of the first Chinese Revolution on the Russian Revolution, the October Revolution, which emerged against the background of the European war, had a deep and visible influence on the Chinese socialist revolution. Lenin's stress on the events of the Xinhai Revolution was guided by his long-term considerations around the problem of the state, the socialist movement, and the people's democratic dictatorship. Yet, only very rarely do we take proper consideration of the following two facts: In the first place, the October Revolution took place after the Xinhai Revolution, and from this, the method of building socialism in one country can, to a very large extent, be seen as a response to the Asian revolutions. From the perspective of the history of the socialist movement, the first modern revolution in China demonstrates that, in Asian social conditions, the European socialist movement in its opposition to capitalism and the nation-state began to move in the direction of a movement for national self-determination. Lenin's theory of the right to national self-determination (1914), and his understanding of the significance of revolution in backward nations in the epoch of imperialism, were both developed subsequent to the 1911 revolution, and had a close theoretical relationship with his analysis of the Chinese Revolution. In the second place, the Russian Revolution had a large, shocking, and lasting impact on Europe. It can be seen as the historical event that separated Russia and Europe from one another. Lenin's evaluation of revolution did not have a fundamental difference from the narrative of Smith and Hegel concerning Asia: they all narrated the history of capitalism as a historical process of turning from the ancient Orient to the modern West, of a necessary development from a means of production based on agriculture and hunting to those based on commerce and industry. Yet, for Lenin, this framework of world history came to include a double significance. On the one hand, world capitalism and the Russian Revolution of 1905 to which world capitalism gave rise were the main forces that served to awaken Asia, as a land that had been stagnant for a long period of time and had no history. On the other hand, the Chinese Revolution represented the most advanced forces in world history, and so for socialists it signified a site of rupture within the imperialist world-system. Among Russian intellectuals and revolutionaries, there had for a long time been lasting debates between Slavophiles and Westernizers. Lenin himself, speaking from the position of a Westernizer, was able, by means of a dialectical comparison between "advanced Asia" and "backwards Europe," to construct a new logic, one of "leaving Europe" (imperialist Europe) and "entering Asia" (the progressive content of revolution in a backward region). From the perspective of seeking modernization via capitalist development, this line of "leaving Europe and entering Asia" still existed within the logic of "leaving Asia." Under this logic, the Chinese Revolution provided a unique road that united the movement for national liberation with socialism—this unique road provided the premises for the emergence of a new revolutionary subject, by which I mean the union of workers and peasants that took the Chinese peasantry as its subject.

From the perspective of the revolutionary movement of 1911, and, one might say, from the perspective of a program that "stands for complete democracy and the demand for a republic,"[11] the republic of the capitalist class and the independent nation-state are the political outer shell for the development of capitalism, and there are several factors that might impede the formation of this outer shell: the attempts of imperialism to carve up China, the conservative forces of the Chinese countryside, and the so-called backward north, represented by the Qing court and the Northern military clique. The *backward north* is a term used by Lenin in a judgment about the 1912 conflict between the north and the southern regions of China: "Yüan Shih-k'ai's [Yuan Shikai's] parties are based on the backward north of China," that is, "the capitalists, landlords and bureaucrats of China's most backward region" (Lenin [1960] 1977h: 41:281–82). As early as 1912, Lenin predicted that Yuan Shikai would seek to have himself declared Emperor, and he linked this problem to the "problem of the north" faced by the Chinese Revolution. Yet, Lenin's understanding of the "backward north" was concentrated entirely on class analysis, especially the collective interests represented by Yuan Shikai and his clique, and so Lenin ignored the factors of territory, ethnicity, and religion as they related to "the most backward region," that is, this region that stood as an impediment to capitalist development. From the perspective of the theory on the right to national self-determination that Lenin came to develop afterward, he took the nation-state as the "norm" of capitalism, and he maintained that since the multinational empire impedes capitalist development it must be eliminated. Under his leadership, the support given by the Bolsheviks to the independence of Poland and Ukraine on the basis of the right to national self-determination was an extension of this political logic.

Given this position, why did Lenin, in the context of discussing the Chinese Revolution, not only give a high estimation of Sun Yat-sen's program for national construction but also not put forward demands to support the independence of Mongolia, Tibet, and the Muslim areas and, instead, take the "backward north" as a barrier for the revolution? From the perspective of method, Lenin's attitude toward the national question was not an "answer to be sought in legal definitions deduced from all sorts of 'general concepts' of law" but was rather an answer "to be sought in a historico-economic study of the national movements" (Lenin [1960] 1977f: 20:395). The economic basis of national movements was that "for the complete victory of commodity production, the bourgeoisie must capture the home market, and there must be politically united territories whose population speak a single language, with all obstacles to the development of that language and to its consolidation in literature eliminated" (396). On the basis of this meaning "the tendency of every national movement is toward the formation of *national states*, under which these requirements of modern capitalism are best satisfied" (396). Having taken this position, Lenin not only rejected the support of Austrian Social-Democrat Otto Bauer for "national-cultural autonomy" but also critiqued the positions put forward by Luxemburg in her opposition to the slogan of Polish independence. Lenin pointed out that the primary mistake of Luxemburg lay in her having "lost sight of the most important thing—the difference between countries, where bourgeois-democratic reforms have long been completed, and those where they have not" (405). That is to say, following the European democratic revolutions over the period 1789–1871, Western Europe had already "been transformed into a settled system of bourgeois states, which, as a general rule, were nationally uniform states. Therefore, to seek the right to self-determination in the programmes of West-European socialists [nowadays] is to betray one's ignorance of the ABC of Marxism." Moreover

> in Eastern Europe and Asia the period of bourgeois-democratic revolutions did not begin until 1905. The revolutions in Russia, Persia, Turkey and China, the Balkan wars—such is the chain of world events of *our* period in our 'Orient.' And only a blind man could fail to see in this chain of events the awakening of a *whole series* of bourgeois-democratic national movements which strive to create nationally independent and nationally uniform states. It is precisely and solely because Russia and the neighbouring countries are passing through this period that we must have a clause in our programme on the right of nations to self-determination." (406)

As a result, for Lenin, the principle of nation was not absolute, and whether to support any given movement for national self-determination would be determined by whether separation and independence would be beneficial to capitalist development in backward regions, and would at the same time also be determined by the political and geographical environment of a specific nation. For example, in Austria, there was "a striving on the part of the Hungarians and then of the Czechs, not for separation from Austria, but, on the contrary, for the preservation of Austria's integrity, precisely in order to preserve national independence, which might have been completely crushed by more rapacious and powerful neighbours! Owing to this peculiar situation, Austria assumed the form of a dual state, and she is now being transformed into a triple state (Germans, Hungarians, Slavs)" (407). Opposite to this, in Russia, the

> "subject peoples" (which, on the whole, comprise the majority of the entire population—57 per cent) inhabit the border regions; secondly, the oppression of these subject peoples is much stronger here than in the neighbouring states (and not even in the European states alone); thirdly, in a number of cases the oppressed nationalities inhabiting the border regions have compatriots across the border, who enjoy greater national independence (suffice it to mention the Finns, the Swedes, the Poles, the Ukrainians and the Romanians along the western and southern frontiers of the state); fourthly, the development of capitalism and the general level of culture are often higher in the non-Russian border regions than in the centre. Lastly, it is in the neighbouring Asian states that we see the beginning of a phase of bourgeois revolutions and national movements which are spreading to some of the kindred nationalities within the borders of Russia. (408)

From the above analyses, we can derive Lenin's fundamental position with regard to the question of the border regions in China: First, comparable to the regions inhabited by Hungarian and Czech peoples in the Austro-Hungarian empire, the movements seeking independence in the border regions of China would in all likelihood make these regions fall into the hands of "more rapacious and powerful neighbours"—from the first Sino-Japanese War (1895) to the interference of Russia, Germany, and France over the ownership of the Liaodong peninsula, and from the joint repression of the Boxer Uprising to the Russo-Japanese War, we can quite clearly see that Russia, Japan, Britain, France, and other powers sought to divide and control China. Second, not only was the "level of capitalist development and general cultural level" of China's "central regions" higher than that of the border regions, but also "the bourgeois revolution and nationalist movements had already developed," and so preserving the territorial integrity of China would be of benefit to the development of the revolutionary movement (and, as a consequence, of benefit to capitalist development). In these terms, Lenin described Yuan Shikai and the northern regions with which he was allied as the backward north and awaited the overcoming and resolution of this region that had impeded the revolution. He did not more deeply analyze why the radical revolutionaries of China had made compromises that violated the principles of the revolution itself, and this was probably linked to the scope of his political analysis. The "backward north" compelled the revolutionary party of the south to make compromises, and yet this exactly demonstrates that China's revolution could not use the means of division in order to pursue capitalist development; "the problem of the north" was a "problem of the north" within the Chinese Revolution and the development of Chinese capitalism.

The "north" of the problem of the north did not only encompass northeast Mongolia and the areas of Huabei under the control of the Beiyang government but also the southwestern parts of Tibet and the region of the northwest, which were intimately linked with these other areas. That is, the "north" also encompassed the four great non-Han ethnic groups conveyed in the concept of the "Republic of Five Nationalities," as well as their areas of activity. Even following the formation of the People's Republic of China, the process of land reform was carried out far more gradually in the areas of Mongolia, Tibet, and other regions compared to elsewhere, and this demonstrates that the relationship between "concessions" in the process of revolution and the problem of the north persisted over the long term. On January 1, 1912, Sun Yat-sen (1981: 2) in his Declaration of the Temporary President of the Republic of China (and Provisional Constitution of the Republic of China) posed the concept of the "Republic of Five Nationalities":

The foundation of the country lies in its people. To unite the lands of the Han, Manchus, Mongols, Uyghurs and Tibetans into one country is to unite the Han, Manchu, Mongol, Uyghur and Tibetan nations into one subject. This is the meaning of national unification." Compared to his early perspective on the nation, the concept of Five Races Under One Union did not limit the republic to a republic of the Han based on the territory of the Ming dynasty, but, rather, took the Great Empire of the Qing as the expansive and diverse space that was "marching toward a republic. (2)

From this latter perspective, Sun Yat-sen accepted the understanding of China posed by the advocates of Constitutional Monarchy in the late Qing dynasty, but at the same time he also took the Republic as the political replacement for the dynasty. This transformation established a basis for modern political equality and gave rise to the challenge of how, by means of law, system, and practice, it might be possible to maintain balance and manage tensions between conservative and religious traditions (for example, the politico-economic organization of Tibetan religious society) and intense class politics.

The Chinese Revolution received the concept of the right to national self-determination, and yet, with the exception of a brief period, that is, the failure of the Great Revolution in 1927, and the period in which the Red Army built the Soviet base areas in Jiangxi, when the Chinese Communist Party adopted the right to self-determination, with the right to secession as its primary content, as part of its provisional constitutional program, the general course of the Chinese Revolution understood the right to self-determination in terms of the demand for independence against imperialism. This understanding was a fundamental premise for the search to found a new democratic state in transition to socialism. The internationalism of the Chinese Revolution and its later embrace of the Third World followed and developed along this line. The struggle of the Chinese Revolution against imperialism and colonialism did not demonstrate the problem of national secession. On the contrary, the revolution emphasized the problem of the unity of the oppressed. In this sense, the practice of the Chinese Revolution that followed the Leninist line was precisely a Luxemburgist line without Luxemburg. Yet, with respect to the political and historical content of the Chinese Revolution, the most appropriate explanation is exactly Lenin's "Draft Theses on National and Colonial Questions" delivered at the Second Congress of the Communist International ([1960] 1977e: 31). The fundamental content of these theses encompassed the following points: after the First World War and the October Revolution, the national question had become a component of the general problem of the world proletarian revolution, and so it was necessary to forge close links with the socialist revolution that had Soviet Russia as its capital; it was necessary to forge proletarian parties, to unite the broad peasant masses and solve the problem of the land; and it was necessary to form an anti-imperialist revolutionary united front with the national bourgeoisie and the democrats while also maintaining the political and organizational independence of the proletariat and so carry forth the struggle for national liberation to its conclusion.

The Historical Experience of the Dictatorship of the Proletariat

The October Revolution created a workers' state under the leadership of the Bolsheviks. In theory, this state was to be a transition toward proletarian society under the guidance of a proletarian state structure, just as Marx had indicated: the dictatorship of the proletariat. The import of proletarian dictatorship is, first and foremost, that revolution should not be a mere handover of state power or a regime change but, rather, a radical transformation of economic and social relations.

Starting in 1917, however, this new political form was besieged by military attacks and polemics launched by foes of the revolution. More important, though, were the internal critiques and resistance among Marxists and members of the Social Democrat Party, which often reached a fever pitch. These cleavages and disputes, which unfolded principally from interpretations of the experience and theoretical understanding provided by the European labor movements, especially the Paris Commune, posed a series of important questions:

1. Should proletarian revolution be undertaken through a long period of economic transformation to implement self-governance, or should political authority be violently seized in order to directly exercise control of state power?

2. Should a socialist state maintain the achievements of bourgeois democratic revolutions, like universal suffrage or parliamentary democracy? In terms of political form, should a socialist nation adopt a state structure based on a federation of divided powers, or should it centralize power?

3. Is proletarian dictatorship the dictatorship of a class or a political party?

Today, amid the contemporary transvaluation of values that has taken place in relation to the Russian and Chinese revolutions, we can still distinguish the clear lines of that period's fierce debates. In rethinking the goals of our contemporary struggles, there is thus much to be gained from revisiting these nearly forgotten debates.

Karl Kautsky, who saw the Russian Revolution as the result of war and a failed czarist system, believed that Russia did not have the necessary conditions for bringing about a socialist revolution, and thus should not attempt to establish a proletarian dictatorship through an armed seizure of power. The revolution, for Kautsky, should simply stop once the czarist system has been overthrown and a liberal phase implemented in alliance with the capitalist class until the social conditions of the working class can mature (Kautsky [1920] 1973: 81). As Kautsky saw it, the Russian Revolution's victory and the Paris Commune's failure were due to the former winning support from the peasantry and the latter having no way of producing such an alliance. But the role of the peasantry, he maintained, also brought "an economic reactionary element from which the Paris Commune was saved. The Paris Dictatorship of the Proletariat was never founded on Peasants' Councils as was the case in Russia" (66). Kautsky's critique focused on the conflict within the new ruling power between various forms of "local self-government" and the dictatorial authority exercised by workers' councils. He believed that not only elements of the old bureaucratic dictatorship revived but also that "the sprouts of a new form of capitalism" emerged under this new dictatorial power.

Luxemburg ([1961] 1972: 28) critiqued Kautsky's opposition to the dictatorship of the proletariat and saw the connections linking the 1917 revolution, "the very first experiment in proletarian dictatorship in world history," to the 1905 revolution, which demonstrated that the impetus for revolution was not only the urban proletariat but also "the mass of the army, which raised the same demand for immediate peace, and the mass of the peasants, who pushed the agrarian question into the foreground" (31–32). She was critical of the Bolshevik land reform policy as well as its position on the right to national self-determination. Most important, however, is her claim that the Bolsheviks lacked respect for and understanding of democracy: they "showed a quite cool contempt for the Constituent Assembly, universal suffrage, freedom of press and assemblage, in short, for the whole apparatus of the basic democratic liberties of the people" (48–49). She maintained that Lenin and Trotsky committed the same error on the left that Kautsky had made on the right: namely, they established an opposition between democracy and dictatorship. Without democratic conditions, which provided the primary form of political training and education of the masses, Soviet Russia was "a dictatorship, to be sure, not the dictatorship of the proletariat but only the dictatorship of a handful of politicians, that is a dictatorship in the bourgeois sense, in the sense of the rule of the Jacobins" (72). This critique was subsequently extended to assert that the Soviet proletarian dictatorship was no longer class dictatorship, but a dictatorship against the working class by a political party or a minority of leaders.

How should we understand Marxism in terms of proletarian dictatorship and proletarian revolution? Should our explanations be drawn from theoretical texts or concrete experience? As early as 1956, Mao Zedong and the CCP leadership argued for a perspective based on experience. Since, "with the exception of the Paris Commune which lasted only 72 days, Marx and Engels did not live to see for themselves the realization of the proletarian revolution and the dictatorship of the proletariat for which they had striven throughout their lives," debate should take as a starting point the concrete practice of proletarian dictatorship (*People's Daily* Editorial Committee 1959: 26).

The Paris Commune provided one concrete experience of proletarian dictatorship, a dictatorship that establishes the basis for a new democratic system to overcome the limits of constitutional and executive institutions (see Marx [1940] 1962; Engels [1940] 1962). But in the decades following the Commune, the major currents of European Marxism abandoned the idea of realizing a dictatorship of the proletariat. When Germany's Social Democratic Party gained authority, even Engels abandoned the concept; and Eduard Bernstein proposed a transformation of the bourgeois state to achieve a harmony between classes, making unnecessary antagonistic class struggle and thus forsaking any idea of proletarian dictatorship.

Lenin subsequently revived the concept of proletarian dictatorship. As early as 1905, in the midst of the "New *Iskra*" debates, Lenin ([1960] 1977i: 9:81) marked a distinction between the concept of "revolutionary communes" and "the revolutionary-democratic dictatorship of the proletariat and peasantry," denouncing the former as "revolutionary phrase-mongering" and affirming the latter as necessary "to administer . . . *all* the affairs of state." Lenin's views are thus distinct from those of Marx, who repeatedly emphasized an antithesis between the Commune and "all the affairs of state." After the October Revolution, the practice of proletarian dictatorship underwent two major transformations: first, instead of a state that permitted multiparty cooperation, a united executive government was established under a single party; second, the worker-peasant alliance was transformed from being the political structure's foundation into becoming the party state's framework, the authority structure by which it would implement all affairs of the state. The dictatorship of the proletariat was thus no longer imagined to create a form of participatory democracy opposed to the state proper but instead became a state structure with a legal monopoly on violence exhibiting a high degree of centralized power.

When considering the relevance of the practical experiences of proletarian dictatorship in either the Paris Commune or the Bolshevik Revolution for Chinese revolutionary activity, one should keep in mind the dramatically different social characteristics, especially the principally agrarian nature of Chinese society. The emergence of industrial capitalism in Europe took shape through a long-term process. Even though formal democracy did not guarantee the economic and political equality of the working class, it did nevertheless provide certain channels by which the working class could advance its struggles via state and legal frameworks. China's working class, on the other hand, which expanded rapidly in the period following World War I, had little political power or legal security of its own and faced industrial bosses and police forces ready to repress them at will. Although the Chinese revolution was inextricably bound to the strength of the urban proletariat, it was essentially based in the vast, rural populace. In 1941, Liu Shaoqi emphasized the difficulty of relying on European and Bolshevik reference points. On the one hand, the Chinese Communist Party, which was established after the October Revolution, was, from the beginning, modeled according to Lenin's principles and under the guidance of the Communist International. But, on the other hand, "China has not gone through the period of the 'peaceful' development of capitalism, such as was experienced in Europe, which allowed the working classes to engage in a peaceful parliamentary struggle" (Shaoqi [1952] 1982: 197). From the very start, the Chinese working class struggle thus had the dual character of a class struggle and a people's struggle.

The People's Democratic Dictatorship of China took shape after 1928, in the lengthy period of the People's War. The People's War, I should emphasize, was not purely a military concept; it was also a political category. It was the process of creating a new political subject, along with the political structures and forms of self-expression adequate to this subject. This is an important point for understanding the essence of political authority in China's early soviets, as well as its relationship to the party and class. During the People's War, the representative relationship of modern government was fundamentally transformed: the peasantry was taken as its primary content; the People was born in political form as the worker-peasant alliance. In the People's War, the party merged with the military, with red political power, transforming the Communist Party's relationship with other parties and representatives of other social strata.[12] The People's War thus created a political party unlike any other in history and made the peasantry into the primary, constitutive members of this class body. The party government posed land reform and military struggle as fundamental bases of mass movements. The party's integration with the military, its deployment of the military in linking peasant movements to land reform, the management of economic life by the party and its subordinate leaders in the soviet areas, the party launching cultural movements as part of its mass work—not only did all of these transform the substantive content of the revolution as well as its core mission, but they were also executed through myriad linkages between the party, military, political authority, and peasant movements, creating an utterly distinct body of revolutionary politics: a red political power. This was the political foundation of the People's War.

Under the conditions of the People's War, the problems attended to by the Chinese Communist Party and the base area's government were not simply of a military order but included organizational problems of everyday life. The party's and the government's mass line implied, first, that the party's work began and ended with planning for the interests of the vast majority of people and, second, that the border region government was charged with organizing the life of the masses. As such, it was only by taking great pains to resolve the problems of the masses and truly improving their lives that the government could earn the masses' faith. Only when the masses' problems were resolved and their lives improved would they be mobilized to join the Red Army in large numbers, aid in the war, and break the Nationalist encirclement campaigns. The People's War did not, therefore, merely adopt tactics of military struggle as a means of wiping out enemies, but it also sought to resolve the primary problems structuring the very fabric of people's lives, including land, labor, resources, the role of women, schools, the urban concentration of commerce, and even monetary and financial systems. The constant relation between the military and daily life became the central problem of the People's War. The mass line was the base strategy of the People's War. It was party policy as well as a means for reconstituting the party: on the one hand, if we have no organization, then we cannot locate the masses; on the other, if we do not become one with the masses, undergoing a process of learning from the masses, then the organization lacks vital force and is just structure bearing down over the masses. In the vast and not yet industrialized countryside, the party and its mass line, which put the peasantry first, achieved a new mode of political expression.

In these ways, the party and its mass line, under the conditions of the People's War, created a form of class-oriented self-articulation, and from this also created a political understanding of class. Whereas notions of political party, party politics, and the soviet government all had their origins in political phenomena of nineteenth-century Europe and twentieth-century Russia, the People's War is the Chinese Revolution's original invention. Not understanding the People's War thus means being unable to comprehend the distinctiveness of the Chinese Revolution and the historical implications of its unique political categories like mass line and United Front.

If one compares the concrete experiences of the People's Democratic Dictatorship carried out under conditions of the People's War with those of the Paris Commune and the October Revolution, then what might we discover? First of all, the Paris Commune and the October Revolution took place in the economic and political centers of Russia and France, whereas the People's Democratic Dictatorship under conditions of the People's War in China opened up in the rural areas far from the central zones of authority. For any armed uprising that takes place in locus of central power, the key task is to form a revolutionary state authority relying on the central location of the capital and then to ensure its prolongation. In the context of the People's War in China, by contrast, because of its distance from the center, the conditions for the rapid formation of a national structure of political power did not exist. Instead, the soviet base areas under red control positioned the People's War as the struggle for the ongoing and expanding formation of the revolutionary subject.

Furthermore, the subject of the Paris Commune consisted solely of workers, and although the October Revolution did receive the support of the peasantry, it was primarily based on the working class and the soldiers, whereas in China, the subject of the People's War was the peasants and those armed detachments comprising peasants. The relationship between the peasantry and the Chinese Revolution was an important topic of discussion for Chinese revolutionaries even before the October Revolution. For example, in 1908, the Chinese Anarchist Liu Shipei ([1908] 2016: 685) wrote that, since the capitalists of China mainly took the form of landowners, the Chinese people comprised peasants, and the wealth of the Chinese state rested primarily on rent income:

> if you wish to carry out an anarchist revolution, then you have to begin from the point of peasant revolution. This peasant revolution will, by means of resisting taxation and all laws, oppose the state and the landlords. In order to implement a system of the common ownership of property, it is necessary to take the common ownership of land as the foundation, understanding the land here as fields. Only if the peasantry implements the common ownership of land will it be possible for all forms of property to be converted to public ownership.

Shipei found in the peasantry a potential for collective organization and resistance that might otherwise have been ignored, especially the potential link between the peasantry and the communist system of ownership. And in this respect it must be said that he was prophetic.

Yet the Chinese Revolution of 1911 did not succeed in grasping this potential, and it ended in failure. Were it not for the October Revolution, the experience of the Chinese Communist Party in mobilizing workers during the course of the First Great Revolution, and then their subsequent pursuit of guerrilla war in the countryside, then it would have been very difficult for the peasantry to assume the task of carrying out proletarian revolution.[13] The tension between the economic position of the peasantry and revolutionary political consciousness generated a unique landscape for the formation of a political proletariat—the redistribution of land became the political moment for the political mobilization of the peasantry, their participation in the construction of the soviet base areas, their learning of self-administration and their formation into organizations under the leadership of the party. The People's War served to educate and train the people, and it forged an organic relationship between the party and the people. The movements for literacy, cooperation in production, social organization, overturning patriarchy, freedom of marriage, the cultivation of hygienic habits, neighborhood relations, relationships between the masses and cadres—all of these were the new values and quotidian forms of a new mode of collective living, and they entered into people's daily lives and political consciousnesses during the process of the People's War and land reform.

Marx imagined that proletarian dictatorship would imply a state of war between the proletariat and the capitalist class, and yet he did not consider that this would take the form of a People's War unfolding in rural conditions. The form of military struggle, the asymmetrical balance of forces, the sharpening of conflict between oneself and the enemy, the modifications of the concept of class in the transformation of the political attributes of the revolutionary subject, the level of education and training of the cadres and soldiers of the Red Army, the absence of a timely means of communication and transmission, the problems of sectarianism and the military method of work arising from the direct amalgamation of military force and internal party struggles, the influence of the Stalin-era purges on the Chinese Communist Party, and the lack of a strict system of democratic supervision and a tradition of law inside the party all led the early Red Army and the Communist Party to commit severe political errors resulting in violent tragedies. The most famous and brutal of these included repressing the Anti-Bolshevik

Clique between 1930 and 1932 in the Jiangxi Soviet era, the 1931 movement to eliminate the "social democratic party" in the Minxi base area, and the whole purge movement that extended up to 1935. During the Yan'an period, the party, taking account of these experiences, sought to reduce mistaken accusations, and yet even in the period following the formation of New China, under conditions of relative peace within China, mistaken accusations resulting from conditions formed by intraparty struggle and the over-extension of the concept of class continued to occur: in the 1950s, the case of the Hu Feng Counter-Revolutionary Clique, the Anti-Party Clique of Gao Gang and Rao Shushi, the expansion of the Anti-Rightist Campaign, the Anti-Party Clique of Peng Dehuai, Huang Kecheng, Zhang Wentian, and Zhou Xiaozhou, and then, in the 1960s, the overthrow of Liu Shaoqi, Deng Xiaoping, and Tao Zhu, together with the early-1950s excesses committed in the course of the Campaign to Repress Counter-Revolutionaries, and the mistaken accusations that were committed subsequently at different levels across the whole country. All of these testify to the real need to carry out a reexamination of the practice of proletarian dictatorship and people's democratic dictatorship.

How then should one go about evaluating the historical experience of proletarian dictatorship? In 1956, when New China had been in existence for less than seven years, Khrushchev made his famous report "On the Cult of Personality and Its Consequences" at the twentieth Congress of the Communist Party of the Soviet Union. In the same year, Mao Zedong, who on many occasions led the Politburo in the discussion of questions raised by the Khrushchev report, published, with the *People's Daily* Editorial Committee, two articles that evoked strong responses: "On the Historical Experience of the Dictatorship of the Proletariat" and "More on the Historical Experience of the Dictatorship of the Proletariat." Mao Zedong and the party leadership analyzed Stalin's mistakes with regard to the expansion of the purges, the lack of awareness vis-à-vis the threat of German invasion, and his ignoring the interests of the peasants and the international communist movement, arguing that "on these issues, Stalin fell victim to subjectivism and one-sidedness, and divorced himself from objective reality and from the masses" (*People's Daily* Editorial Committee 1959: 9) and that he "impaired to a certain extent the principle of democratic centralism both in the life of the Party and in the state system of the Soviet Union" (33). We should note that, although Mao and his comrades criticized Stalin, at no point did they follow Kautsky and Luxemburg in appealing to elements of formal democracy arising from the experience of the European bourgeois revolutions, such as the electoral system or parliamentary democracy. Instead, they returned to the "mass line" that had been posed in the context of the People's War and sought to understand the problem of democracy under the conditions of proletarian dictatorship. In "On the Historical Experience of the Dictatorship of the Proletariat," the authors described the decision taken at the meeting of the Central Committee concerning methods of party leadership in June of 1943, in which it was argued that "in all practical work of our Party, correct leadership can only be developed on the principle of 'from the masses, to the masses'" (13). This means, after careful study, coordinating and systematizing the scattered and unsystematic views of the masses and then taking the resulting ideas back to the masses for them to test in practice. Departing from the masses makes it easy to commit errors of dogmatism, and the error of expanding the purges in the base areas of the Red Army over the period 1927–36 were the consequences of errors of exactly this type.

In addition to the destruction of the system of democratic centralism and departure from the masses, a further error on the part of Stalin was in taking the "middle forces" rather than the chief enemy as the primary target of attack (*People's Daily* Editorial Committee 1959: 15). During the civil war from 1927 to 1936, the authors note, some comrades crudely applied Stalin's formula to the Chinese Revolution and attacked the middle forces as the primary enemy. In response to this error, the Central Committee of the Chinese Communist Party formulated a policy of "developing the progressive-forces, winning over the middle-of the-roaders, and isolating the die-hards." The progressive forces in question consisted of the workers, peasants, and revolutionary intellectuals; the middle forces included the national bourgeoisie, the democratic parties, and democrats without party affiliation; and the die-hards were the comprador-feudal forces led by Chiang Kai-shek (16).

This discussion concerning the middle forces also related to the question of how to distinguish between two different types of contradiction. One type of contradiction poses the relationship between enemies, including that between antagonistic classes and between imperialists and the oppressed nations of the world. The other type of contradiction refers to differences among various sectors of the people, among party comrades, and between the governments of socialist countries. The solution of this second type of contradiction must be subordinated to the overall interests of the struggle against the enemy: "In a word, anyone who adopts the standpoint of the people should not equate the contradictions among the people with contradictions between the enemy and ourselves, or confuse these two types of contradiction, let alone place the contradictions among the people above the contradictions between the enemy and ourselves" (*People's Daily* Editorial Committee 1959: 26). Yet even if this question was clearly understood in theoretical terms, socialist China committed various kinds of mistakes in the actual practice of distinguishing the two kinds of contradiction, including the anti-rightist movement of 1957 and the whole period of struggle against "power-holders taking the capitalist road" in the 1960s and 1970s, which exhibited the phenomenon of expanding the scope of violence.

When the socialist state was created, and when the governing position and monopoly on power of the revolutionary party became a fundamental feature of politics, there emerged two groups of problems. The first regarded how to manage the relationship between the leadership position of the political party of the proletariat via-à-vis the legislative and executive mechanisms of the state. As Max Weber observed, in a historical period in which the division of labor has developed to a definite level, no political form can definitively escape the constraints of the bureaucratic system. Simply to point out that the socialist state preserved the bureaucratic form of the state, then, does not possess much depth of analysis. The fundamental question is this: How can a revolutionary party that styles itself as the leader of the masses avoid the problem of its own bureaucratization? And furthermore, how can the state be transformed into a political form that engenders the conditions for its own negation and becomes a vehicle of democratic participation? Lenin himself asserted the importance of maintaining a strict separation between the Bolshevik party and the Soviet state, and, similarly, Mao (1938) noted that a distinction must be maintained between class dictatorship and the dictatorship of the party, that the party should not and cannot enact dictatorship on behalf of the class. Yet the socialist state, did, in the end, develop into a unique party-state, in which "all fundamental directions, policies and plans must receive the unified decision of the party centre" (Mao [1952] 2004). The "stratification" of the governing party led, on the one hand, to the concentration of power in the hands of the governing party and, on the other hand, to the growing alienation of the party from the masses. Following the change in the role of the party, the socialist state system became ossified, and the self-negation of the state anticipated by Marx almost disappeared into oblivion.

The "Great Proletarian Cultural Revolution" was a response to this stratification of the governing party. The revival of social mobilization, the activation of a political realm and political value beyond the constraints of the party-state, and the formation of a system of mass democratic participation comprised specific features of the Cultural Revolution during its early stages. Mao Zedong attempted to break the absolute power of the state and governing party by means of social movements and political debate, with the aim to form a social system that contained the potential for the self-negation of the state and the governing party. In the early stages of the Cultural Revolution, there emerged, for a brief period, and in many different locales, schools, and factories, social experiments in self-governing organization (including those later instances of social organization named the "three representative committees," consisting of worker representative committees, peasant representative committees, and army representative committees). These experiments took the Paris Commune as their model and comprised experimental attempts to transform the old state apparatus and transcend the state apparatus itself. They contained various elements of a commune movement, as when workers, peasants, and soldiers were elected to serve at various levels and within leadership organs of the party and the state, as well as the requirement that each party member and state officials periodically enter factories and the villages in order to expose themselves to social practice. Despite the fact that these workers, peasants, students, and soldier representatives had no means by which to respond to the demands of the state-party system, and so ultimately came to be pushed to the margins of power,[14] the challenges and forms of reimagining posed to the state during this period were very significant.

A second group of problems that the socialist state needed to resolve was the relationship among the governing party, the socialist government, and the economy. The meaning of proletarian dictatorship does not consist in passing political power from one group to another, but, rather, a total transformation of the relations of production. This problem has often been simplified in terms of an opposition between a market and a planned economy, but its nucleus lies in the relationship between the economic and the political. The state of proletarian dictatorship, in other words, is not a political form divorced from economic relations but, instead, a translational form of state created on the basis of a fundamental social revolution. When explaining the phenomenon of the bureaucratic system within the socialist state, many link the bureaucratization of the Communist Party and the state to the problem of economic management. In this regard, Mao Zedong and the editorial committee of the *People's Daily* addressed in 1956 whether Stalin's mistakes were due to the fact that the political system of the Soviet Union could not meet the needs of economic development. Their response was that Soviet economic development showed that Stalin's errors did not originate in the socialist system or in the fact of state administration of economic affairs. Adjustments had to be made to the socialist economy, but fundamental changes were not necessary (*People's Daily* Editorial Committee 1959: 35). In 1962, when the Sino-Soviet Split was coming into the open, Mao ([1962] 1978) reminded the whole party: "our country, if it does not found a socialist economy, then what kind of situation would this be? We would transform into a revisionist country, we would actually transform into a capitalist country, the dictatorship of the proletariat would transform into the dictatorship of the bourgeoisie, and this would be a reactionary, fascist dictatorship." It is impossible to conceive of a "proletarian dictatorship" or a "socialist state" that is divorced from the process of constructing a socialist economy. From this perspective, the failure of socialist states can be traced back to the point when, within socialist states, the economic system became separated from the political form. When the working class is restricted to the economic realm, its members considered only as laborers, and does not have control of political decision-making, then claims that the working class has a leadership role in politics, as well as claims of a people's democracy, are completely hollowed out.

Lessons of the Past

In contemporary intellectual discourse, the debates between the Left and liberals concerning the failure of socialism in the twentieth century revolve around three poles: the party, the state, and the economy. With respect to the seizure and solidification of political power, the party demonstrated great strength but lost its ability to construct a transitional state. With respect to the development of the economy, the socialist state has some formidable accomplishments (although by no means in all cases), and yet it made constant concessions with regard to the negation of the system of private ownership. Following the failure of the planned economy, the market economy has once again come to occupy a central position in Russia, China, and other countries, and as a result the state has been reestablished as a controlling mechanism that is separated from civil society. These developments signify a radical departure from the summary posed by the authors of "More on the Historical Experience of the Dictatorship of the Proletariat" with regard to the experience of the October Revolution. In the perspective of this important document, the governing party, political power, proletarian dictatorship, the nationalization of industry and collectivization of agriculture, the planned development of a socialist economy and a socialist culture, the upholding of the principles of socialist internationalism—all of these and more are key achievements of the October Revolution. The historical conjuncture of 1956 is very different from that of today, and yet, it also cannot be denied: Mao and his comrades—while recognizing the setbacks and lessons of the experience of socialism in the Soviet Union, and seeing clearly the serious errors committed by the party and the state in the course of the socialist movement—never attributed these problems to the form of the party and the form of the state. From the beginning they considered the socialist state a transitional form aimed toward its own negation. They thus focused instead on the political line and the strategies of the party and the state, maintaining the logic of the state's self-negation while, at the same time, fighting for their immediate objectives. That is why they mobilized people to struggle against "bourgeois tendencies within the party." In working through the experience of the Chinese Revolution in order to consider the problems of "proletarian dictatorship" and the "socialist state," Mao sought to elucidate the strategy of armed struggle, the direction of the mass line, the policy of the United Front, the method of building the party, the dialectical method of distinguishing different kinds of contradictions, unified politics, methods of economic and cultural struggle, and so on. However, the failure of the Cultural Revolution marked the beginning of the end of the entire long process of revolution in twentieth-century China.

Communism not only constitutes a philosophical hypothesis but also possesses a rich body of experience that still has the capacity to inspire. The search for a socialism of the twenty-first century not only should, but indeed must, learn from the experiences of the Russian Revolution, the Chinese Revolution, and other people's revolutions of the Third World so that, following the revolutionaries of those eras, we might not only consider the principles of revolution but also, according to the concrete conditions of individual countries, carry out a summation of the theoretical and historical lessons of the past. Indeed, this is not in order to return to the past but to aspire toward the future—not an abstract movement toward the future, whereby our hands clutch at phantoms in the air, but rather a search for a new road that carries a body of rich experience and painful lessons in its confrontation with the present.

—Translated by Benjamin Joseph Kindler and Harlan David Chambers

Notes

Portions of this essay have appeared in Chinese as Wang Hui. 2008.《去政治化的政治》三联书店 (*Depoliticized Politics*). Beijing: Sanlian Bookstore and Wang Hui. 2015.《短二十世纪：中國革命與政治的邏輯》香港:牛津大学出版社 (*The Short Twentieth Century: The Chinese*

Revolution and the Logic of Politics). Hong Kong: Oxford University Press. Those publications have, in turn, also been published in English elsewhere, in Wang Hui. 2016. *China's Twentieth Century: Revolution, Retreat and the Road to Equality*. Edited by Saul Thomas. London: Verso and *The Politics of Imagining Asia*. 2011. Edited by Theodore Huters. Cambridge, MA: Harvard.

The translators would like to thank Rebecca Karl, Michael Hardt, and Wang Hui for making this opportunity available. They also extend their individual thanks to Zhen Zhang for his assistance with Russian citations and to Chen Yedong and Minh Ha Nguyen for some individual translation queries.

1   [Trans.] Wang Hui refers here to an influential book published by the liberal intellectuals Liu Zehou and Liu Zaifu (1996) in which the authors sought to demarcate the present from the revolutionary legacy.

2   See Filatov 1995. This article draws on the Chinese translation, Filatov and Volobuev 1997.

3   This article cites the Chinese translation of a recorded interview by E. Bushuyev, editor of the history section in the Soviet publication *Communists*, with Indiana University Professor and Vice Chair of the International Committee on the History of the October Revolution Alexander Rabinowitch. It was published in 1990 in *Communists*, issue no. 16.

4   This is the view of University of Luhansk professor Anatolii Ivanovich Fomin, from "Reflections on the Major Incidents of the Revolutionary Period," published in Russia's *Free Thinking* magazine in issue no. 10, as well as drawn from *The "October" Choice* cited in note 2.

5   This is an original quotation by Lenin, but the author used it to advance his own argument. See Fomin 1997: 352.

6   Lenin ([1960] 1977g: 31:439) had already said: "Brest-Litovsk was significant in being the first time that we were able, on an immense scale and amidst vast difficulties, to take advantage of the contradictions among the imperialists in such a way as to make socialism the ultimate gainer."

7   Official statistics from 1889 show that various "dues and obligations" comprised 70 percent of the net income of a typical peasant household and that they totaled more than twice the net cash income of the peasantry; "the corvee payments due under the serf system were not necessarily this high." Bankrupt peasants, even when they wanted to abandon their land, also had to pay a special "quit rent" fee on the land.

8   For a discussion of Russian agrarian reform, see Lü 2004: 143–215.

9   Lenin's "Agrarian Program of Social-Democracy in the First Russian Revolution, 1905–1907" was written during November and December of 1907 and printed in St. Petersburg in 1908 but was not published because it was confiscated and destroyed by the czarist secret police. Only one copy, lacking a conclusion, survived. In September of 1917, it was published as a single volume, with the addition of a conclusion. In summer 1908, however, Lenin, acting as an author, responded at the invitation of the Polish Social-Democrat Party and published a summary introduction in the Polish journal *Kritika*. See Collective of the Marxist-Leninist Academy of the Central Committee of the Communist Party of the Soviet Union 1960: 204.

10 According to Lenin ([1960] 1977f: 20:407), the problem of Asia was closely bound up with the nation-state. He said that in Asia "the conditions for the most complete development of commodity production and the freest, widest and speediest growth of

capitalism have been created only in Japan, i.e., only in an independent national state? [Japan] is a bourgeois state, and for that reason has itself begun to oppress other nations and to enslave colonies."

11   The perspectives of Russian intellectuals on Europe and Asia were clearly influenced by contemporary political developments in Western Europe as well as the Enlightenment view of history. In Lenin's usage, Asia, as a concept closely linked to absolutism, is derived from the political and historical perspectives of contemporary Europe. Concerning the debate between Slavophiles and Westernizers, see Berdyaev 1995: 1–70.

12   [Trans.] Red political power here refers to Mao's understanding of the base areas established in Jiangxi during the late 1920s as part of the Communist Party's early efforts in rural mobilization. For a discussion of the conditions that enabled the formation of these base areas and the policies pursued therein, see Mao 1928.

13   [Trans.] The First Great Revolution here refers to the period 1925–27, during which the Chinese Communist Party formed its first alliance with the Nationalists and had a primarily urban base of operations. The eruption of the White Terror in April 1927 signaled the end of this urban period and largely severed the direct links between the party and the urban working class.

14   As a backlash against this phenomenon, in the late 1960s in certain locales (for example, Wuhan) there appeared a mass "movement against a return to the old order," which took the implementation of the "three combinations" as their demand—this "opposition to a return to the old order" meant opposing a return of the revolutionary committees to the party-state bureaucratic system.

References

Badiou, Alain. 2008. "The Communist Hypothesis." *New Left Review*, no. 49: 29–46.

Badiou, Alain. 2010. *The Communist Hypothesis*. Translated by David Macey and Steve Corcoran. London: Verso.

Berdyaev, Nikolai. 1995. *Russian Thought*. [In Chinese.] Translated by Lei Yongsheng and Qiu Shoujuan. Beijing: Sanlian.

Collective of the Marxist-Leninist Academy of the Central Committee of the Communist Party of the Soviet Union. 1960. *Biography of Lenin*. [In Chinese.] Vol. 1. Beijing: Sanlian.

Borodin, E. T. 1997. "What Happened in My Country in 1917?" [In Chinese.] In *The "October" Choice: 90's Discussion of the October Revolution by Scholars Abroad*, edited by Liu Shuchun, Zhai Mingang, and Wang Lihua, 129–47. Beijing: Central Compilation and Translation.

Bushuyev, B., and Alexander Rabinowitch. 1997. "Russia of Autumn 1917." [In Chinese]. In *The "October" Choice: 90's Discussion of the October Revolution by Scholars Abroad*, edited by Liu Shuchun, Zhai Mingang, and Wang Lihua, 20–32. Beijing: Central Compilation and Translation.

Engels, Frederick. (1940) 1962. Introduction to *The Civil War in France*, by Karl Marx. New York: International.

Filatov, Sergei Aleksandrov. 1995. "October of 1917 and Russia's Bolshevik Experiment." [In Chinese.] In *The "October" Choice: 90's Discussion of the October Revolution by Scholars Abroad*, edited by Liu Shuchun, Zhai Mingang, and Wang Lihua, 304–13. Beijing: Central Compilation and Translation.

Filatov, Sergei Aleksandrov, and P. V. Volobuev. 1997. "Regarding Debates on the Bolshevik Experiment." [In Chinese]. *The "October" Choice: 90's Discussion of the October Revolution by Scholars Abroad*, edited by Liu Shuchun, Zhai Mingang, and Wang Lihua, 304–13. Beijing: Central Compilation and Translation.

Fomin, Anatolii Ivanovich. 1997. "Reflections on the Major Incidents of the Revolutionary Period." [In Chinese]. *The "October" Choice: 90's Discussion of the October Revolution by Scholars Abroad*, edited by Liu Shuchun, Zhai Mingang, and Wang Lihua, 345–68. Beijing: Central Compilation and Translation.

Kautsky, Karl. (1920) 1973. *Terrorism and Communism: A Contribution to the Natural History of Revolution*. Translated by W. H. Kerridge. Westport, CT: Hyperion.

Lenin, Vladimir I. (1960) 1977a. "Agrarian Programme of Social Democracy." Vol. 13. *V. I. Lenin: Collected Works*. Moscow: Progress.

Lenin, Vladimir I. (1960) 1977b. "Backwards Europe and Advanced Asia." Vol. 19. *V. I. Lenin: Collected Works*. Moscow: Progress.

Lenin, Vladimir I. (1960) 1977c. "Declaration of Rights of the Toiling and Exploited People." Vol. 26. *V. I. Lenin: Collected Works*. Moscow: Progress.

Lenin, Vladimir I. (1960) 1977d. "Democracy and Narodism in China." Vol. 18. *V. I. Lenin: Collected Works*. Moscow: Progress.

Lenin, Vladimir I. (1960) 1977e. "Draft Theses on National and Colonial Questions." Vol. 31. *V. I. Lenin: Collected Works*. Moscow: Progress.

Lenin, Vladimir I. (1960) 1977f. "The Right of Nations to Self-Determination." Vol. 20. *V. I. Lenin: Collected* Works. Moscow: Progress.

Lenin, Vladimir I. (1960) 1977g. "Speech Delivered at a Meeting of Activists of the Moscow Organization of the R. C. P. (B.)." Vol. 31. *V. I. Lenin: Collected Works*. Moscow: Progress.

Lenin, Vladimir I. (1960) 1977h. "The Struggle of Parties in China." Vol. 41. *V. I. Lenin: Collected Works*. Moscow: Progress.

Lenin, Vladimir I. (1960) 1977i. "Two Tactics of Social-Democracy in the Democratic Revolution." Vol. 9. *V. I. Lenin: Collected Works*. Moscow: Progress.

Liu, Shaoqi (Liu Shao-ch'i). (1952) 1982. "On the Intra-Party Struggle." In *Mao's China: Party Reform Documents, 1942–1944*. Translated by Boyd Compton. Westport, CT: University of Washington Press.

Liu Shipei. (1908) 2016. "Anarchist Revolution and Agrarian Revolution." [In Chinese.] *Natural Justice-Equity*. Vol. 2, edited by Wan Shiguo and Liu He. Beijing: People's University.

Liu Zehou, and Liu Zaifu. 1996. *Farewell to Revolution (Gaobie Geming)*. Hong Kong: Cosmos Books Ltd.

Lü Xinyu. 2004. "Agricultural Capitalism and the Modernization of the Nation State." [In Chinese.] *Shijie (Horizon)*, no. 13: 143–215.

Luxemburg, Rosa. (1961) 1972. *The Russian Revolution and Leninism or Marxism?* Ann Arbor: University of Michigan Press.

Mao Zedong. 1928. "Why Is It That Red Political Power Can Exist in China?" In *Selected Works of Mao Tse-Tung*. Maoist Documentation Project. www.marxists.org/reference /archive/mao/selected-works/volume-1/mswv1_3.htm.

Mao Zedong. 1938. "A Chat with Qi Guang, Reporter with Yan'an Xinhua Daily." [In Chinese]. *Jiefang (Liberation Newspaper)*, February 2.

Mao Zedong. (1952) 2004. 'The Leadership Responsibilities of the Party toward Government Work." [In Chinese.] *Collected Works of Mao Zedong.* Vol. 6. Beijing: People's Press.

Mao Zedong. (1962) 1978. "Talk at the Lecture Central Work Meeting." [In Chinese.] *Renmin Ribao (People's Daily)*, July 1.

Marx, Karl. (1940) 1962. *The Civil War in France.* New York: International.

People's Daily Editorial Committee. 1959. *The Historical Experience of the Dictatorship of the Proletariat.* Peking: Foreign Languages Press.

Sun Yat-sen. 1981. "Zhonghua Minguo linshi da zongtong xuanyan shu" ("Declaration of the Temporary President of the Republic of China"). Vol. 2. *Sun Zhongshan quanji (Collected Works of Sun Yat-sen).* Beijing: Zhonghua shuju.

Giso Amendola

The Abolition of Law or Law of the Common(s)?
Pashukanis and the Revolution

After exploring numerous historical examples of grassroots production of the "common" and autonomous spaces independent of private property and exploitation, Pierre Dardot and Christian Laval conclude their book *Commun* (2014) with a *postscriptum* that questions the current relevance of revolution. Neoliberal reason has excluded everything that can be considered revolution—in other words, the radical transformation of the present in its totality—from the field of political thought. Yet neoliberal reason itself constitutes a totality that organizes, or purports to organize, the whole of the social. The radical transformation of the social and not only the political order must therefore be recognized as the ultimate goal of any struggle against neoliberalism. A book that provides a resolute defense of the continued relevance of the mutualist-associative and federalist traditions ends therefore with a reflection on revolution and on the need to retain the concept. The synthesis between the mutualist tradition and the revolutionary option is found in the idea, inspired by Cornelius Castoriadis (1987), of revolution as a self-instituent practice of society. It is significant that the languages of instituent practices and revolution are reconciled here: revolution is a radical

The South Atlantic Quarterly 116:4, October 2017
DOI 10.1215/00382876-4234961 © 2017 Duke University Press

transformation of the whole of society, but at the same time it is the production of singular institutions in the present. This copresence, within the development of an oppositional strategy to neoliberalism that seeks to generalize experiences and inquiries that have arisen from the movement of commons, is certainly not easy or without problems.

On the one hand, the revolutionary perspective persists, while, on the other, the idea of instigating change within neoliberalism itself has taken hold, albeit with a view to its radical transformation. As Sandro Mezzadra and Brett Neilson (2014: 780) have written, the "abolition of the present state of things"—citing a definition of *communism* by Marx and Engels—insists on the present time of transformation, thus averting the risk that communism is embraced as a regulative ideal, which remains an ever-unreachable point on the horizon. Nevertheless, this act of abolition continues to indicate an essentially negative activity. The affirmative moment of the production of commons that is brought about by instituent practices, for its part, risks being weakened: for although such micropolitics operates in the present and certainly does not hold off for a future "horizon of expectation," it forgoes focusing attention on the diverse but nevertheless all-encompassing theme of exploitation.

The communist question is reproposed today in a diverse spectrum of practices and *dispositifs* that range from the production of *commons* to the affirmation of the *common* in the singular, from the invention of new institutions to revolution, but also, from a temporal point of view, they are situated between transformation in the present and the horizon of expectation. Alongside the heterogeneity of the *dispositifs* of exploitation and extraction sits the corresponding heterogeneity of struggles, practices of resistance, and production of commons, a heterogeneity that is already an essential characteristic of the subjectivities engaged in these practices. Radical transformation, the construction of effective power, and the production of critical mass need continually to come to terms with this constitutive heterogeneity, which makes it difficult to imagine radical transformation according to the classic tenets of revolution. On this note, Gilles Deleuze's caustic remark that the "future of revolution" is not at all the same as the actual "revolutionary becoming" (Deleuze and Parnet 2002: 2) still holds true. On the other hand, by eliminating the question of revolution, micropolitical, interstitial, and "light" practices run the risk of being rapidly mobilized by neoliberal *dispositifs* or, in the least, of establishing acts of resistance on merely defensive and neocommunitarian grounds that are illusorily conceived to be outside the relation of capital.

Besides the difficult relations between practices and totality, between singularity and the common, and between micropolitics and the construction of power, the practices of building commons and producing institutions, or the self-institutionalization of society, also raise the specific problem of the relation with forms of legal regulation. These plural and heterogeneous practices often use the languages and instruments of law and rights. They are obviously able to do this either instrumentally or tactically: they can use the law within specific struggles and use it as it is used daily in the management of one's own affairs. The instituent practices and the production of commons have, however, also a more narrow/intimate and problematic relationship with law. Law is used as a specific instrument for the production of commons and, as such, is considered part of the instituent practices themselves. The production of commons can be imagined as a means to produce another, if not an alternative, law to the institutionally recognized sources. The production of institutions, the liberation of spaces from private property, the creation of places, moments and procedures of collective bottom-up decision making—such practices, which have characterized social movements especially since 2011 and the Occupy movement, have been interpreted as instituent *social* practices and, at the same time, as sources of an alternative legality, independent from the public monopoly of the sources of production of law. From the production of common goods would be reborn a true *law of the commons*, as would, in the long run, an all-encompassing, alternative legal practice, a *law of the common*. As Sandro Chignola (2012: 7–8) has written, "If the criticism of law was at one time simply the criticism of the hypocrisy with which the legal system concealed the domination of the State, as this emphasis has since faded . . . , law can be appropriated, traversed and used as part of a more general project for the transformation of reality."

Is it, however, possible to imagine a legal form so supple and versatile as to become instrumental also for a process of radical transformation? Just as the relationship between the production of commons and radical transformation based on the common still requires clarification, the relation between another alternative legal production to the State and revolution is also very problematic. The question of the law of the common and revolution raises some classic Marxist themes, starting, clearly, from that of "transition from socialism to communism." One classical way of thinking of these problematic issues through the trajectories of a possible law of the common could be to reconsider one of the most dramatic confrontations between legal theory and revolution: the question of the abolition or extinction of law that was addressed in the 1920s by the Soviet legal scholar Evgeny Pashukanis, whose reflection focused precisely on the relation between legal form, transition, and communism. Had the October Revolution produced a new form of law, or had it introduced new class relations into old forms that allowed for a revolutionary use of the law? Moreover, could the revolution be interpreted as the foundation of a proletarian State?

Beyond the Critique of Law as a Critique of Ideology

Current interest in Pashukanis's general theory of law resides in the fact that it represents an example of a materialist critique of law, which refutes the critique of law as just ideology or superstructure.[1] Law is not a mystification that conceals authentic power relations, nor is it a *false* normative form that encompasses an *authentic* factual content. In other words, it is not the mystification of formal equality in the abstract norm of a specific concrete content that is to be found in the domination of the bourgeois class. Abstraction for Pashukanis is not the falsification of concrete truth. From the perspective of method, he pursues a rigorously Marxian approach: abstraction is an indispensable instrument for the understanding of things (Pashukanis 2002: 66). This is, however, an abstraction that, in turn, is rendered possible by precise historical circumstances: a *determinate abstraction* allows one to know the concrete, but it is in turn produced by material conditions that constitute the premise. It is necessary to proceed from the most basic abstraction to the most complex one: the most basic abstraction, however, is not a given, but the product of necessary material conditions that make it possible (67). In terms of method, Pashukanis moves perfectly within the instruments of the Marxian critique of political economy. Rather than considering concepts as abstractions to be eliminated by shifting analysis to an alleged empirical concreteness, Pashukanis considers conceptual abstraction the principle that allows for the analysis of social phenomena. The same abstraction, however, must be reconnected to the historical material conditions that produce it. The concept of labor in general is clearly an abstraction, but it is an indispensable abstraction because only labor in general—labor as an economic abstraction—can explain the historical reality of the concrete and determinate forms of labor (67). In turn, however, labor in general is a concept that develops exclusively thanks to industrial production, which made labor homogenous as a means of production, allowed its measurement, and rendered the specific and qualitative differences between the different concrete types of labor irrelevant. Finally, and still entirely within the Marxian method, Pashukanis reminds us how concepts such as determinate abstractions, while chronologically taking shape in an advanced phase of historical development, can be used to explain previous stages. So if one wants to understand tithes and feudal tributes, it is necessary to possess the concept of land rent. Bourgeois society develops concepts with which it is possible to understand the relations of production of past societies; from a Marxian perspective, the anatomy of the human explains that of the ape.

The Marxian method of determinate abstraction is at the heart of Pashukanis's general theory of law: *law* is the relation between legal subjects. Pashukanis, in fact, offers a formal definition of *law*: it is the (abstract) relation between legal subjects, which are themselves a product of abstraction. In turn, however, abstraction is a determinate abstraction: the legal form—the relation between legal subjects—is produced by specific relations of production. The relation between subjects is the legal form produced by the economy of commodities founded on free commodity exchange. The legal subject, in turn, is the owner of commodities, endowed with his or her freedom, first and foremost the freedom of contract. Pashukanis does not linearly derive the legal superstructure from the economic structure, nor does he consider the former to be an ideological deformation that conceals the material relations that are expressed in the structure. The *commodity exchange theory of law* instead underlines the structural analogy between commodity-capitalist society and the legal form.[2] The former is the circulation of commodities, and the commodity is the form of exchange value, an abstraction with respect to the particularity of use value. The latter, the legal form, is the constitution of the abstract subject of law and of the relation of (formal and abstract) equality between these subjects. The reference to the form is not only necessary to unmask bourgeois ideology: it is also needed, as Pashukanis writes, "to throw light on the fundamental characteristics of the legal superstructure as an objective phenomenon" (40). Following straight on from this, Pashukanis adds: "The principle of legal subjectivity (which we take to mean the formal principle of freedom and equality, the autonomy of the personality, and so forth) is not only an instrument of deceit and a product of the hypocrisy of the bourgeoisie, insofar as it used to counter the proletarian struggle to abolish classes, but is at the same time a concretely effective principle which is embodied in bourgeois society from the moment it emerges from and destroys feudal-patriarchal society" (40).

The subject is an abstraction: but a determinate abstraction is an abstraction that has an effectively functioning, constitutive force. The legal subject is the principal abstraction: the "person" is the center of relations in the field of private law, and it is an abstract construction that is possible only because, in the specific relation of production that is the commodity-capitalist economy, the individual is characterized as an owner of commodities.

These fictions consent to free relations based on the free will to contract: as such, the legal form is established as analogous to the commodity fetishism that characterizes the society of exchange. Yet just as commodity fetishism is not a distortion, a falsehood, or an ideological corruption, but instead reflects the specific commodity-form that characterizes capitalist society, so in turn the legal form is the specific form of the social regulation in this determined relation of production.

Pashukanis's position in relation to much of the legal tradition, as well as to much of the critique of law that in any case is connected reverts back to this tradition, is characterized very clearly by a definite relativization of the role of legal coercion, of command, and of the State. As Antonio Negri (2012: 221) notes, the imbalance between the moment of the organization of exploitation and the moment of command in Pashukanis would appear to be, on first sight, clear. The marginalization of public law, and the respective elevation of private law to the center of the legal experience, is clearly the consequence of this absolute privilege for the horizontal moment in the construction of legal form. For Pashukanis, the moment in which formal equality is established is central, as is the contractual relation between equal free wills, as a form of exploitation. This is not, however, a defense of bourgeois society. The logic of the relation between equals is not ideology because it is the real function or effective *dispositif*, but it is, nevertheless, the logic that produces the exploitation of one class over another. Pashukanis does not downplay exploitation: however, he sees it deriving directly from the legal form of equality between legal subjects, rather than from the content of class that the legal form is called on to protect. Pashukanis does not privilege the form of equality over the concreteness of command because, according to Karl Korsch's (2002) malicious reading, he is interested more in the reformist regulation of circulation than in entering into the laboratories of production from a Marxian perspective. His entire discussion is a critique of bourgeois regulation and of the legal form that makes this possible. His aim, however, is to demonstrate how exploitation emerges directly and principally from the legal form of equality: and here commodity-exchange theory is effectively the real parallel, in the field of legal theory, to the Marxian critique of political economy. The commodity is an abstraction, while the legal subject is the abstraction coined in parallel to the figure of the owner of commodities: but the specificity of the commodity labor power, of its establishment as such, and the mechanism of the extraction of surplus value enter very marginally into Pashukanis's theory. The focus of his analysis is how commodity fetishism is reflected in the legal relation between owners of commodities, much more than the buying and selling of labor power and its direct effect of exploitation.[3]

Although the command over labor power has a marginal role, it is nevertheless the case that for Pashukanis the legal form—the relation between formally equal subjects—contains itself the secret of exploitation. The secret is in the form and not in the content of class: not because the materiality of the class content of law does not matter, but, on the contrary, because class exploitation already exists entirely within the legal form that is specific to capitalist market society. Exploitation emerges in the legal form of the equivalent, in the apparently formal balance of the legal relation. The consequence of this formalism—which is in fact not very formal at all because it is itself the engine of exploitation—is clear: law is not a neutral instrument (already due to its form and not for its contingent content) with respect to class conflict. It is not possible, therefore, to eliminate its class content and make it function as an instrument of other relations of material forces. There is no proletarian law: law is, already in its form, bourgeois and cannot be made functional for anything else (Pashukanis 2002: 61).

The consequences of the analysis of the relation between law, revolution, and transition are now clear: if law is indissolubly tied, in its form, to mercantile-capitalist society, then revolution, by destroying the relations of capitalist production, can only lead to the abolition of law. By destroying the exchange of equivalents, there is no longer a legal form, which is the form of the exchange of equivalents. The revolution brings about the extinction of law and not a revolutionary law: and until it is abolished, law will be nothing else but the regulation of exchange and, therefore, bourgeois formal law.

No Law Is Proletarian

The object of Pashukanis's polemic is very clear: the idea of a "proletarian law" that is established during the phase of transition. The legal form as a specific form of capitalist society based on commodity exchange cannot be maintained by using it as a neutral instrument for the organization of the abolition of exploitation, because exploitation is itself intrinsic to this form. Pashukanis therefore adopts a position that is clearly anti-legal: the struggle for transformation is always a struggle against the legal form. It is inevitable that the legal form persists, even for an extended period: but this derives from the fact that the relations of exchange of equivalents nevertheless remain, or, to be more precise, a number of relations continue to conserve the form of an exchange of equivalents. What remains, therefore, is always bourgeois law: it is not a question of transforming bourgeois law into a new "proletarian" legal form.

Pashukanis refers to Marx's analysis in *Critique of the Gotha Program.* Let us imagine that the means of production already belong to the whole of society and that producers do not exchange their products: the relations of the market, in other words, have been fully replaced by the relations of organization. In such a situation, mercantile exchange is eliminated. Individual labor is no longer a part of overall labor in an indirect way through the law of value and the relation of exchange, but it is organized directly. In this case as well, as Pashukanis notes following Marx, the principle that dominated in the exchange of commodity equivalents, despite being completely transformed in form and content, continues to exist as the principle of distribution. As Pashukanis comments, citing once again *Critique of the Gotha Program*, every producer "receives back from society—after the deductions have been made—exactly what he gives to it." It is "the birthmarks of the old society" that cannot be eliminated in the new society, even after the elimination of mercantile exchange (Pashukanis 2002: 62). In order for this principle of distribution to be overcome once and for all, it is necessary to overcome for good the relation of equivalence, which has outlived the elimination of class divisions. In other terms, as Pashukanis emphasizes, labor must no longer be a means of subsistence. The relation of equivalence is overcome only when the productive forces grow together with the all-around development of the individual, when everyone works spontaneously according to his or her abilities, or—as Lenin puts it—when one will no longer be forced to "calculate with the heartlessness of a Shylock whether one has not worked half an hour more than somebody else" (63).

It is true that the abstraction of the legal form is the determinate abstraction that corresponds to a certain stage of relations of production: that of mercantile-capitalist society. Its form, however, even if in clear tension with the transformation both of the form and of the content of the principle of the exchange of equivalents, persists as long as the organization of labor conserves an analogous principle. The legal form that survives is not an "alternative" legal form: it is the only legal form thinkable, which gives shape to the exchange, even if it now finds itself having to survive after the removal of mercantile-capitalist exchange. Pashukanis's position is clearly and consciously "anti-legal": the insistence on the survival of bourgeois law in its legal form—bourgeois insofar as it is formal, indeed bourgeois precisely because it is law—seeks to avoid any idealistic attempt to eternalize the legal form and any possibility of thinking that the legal form can be filled with other contents and made to function outside of the capitalist relation. This argument is directed obviously against those who asserted the need for a proletarian law in the phase of the transition from socialism to communism; in other words, those who argued that if legal mediation is necessary, and as long as it is necessary, this can only be produced by the form inherited from the society of commodity exchange. These "revolutionaries" who think they need to construct a proletarian law are precisely those who fall into the worst form of legalism. They end up proclaiming "the immortality of the legal form, in that it strives to wrench this form from the particular historical conditions which had helped bring it to full fruition, and to present it as capable of permanent renewal" (61). The dispute with those Soviet legal scholars who strove for a proletarian legal science was inevitably extremely bitter: P. I. Stuchka (1988: 223), who initially shared similar positions, ultimately claimed that Pashukanis overestimated the bourgeois legal form and was essentially incapable of analyzing the material, class contents that determined the legal system (Beirne and Sharlet 1980: 20–23). A. J. Vyshinsky (1954: 53–57; Beirne and Sharlet 1980: 34–37) was far more severe in judgment, accusing Pashukanis of having betrayed the revolution, of being an apologist of bourgeois law, and of having reduced all law to private law (a criticism that, significantly, was similar to one made by Hans Kelsen). Furthermore, according to Vyshinsky, Pashukanis rejected the possibility of constructing a new Soviet law and instead reduced the law of the Soviet state to a simple expression of bare political force, denying it of its scientific autonomy. Yet from Pashukanis's point of view, it was these positions that were precisely formalist: by lacking an analysis of the specificity of the form of bourgeois law, they ultimately considered law as a neutral form, adaptable to any class interest (Stuchka), or saw it as a complex of norms pliable to the will of any subject and usable for any political goal (Vyshinsky).

On the contrary, Pashukanis's position, precisely due to his rigorous attention to the specific material determination of the legal abstraction, inevitably identifies the law only and exclusively as the form of the exchange of equivalents. As long as there is some form of such an exchange, there will be law: bourgeois law, because there is no other law. The "law" of precapitalist societies is explained only as the first moment of the formation of the modern legal form, which then fully unfolds only in mercantile-capitalist society: since the human anatomy explains the anatomy of the ape, the legal form that develops in bourgeois capitalist society allows us to understand, for example, the legal form that appears, in its primordial state, in ancient Roman society. In the same way, the law "that comes after" mercantile-capitalist society is a residue, one that is increasingly unable "to veil and conceal the social relations from which it emanated" (Pashukanis 2002: 64). It is, in other words, a dying ideology, although, as we know, ideologies for Pashukanis are nevertheless concrete and determinate abstractions: even when they no longer coincide with the social relations that generated them, they conserve a real formative capacity. But in the transition, this formative capacity, precisely because it is analogous to the society of commodity exchange, as commodity-exchange theory explains, cannot be "used" for proletarian goals: it is a residue, a "birthmark" that cannot be eliminated straight away, but which certainly must not be consecrated. No new legal form needs to be created: the objective is only to accelerate, as far as possible, the abolition of the legal form in itself. As Pashukanis notes, "Marx conceives of the transition to developed communism not as a transition to new forms of law, but as a withering away of the legal form as such, as a liberation from that heritage of the bourgeois epoch which is fated to outlive the bourgeoisie itself" (63).

The abolition of law is therefore against what, by definition, are impossible, new forms of law. This clearly represents a very firm stand against any form of state socialism.[4] Moreover, one can detect, "in the watermark," as Negri writes, a criticism not only of state socialism but also of all theories of state monopoly capitalism. Interpreting law as a determinate abstraction connected to the same form of bourgeois exchange clearly confounds any attempt to use the legal form as an instrument for proletarian organization. In other words, the state is not something neutral that can be seized. Critique needs to understand it in its difficult relation with the moment of legal construction, but must also recognize that exploitation is in the legal form itself, without excluding the difficult relation between this form and the severe and "exceptional" violence of command. The organization of struggles needs to recognize that the State cannot be occupied and reused, as Lenin insisted in *State and Revolution*, a text that was obviously a key source for Pashukanis. On the contrary, the State needs to be abolished along with the entire legal form.

The Abolition of Law between the Administration of Things and Class Struggle

Pashukanis therefore clearly represents an antidote to an overly simple pacification between legal instruments and struggle: not "other forms of law," but the abolition of law. It is no coincidence that he has been recently reread as a means of reviving a radical stance with respect to the "legal routes" to struggles, by those who have wanted to warn against the risks for struggles being neutralized within a sort of new legal formalism or new institutionalism. More radically, he has been read as the antidote to every form of "legal Marxism," to every reconciliation between class struggle and legal form.[5] The radicalness of the "Pashukanis moment" has evidently many merits, namely, its decisive break with the worst syntheses of a socialist stamp between state, law, and the centralization of production. Moreover, the socialist state and its late-capitalist centralizing twin were the effective targets of Pashukanis's thought. If the clarity with which Pashukanis configures the transition as the moment of the abolition of the legal form, and not its conservation under false pretenses, has great critical force in opposing the statism and various forms of fetishism of law that also emerge within struggles, it is necessary nevertheless to analyze more closely what the process of abolition or extinction of law means for Pashukanis, how it happens, and what drives it. A critical analysis of Pashukanis's approach to understanding the abolition of law allows us in fact to rethink the idea of a clear-cut opposition between the "abolition of law" and the invention of "new forms of law." In other terms, in certain conditions the abolition of law does not entirely remove, as Pashukanis would wish, space for the imagination of new institutional forms. The "law of the common" might not be affected by Pashukanis's interdiction.

What does Pashukanis mean, then, by abolition of the law? Here the legal scholar's argument is less coherent: indeed, two very different conceptions, which are not easily reconcilable, appear to be confused.

A first conception sees the abolition of law as a linear consequence of the productive forces. Initially, as we have already seen, the legal form endures, because, even after the seizure of political power on the part of the proletariat, "so long as the task of building a unified planned economy has not been completed, so long as the market-dominated relationship between individual enterprises and groups of enterprises remains in existence, the legal form too will remain in force" (Pashukanis 2002: 131).

But this regulation of the relations through the legal form, or, in other words, through the survival of contractual instruments, ends with time, thanks to the advance of the organized planning of production and distribution and to its replacement by a different, technical-administrative system of regulation. Two tendencies, therefore, overlap for a period but in the end are resolved by the prevalence of the second. The contractual legal regulation, a parallel form to the circulation of commodities that has survived the disappearance of mercantile-capitalist society, is progressively replaced by a direct social regulation, which is not hidden behind the contractual form. The legal rule thus gives way, as Pashukanis argues, to "direct" prescriptions or, to be more precise, to technical directives that constitute an engineering-based and highly technocratic approach to planning possessing characteristics that today would be described unmistakably as "postpolitical."

Clearly, this description of the abolition of law in the technical-economic management of society betrays a degree of optimism and probably also a good dose of illusion about the development of the productive capacities and centralized planning in the Soviet Union in the first half of the 1920s: good, avant-garde faith in communism as the product of electrification, much more than the soviets, to recall the Leninist motto. It also reflects that evolutionism, of an almost social-positivist bent, that many have claimed to read in Pashukanis.[6] It is clear that, in part, the opposition to the "proletarian State" or to state capitalism is based here on a certain proximity to the socialist tradition of the self-administration of society as a process of technical self-regulation, to Henri de Saint-Simon's positivist formula that saw the abolition of political government precisely in the "administration of things." In sum, according to this approach, abolition of the legal form means the *withering away* of the legal form thanks to the growth of technological-industrial capacity and to the respective transition from the legal form of the contract to the technical regulation of standards and directives.

However, it is essential to avoid a one-dimensional evolutionary and positivist reading of the question of the abolition of law. Pashukanis in fact also provides another interpretation that derives from the consideration of the relation between the legal contractual form and the state, between legal relation and processes of centralization: or, following Negri's reading, for the introduction, alongside the legal form, of the theme of command. The *vertical* dimension of the exploitation of labor power and of the extraction of surplus value is not in fact absent in Pashukanis, even if most of the time it appears hidden in the analysis of exploitation as the product of the same legal equality and the consequence of the legal relation between equal subjects. This dimension of command reemerges continuously, however, as the conflict between "pure" legal form, that is, in the analogous contractual form to commodity exchange of mercantile-capitalist society, and the process of progressive centralization on the part of the state. For Pashukanis, it remains the case, obviously, that law is only private law, as Kelsen lamented (1955: 89–93): but this does not mean that the public has no role. It means that the public, that is, the State, is not the ultimate, reconciled place of the general regulation of society: it does not constitute top-down the space of property, as in the classic readings that focus their analysis of the legal phenomenon on the Law and Sovereignty. On the contrary, it depends originally on property, but it triggers off an intrinsically contradictory dynamic. The reciprocal recognition of legal subjects, in fact, calls into question the existence of a guarantor. Nevertheless, and as Pashukanis consistently notes on different occasions, this authority from a legal theory perspective is completely external. It is external because it is rooted in a relation of domination, which is not reducible to the horizontal nature of the relations between free owners, but is de facto domination that allows for exploitation and renders it stable. The State is command that is external to organization: not in the sense that it is destined to wither away in the technical organization of society, but rather because it remains intensely conflictual and absolutely irreconcilable with the rule of law. Instead of evolution and atrophy, here the abolition of law clearly becomes the expression of a contradiction intrinsic to the relation between the logic of exchange and the logic of command. By stressing this impossible relation between exchange and authority, between organization and command, and, ultimately, between legal form and the State, Negri has been able to read the abolition of law in Pashukanis precisely as a field of contradiction, rather than a process of evolution/atrophy.

Furthermore, and crucially, this field of contradiction is animated in subjective terms: the relation between legal form and the State is exactly the point in which class struggle appears decisive in Pashukanis (Negri 2012: 262–63). The State is always command that is external to the legal form, and it can never be integrated into any complete legal theory. A legal theory of the State is, for the bourgeoisie, the perfect utopia because it would mean being able to connect the legal form of the contract with sovereign command. This is what natural law theory would seek to resolve, with the goal of logically separating the *pactum subjectionis*, the submission to command, from the *pactum unionis*, the relation between subjects. But there is no possible mediation between the value of exchange (which, according to Pashukanis, is the only true substance of law) and command (for Pashukanis, the State is always an external domination to the legal relation). Whether it is the Western capitalist State, produced by the centralization of the function of command, or the proletarian state that, in these terms, is only an ideological mystification deployed during the transition, any attempted mediation breaks down precisely due to the impact of class struggle. Class struggle forces command to reveal its radical externality to the logic of exchange, as the violent "guarantor" of exploitation that does not terminate in the world of exchange value but which asserts itself to create the conditions of expropriation of surplus value that the mere relation of exchange presumes but is unable to maintain. The rule of law as a legal form of exchange ends, writes Pashukanis, at the moment when the outbreak of class struggle forces state command to appear in all its violence, but also in all its radical externality to the measure of the legal relation. "The more the hegemony of the bourgeoisie was shattered, the more compromising these corrections became, the more quickly the 'constitutional state' was transformed into a disembodied shadow, until finally the extraordinary sharpening of the class struggle forced the bourgeoisie to discard the mask of the constitutional state altogether, revealing the nature of state power as the organized power of one class over the other" (Pashukanis 2002: 150). Class struggle breaks every ostensible legal synthesis: it breaks up the capitalist and monopolist state, just as in the transition it breaks up all pretense of a proletarian state, leading command back to its external position of domination. Any attempt at social property is abandoned under the divisive pressure of class struggle, for social property is only another way of organizing exploitation. No "legal" bridges can be constructed between the logic of private owners (the true legal logic), the logic of exchange, and the (violent) logic of command, that is, pure domination that is de facto in the hands of the State. Here the anti-legalism of Pashukanis is reaffirmed: law is only bourgeois law. But the abolition of this bourgeois legal form becomes a battlefield, a contradiction exposed to the onset of class struggle and to its separation from any ostensible legal "synthesis," be it of the statist or socialist variety.

The Law of the Common

Let us recap: the abolition or extinction of law presents us with two options. The first option is where abolition is conceived as a progressive erosion of the legal form that gradually withers away to open up space for the economic-technological management of society. Here evolutionism and positivist progressivism prevail, and the basic norm marks the linear trajectory of development. The second option is where the abolition of law is the arena of class struggle. Class struggle abolishes law by precluding the mystified synthesis of both the capitalist state and the proletarian state. Public and private, authority and exchange, organization and command continually reproduce, through class struggle, an unsynthesizable dualism that clashes against any stabilization of the relations of exchange and attempts continuously to destroy the *dispositifs* of free appropriation of surplus value that lie behind the egalitarian logic of law and exchange. Class struggle always responds, in the face of an "alternative" law that tries to transfer a new content of class within the old legal form, by separating these ideological syntheses. But once the pretense of legal and state monopoly is broken, one that seeks to occupy the whole arena of transition in a brutally socialist way, this very transition remains an antagonistic, contradictory terrain traversed by class subjectivities.

The abolition of law is presented here also as an antagonistic arena traversed by class subjectivities. In this sense, the possibility arises that the abolition of law, that is, a radical transformation beyond property law, arises also through the organization of *dispositifs* of reappropriation that mark the phase of transition. In fact, these *dispositifs*, precisely because they are subjectively animated and constituted, cannot be assimilated to simple residues of the logic of bourgeois law, or impermanent marks that the final abolition of law will free us from, as Pashukanis at times appears to suggest.

Indeed, for Pashukanis, struggle during the transition, when it frees itself of the excessive positivist linearity that reduces the abolition of law to its gradual withering away through technical planning and directives, is always a dualistic and antagonistic arena. However, this antagonism in Pashukanis always meets a limit: the dualism is confined to the struggle between, on the one hand, the public and state demand, which proves to be increasingly external and which is sheer, violent domination, and, on the other hand, the reappropriating capacities of private subjects, owners of commodities, that nevertheless remain the only subjects that inhabit Pashukanis's world. As such, class struggle inevitably assumes a destituent and destructive quality: certainly a destruction of great significance, because it is the struggle against the presumption of reconstructing a mystified unity of organization and command through the fraud of a socialist legal form, something that Pashukanis never ceases to denounce. But things change, and this solely destituent sense of struggle for abolition can be overcome, if we imagine the struggle for the abolition of law updated to the present, to an era of diffuse and cognitive socialization of production. When subjects are no longer the masks that are created through exchange and the centers of imputation of exchange values, but have incorporated the means of production itself, when subjects are at the core of socialized and cooperative production, the dualism is animated by a logic that is not only destituent. Indeed, it is no longer just a struggle against the hardening of command but is also an act of reappropriation that can be socialized and collectivized.[7] The abolition of law is thus no longer a linear struggle: if it continues to struggle against every legal mythology, every statism, every adoration of an improbable socialist law, to struggle to abolish law now also means experimenting with the reappropriation of the functions of command. These are not new legal forms because the goal is, precisely and with good reason, the abolition of the legal form. Rather, they signal new organizational forms and the creation of counterpowers, within a dualism that class struggle always leaves open, thus in turn destroying any attempt at reconstructing a unitary law, be it socialist or property-based.

We can now sum up the different positions encountered through Pashukanis. First of all, he confronts a technological and linear conception of the abolition of law. If the common is understood exclusively as the overall organization of the productive forces, the law of the common would coincide with the *dispositifs* of regulation of this organization. It would be the technocratic dream under a communard mask: a common generated immediately by the evolution of the productive forces. The common would be absolutely consistent with the evolution of productive forces within capitalism: the law of the common would be nothing more than the administration of postcapitalism, an objectivist and evolutionary dream that Pashukanis himself shared. The abolition of law and the law of the common here would coincide perfectly: the bourgeois legal form withers away in the technological management of social cooperation.

From a second perspective, the law of the common—or, more precisely in this case, the law of commons—would be identified with the creation of non-property-based institutions. It would be the logic of the instituent act that produces qualified uses, the self-institutionalization of society, in accordance with the development of mutualist and cooperative traditions.[8] At the political level, it would produce a dualistic logic that is marked by the permanence of functions of command alongside the production of new modes of self-organization and self-management. Here the law of the common is produced interstitially between the public and the private, by liberating spaces and through experiments of reappropriation in the name of social property. The instituent logic opens up spaces for experimenting with a new legal form, which can transform bourgeois law, by being situated both inside and against it. The law of the common appears here more as an innovator of institutional logic and of the legal form, separating the latter from its property content, while the abolition of law is relegated to the realm of utopia. The risk is that of reproducing an institutionalist logic that liberates pluralist spaces but does not produce a complete transformation, stalling at the balance between property law and the spaces of the law of commons and, as such, not advancing to the level of a law of the common in the singular. Everything is staked here in the encounter with productive transformations, or, put another way, in the construction of an effective relation between these institutional experiments and the struggles for reappropriation.

The dynamic between these two positions effectively opens up the third position: the law of the common that develops in the antagonistic arena of class struggle. Reappropriation involves the whole of social cooperation, and the creation of commons, together with a corresponding law of the commons, is used to produce the overall plan of the common. The establishment of institutions coincides with the planning activity of cooperative capacities: here as well, appeal is made to the logic of administration, beyond private property and state command, but the administration of cognitive, intellectual, and affective capacities has nothing to do with the positivist dream of the "administration of things." The institutions of the common, however, are tested in a logic that is openly dualistic and traversed by class struggle. The plurality of institutions of the common is not simply an interstice, between public and private, but is aimed at the creation of counterpowers that create another principle of legitimacy that is irreducible to private law and state law. Understood as such, the law of the common and the abolition of the law are two aspects of revolutionary transformation. The abolition of law marks the moment of confrontation and destabilization with regard to any legal figure of exploitation, be that figure public or private, and the principally negative and destituent aspect of class struggle; the law of the common marks the moment of reappropriation, the production of a higher level of cooperation, and the invention of enduring counterpowers, albeit always partial and open to transformation.

—Translated by Nick Dines

Notes

1   Pashukanis (1891–1937) studied at the University of Saint Petersburg and later in Munich. He returned to Russia in 1914, and, close to the Bolsheviks, he later took part in the October Revolution. In 1920 he joined the People's Commissariat for Foreign Affairs as legal adviser. As vice president of the Communist Academy, he organized with P. I. Stuchka the section on the general theory of law and the state. In 1924 he published his key work, *The General Theory of Law and Marxism*. He went on to hold many public posts and participated in the projects for a new criminal code, but he was increasingly marginalized with the rise of Stalinism and, in particular, was subject to ferocious criticism from A. J. Vyshinsky, procurator general at the time of the Stalinist trials. He disappeared suddenly in January 1937 at the hands of the secret police. He was "rehabilitated" by the Communist Party of the Soviet Union in 1956.

2   This theory has been termed elsewhere the "commodity form theory of law." The origin of this terminology is not clear and does not come from Pashukanis (Koen 2011: 115n27).

3   The privilege of circulation is also inevitable, since Pashukanis elaborates a general theory of the legal form: the form (abstraction) regards the moment of exchange and circulation, precisely because it is abstracted from the productive process in general. This point is explained well in Koen 2011.

4   Vyshinsky brutally states what is fundamentally at stake: these interpretations weaken the state's authority at a time when there is a need to intensify it. To claim that Soviet law is nothing other than "assimilated" bourgeois law is, for Vyshinsky, essentially an anarchist position, which is the same position held by Pashukanis: "The withering away of the state will come not through a weakening of the state authority but through its maximum intensification" (Vyshinsky 1954: 62). Despite conceding some formal niceties, Pashukanis remained steadfast in the essential points. As he writes in response to Stuchka, in the foreword to the second edition of *The General Theory of Law and Marxism*: "Another of the things with which Comrade Stuchka reproaches me—namely that I recognise the existence of law only in bourgeois society—I grant, with certain reservations" (Pashukanis 2002: 44).

5   Regarding the specific Italian case and legal scholars close to the Italian Communist Party, see Nivarra 2015. Here Pashukanis is used as an example of the impossibility of a legal Marxism.

6   For an evolutionist and realist Pashukanis, see Guastini 1971.

7   On the emergence of this new affirmative sense of reappropriation, see Cava 2013: 24.

8   For an essential study of the common as a product of instituent action and on its use as the administration of the common, see Napoli 2014.

References

Beirne, Piers, and Robert Sharlet. 1980. "Editors' Introduction." In *Pashukanis: Selected Writings on Marxism and Law*, translated by Peter B. Maggs, 1–37. London: Academic Press.

Castoriadis, Cornelius. 1987. *The Imaginary Institution of Society*. Translated by Kathleen Blamey. Cambridge, UK: Polity.

Cava, Bruno. 2013. "Pashukanis e Negri: Do antidireito ao direito do comum" ("Pashukanis and Negri: From Anti-Law to the Law of the Common"). *Direito e práxis* (*Law and Practice*) 4, no. 6: 2–31.

Chignola, Sandro. 2012. "Introduction." *Il diritto del comune: Crisi della sovranità, proprietà e nuovi poteri costituenti* (*The Law of the Common: Crisis of Sovereignty, Property, and New Constituent Powers*), edited by Sandro Chignola, 7–14. Verona: Ombre Corte.

Dardot, Pierre, and Christian Laval. 2014. *Commun: Essai sur la révolution au XXIe siècle* (*Common: An Essay on Revolution in the Twenty-First Century*). Paris: La Découverte.

Deleuze, Gilles, and Claire Parnet. 2002. *Dialogues II*. Translated by Hugh Tomlinson and Barbara Habberjam. London: Continuum.

Guastini, Riccardo. 1971. "La 'teoria generale del diritto' in URSS: Dalla coscienza giuridica rivoluzionaria alla legalità socialista" ("The Jurisprudence in URSS: From Revolutionary Legal Consciousness to Socialist Legality"). *Materiali per una storia della cultura giuridica* (*Materials for the History of Legal Culture*), no. 1: 329–508.

Kelsen, Hans. 1955. *The Communist Theory of Law*. London: Stevens and Sons.

Koen, Robert. 2011. "In Defense of Pashukanism." *Potchefstroom Electronic Law Journal* 14, no. 4: 103–69. doi.org/10.4314/pelj.v14i4.5.

Korsch, Karl. 2002. "Appendix: An Assessment by Karl Korsch." In Pashukanis, *General Theory of Law and Marxism*, 189–95.

Mezzadra, Sandro, and Brett Neilson. 2014. "The Materiality of Communism: Politics beyond Representation and the State." *South Atlantic Quarterly* 113, no. 4: 777– 90.

Napoli, Paolo. 2014. "Indisponibilité, service public, usage: Trois concepts fondamentaux pour le 'commun' et les 'biens communs'" ("Unavailability, Public Service, Use: Three Fundamental Concepts for Theorizing the Commons"). *Tracés*, no. 27: 211–33.

Negri, Antonio. 2012. "Rileggendo Pashukanis: Note di discussione" ("Rereading Pashukanis: Discussion Notes"). In *La forma stato: Per la critica dell'economia politica della Costituzione* (*The State-Form: For a Critique of the Political Economy of the Constitution*), 213–63. Milan: Baldini Castoldi Dalai.

Nivarra, Luca. 2015. *La grande illusione: Come nacque e come morì il marxismo giuridico in Italia* (*The Great Illusion: The Birth and Death of Legal Marxism in Italy*). Torino: Giappichelli.

Pashukanis, Evgeny. 2002. *The General Theory of Law and Marxism*. Translated by Barbara Einhorn. With a new introduction by Dragan Milovanovic. New Brunswick, NJ: Transaction.

Stuchka, P. I. 1988. *Selected Writings on Soviet Law and Marxism*. Edited and translated by Robert Sharlet, Peter B. Maggs, and Piers Beirne. Armonk, NY: M. E. Sharpe.

Vyshinsky, A. J. 1954. *The Law of the Soviet State*. Translated by Hugh W. Babb. With an introduction by John N. Hazard. New York: Macmillan.

Martín Bergel

José Carlos Mariátegui and the Russian Revolution: Global Modernity and Cosmopolitan Socialism in Latin America

As in many other regions of the world, the Russian Revolution had a profound impact on Latin America. Not only was it a decisive motivating factor in the gradual configuration of communist parties and worker organizations, but in more general terms it also incentivized the expansion of leftist culture and the desire and yearning for social redemption. Instilling both fear and admiration, the news of its development and the fate of its protagonists captured the imagination of an urban public that at the time was undergoing a sustained process of growth and increased complexity. One of the figures on the South American continent most actively involved in analyzing the new framework presented by the Soviet experience was Peruvian José Carlos Mariátegui. In 1928, in response to Belgian Social Democrat Henri de Man's book *Au-delà du marxisme* (*Beyond Marxism*), which, from within Europe, purported to declare the "liquidation of Marxism," he wrote: "Whether the reformists accept it or not, the Russian Revolution constitutes the dominant event of contemporary socialism" (Mariátegui [1934] 2015: 9). It is interesting to note that the notion of event employed here conjures up the concept that has since acquired theoretical

The South Atlantic Quarterly 116:4, October 2017
DOI 10.1215/00382876-4234972 © 2017 Duke University Press

status in contemporary political philosophy. Mariátegui, who had begun declaring himself socialist in ideology shortly after the first reports of October 1917, inevitably located himself—from then until his premature death in 1930—within a revolutionary Marxist milieu, which he would seek to enrich and expand through a variety of intellectual and political initiatives.

However, a general reading of the work and intellectual praxis of the man distinguished as the "first Latin American Marxist" (an appellation coined by Antonio Melis [1967]) reveals that the Russian Revolution represented much more to him than a mere chapter in the discussion of the nature of socialism. Along with the Great War of 1914, it was the fundamental impetus for his insertion into an irrevocably global horizon of action and reflection from his base in Lima. Mariátegui was one of the Latin American intellectuals who most determinedly pursued a particular premise: that of being contemporary to his time. He was also the continent's most successful figure at melding aesthetic vanguardism and political vanguardism. From these positions, he developed an avid curiosity for a wide range of cultural and political phenomena around the globe. And it was above all the Russian Revolution, beyond the factual minutiae of its evolution, that inspired in the Peruvian this insatiable *vocation for the world* that would accompany him throughout the rest of his life.

The consensus, for some time now, has been to interpret the First World War and the Bolshevik Revolution as the inaugural moments of the twentieth century. In contrast, the need to read both of these processes within an effectively global perspective, capable of contemplating the multiple resources and connections between events, actors, and collective imaginaries across all continents, is much more recent. At the same time, studies of Mariátegui have tended to privilege a vision that emphasizes his role in nationalizing Marxism. According to this view, if Mariátegui was indeed the first Latin American Marxist, it was due to his translation and adaptation of Marx's doctrine to Peruvian circumstances, given the important role the national question plays in his work. This is the guiding premise that the most outstanding generation of Mariátegui scholars from the 1970s and early 1980s used in their approach, most notably Melis, José Aricó, Oscar Terán, Robert Paris, Carlos Franco, and Alberto Flores Galindo, among others.[1] This perspective, corroborated and popularized through several references extracted from Mariátegui's work and used as a supposed essential synthesis of his thinking (especially the dictum "we certainly do not wish socialism in America to be a carbon copy or an imitation. It must be a heroic creation"), found a warm welcome in the Latin American progressive political cycle of the past decade and a half, which made regional and national particularisms one of the touchstones of the so-called cultural battle. Within this context, the overall trend of the works produced during this period has sustained the general analytical framework of the generation of the 1970s, though lacking its brilliance and interpretive findings (see, e.g., Mazzeo 2013; López 2016). Ultimately, the predominance of this reading has meant that Mariátegui is often located within the powerful national-popular political and cultural tradition of the continent and even positioned as one of its pioneering figures.

This essay presents a departure from that perspective and offers an alternative reading of the figure of Mariátegui, in my view more faithful to the totality of his intellectual trajectory. Through a series of approaches to various aspects of his career, I argue that the Russian Revolution not only drew him closer to a belief in socialism but, more specifically, led him to adopt a cosmopolitan socialism. Cosmopolitanism had been one of the key ingredients in his earlier writing (which he later referred to as his "Stone Age"), even though an exploration of his vast production during this period shows that the majority of the texts are dedicated to Peruvian topics. However, in his mature stage, which began with the Bolsheviks' rise to power and was consolidated between 1919 and 1923, the years Mariátegui spent in Europe, the socialist outlook and cosmopolitan sensibility act in constant reaffirmation of each other. And just as aesthetic and political vanguardism overlap and are intertwined in his work, socialism and cosmopolitanism— along with related topics Mariátegui explores—function in mutual interaction. The Russian Revolution opened up a perspective onto the global revolution, the advance of the international proletariat, and in doing so brought into view a multiplicity of cultural objects and political events from all latitudes (to which he would make constant allusion in an extended series of articles he published in the weekly *Variedades*). Conversely, Mariátegui would delve into literature, psychoanalysis, film, and other phenomena of cultural modernity to find elements that provided keys to understanding the social and political dynamics and the situation of the socialist forces. And all this was in relation to a continuous effort to clarify the emerging and declining elements of the "epoch," a central notion in the Mariateguian matrix that held the Russian Revolution as one of its foundational events and that served as the scenario for the fusion of his socialist and cosmopolitan endeavors.

Journalism and Global Modernity

"Journalism is the daily, episodic history of humanity. Before, human history was written from interval to interval. Now it is written from day to day" (Mariátegui [1955] 1994: 1391). Around 1923, having recently returned from

Europe, Mariátegui thus refers to the milieu that had decisively molded the cadence of his writing and his intellectual style, a unique type of work linking essayistic reflection to current events. In some passages in his work, Mariátegui makes direct allusions to this approach. In the prologue of his first book, *The Contemporary Scene* (*La escena contemporánea*), he writes:

> I do not think it is possible to imagine the entire panorama of the contemporary world in one theory. It is not possible, above all, to set in theory its movement. We have to explore it and know it, episode by episode, facet by facet. Our view and our imagination will always be delayed in respect to the entirety of the phenomenon.
>
> Therefore, the best way to explain and communicate our time is one that is perhaps a little bit journalistic and a bit cinematographic. (Mariátegui 2011: 125)

The Contemporary Scene is, in effect, a volume based on insights into aspects of global affairs that Mariátegui published as weekly articles in the "Figures and Aspects of Worldwide Life" section of *Variedades*. (In the book, brief essays are grouped into chapters by theme: "Biology of Fascism," "Facts and Ideas on the Russian Revolution," "Message from the East," etc.) *Seven Interpretive Essays on Peruvian Reality* (*Siete ensayos de interpretación de la realidad peruana*) is based on the same process, composed of—as he describes in the "Author's Note"—"the articles that I published in *Mundial* and *Amauta*" and which acquired book form "spontaneously and without premeditation" (Mariátegui [1928] 1993: 13). The entirety of the Peruvian's work—a few thousand short articles—is indebted in its origins to the formats and rhythms of the journalistic press.[2]

Mariátegui's weekly contributions to Lima's current events magazines, *Variedades* and *Mundial*, were his main means of subsistence during his mature phase. However, beyond this economic role, the modalities of journalism appear to have been remarkably favorable to the style of writing he developed throughout his career. In essence, this journalistic approach lent itself particularly well to the method he announced as "a little bit journalistic and a bit cinematographic" in *The Contemporary Scene*, when setting out to scrutinize the cultural and political dynamics of modernity. As Michelle Clayton (2009: 245–46) has stated, this method was aimed at capturing "snapshots in motion . . . a series of fragments or photos combined to constitute a narrative" with the intention of "keeping readers up-to-date on global events."

Associated with Peruvian newspapers from the time of his adolescence, and without any formal university education, Mariátegui found in his daily work with the press an opportunity for intellectual education as well as a space for literary and essayistic experimentation (Flores Galindo [1980] 1994: 445–47; Bernabé 2006: 63–116). For both of these tasks, he took full advantage of an essential resource that—since its appearance in the last decades of the nineteenth century—had converted the modern newspaper into the perfect form for almost instantaneous construction of episodes with global resonance: the international newswire. As Julio Ramos (1989: 82–111) has astutely observed, in Latin America the snippets of information provided by the telegraph had already supplied materials for a generation of modernist writers who in their chronicles constructed a space of enunciation in newspapers in the late nineteenth and early twentieth centuries. Two decades later, Mariátegui intensified and stylized this characteristic. In a well-known autobiographical letter to the Argentine author Samuel Glusberg in 1928, he summarized: "Since 1918, nauseated by creole politics, I have oriented myself resolutely toward socialism, breaking with my first literary approximations corrupted by decadentism" (Mariátegui [1984] 1994: 1875). What this brief reference does not reveal is that this orientation was in large part due to Mariátegui's contact with international news items related to the new Soviet experiment he commented on in his columns. By the end of 1917, he was already openly declaring his sympathies for the Bolsheviks (Terán 1985: 36). Several months later, in a note titled "Hostile Newswire," he expressed his bitterness at the news transmitted by the agencies regarding the fate of the revolutionaries in their struggle against the reactionary militias. In another piece from that period, published under the title "Bolsheviki, Here," he wrote: "We who are ridiculed as Bolsheviks have not defended ourselves by horror at this nickname, but rather we have embraced it with courage and fervor; we must take pleasure in and be strengthened by the fact that socialism is beginning to acclimate itself among us like a foreign plant that finds love in this soil" (Mariátegui cited in Stein 1997: 189).

However, it was during his time in Europe that Mariátegui began explicitly to play the role of mediator between international information and his Latin American readers. Contemporary world events ended up proving a source of vital inspiration for him, continuously nourishing his thinking. But these events were also constantly held up to the standards of the critic, who situated them within their historical and political contexts and within a particular *philosophy* (understood as an intellectual worldview). Mariátegui did this consciously, pinpointing both the indispensable nature of current world news and the precautions that should be taken with respect to the material mechanisms that delivered it. At a 1923 conference he declared that "the newspaper . . . gathers the daily pulsing and throbbing of indefatigable humanity" (Mariátegui 1997b: 21). Mariátegui seemed fascinated by the possibility of being in contact with what he called "the excitement of the instant" and vehemently encouraged his readers to allow themselves to be captivated by the events affecting the planet. "We must all elevate ourselves above our limited local and personal horizons to reach the vast horizons of world life" (Mariátegui 1997a: 21), he wrote during the same period. However, he also urged caution in adequately digesting this new onslaught of news arriving from around the globe: "Now more than ever, the proletariat needs to know what is going on in the world. And it cannot know this through the fragmentary, episodic, homeopathic information from the daily news—poorly translated and even more poorly edited. It always comes from the reactionary press agencies that are charged with discrediting the revolutionary parties, organizations, and men, discouraging and disorienting the world proletariat" (Mariátegui 2011: 296). The corollary of these statements was the construction and positive appraisal of a position of vigilance and translation assumed by Mariátegui himself. Not coincidentally, in the late 1920s *Mundial* offered the fruitful results of his journalistic production in a section designated "What the Newswires Leave Out."[3]

More generally, from the way these news stories reverberated on a global scale, Mariátegui ([1959] 1994: 905–6) extracted a thesis he would repeat on several occasions: "Internationalism is not only an idea, it is a historical reality." And that is so because "the progress of communications has connected and united the activity and history of nations to an incredible extent":

> Communications are the nervous system of this internationalized and united humanity. One of the characteristics of our epoch is rapidity, the speed at which ideas are disseminated, at which currents of thought and culture are communicated. A new idea that springs forth in Britain is not a British idea except for the time it takes to print it. Once launched into space by the press, if that idea transmits a universal truth, it can be instantly transformed into a universal idea. How long would Einstein have once taken to be popular in the world? In our time, the theory of relativity, despite its complications and technicalities, has traveled around the world in only a few years. All of these facts are merely signs of internationalism and the solidarity of contemporary life. (909)

Following his return from Europe, Mariátegui developed this argument in a series of conferences he delivered at the González Prada Popular University in Lima (the main outcome of the University Reform movement in Peru) before an audience of workers and students. These conferences, he explained when announcing them, were aimed at "spreading awareness of the world crisis among the proletariat" (and, after his death, they would be grouped in a volume titled *History of the World Crisis*). Yet out of the decomposition precipitated by the Great War of the bourgeois nineteenth-century world, a new order emerged. "I share the opinion of those who believe that humanity is living through a revolutionary period" (848), he affirmed in the first of his speeches at the Popular University. And the beacons that had illuminated that era of global agitation came but from the land of the Soviets.

The Excitement of Our Times

In another of his contributions in the same series, Mariátegui ([1959] 1994: 861) presented the Russian Revolution as "a great event, on which the eyes of the universal proletariat converge . . . humanity's first step toward a regime of fraternity, peace and justice." The Bolshevik adventure was at the forefront of new horizons around the world. But in a characteristic that reveals much about the way he observed reality, Mariátegui was interested less in the Russian vicissitudes on the empirical path to constructing a communist society than in the imagined effects of the revolutionary process on the rest of the planet. Of course, in many of the numerous brief essays in which he alludes to distinct facets of the "new Russia," fragments of its recent history can be detected. In a conference at the Popular University dedicated to the circumstances culminating in the storming of the Winter Palace, he began by cautioning his public that he would narrate the revolutionary episodes "as a journalist . . . without erudition and without literature" (Mariátegui [1959] 1994: 862). Later, at distinct points, he sought to communicate with his audience regarding aspects of the process in its unfolding, for instance, to include the fate of Trotsky, whose itinerary he pursued in a series of articles published in 1924, 1928, and 1929. Mariátegui, however, did not deliver sociological essays in the style of the Argentine José Ingenieros, probably the most prestigious and high-profile Latin American intellectual dedicated to disseminating knowledge in the region about the Soviet experience in studies such as "Functional Democracy in Russia," "Comprehensive Education in Russia," and "Economic Lessons from the Russian Revolution," all written in 1920 and later collected in the volume *Los tiempos nuevos* (Ingenieros [1921] 1990). Likewise, and in contrast to his compatriots César Vallejo and Haya de la Torre, Mariátegui did not visit Russia on the trips he took while living in Europe, although he did consider the idea (Paris 1981: 87). In fact, he seemed engrossed more in images of the Revolution—those that inspire literature, for instance—than in the factual chronicling of its evolution.

This Mariateguian privileging of the life of symbols would find its most resonant form of expression in his subscription to the political theory of myths, which he adopted from the figure he believes offered the most thought-provoking fusion of Marxism with contemporary antipositivist and vitalist philosophical currents: Georges Sorel. In one of the brief articles later included in "The Excitement of Our Times," he writes:

> All modern intellectual investigations on the global crisis lead to a unani-
> mous conclusion: bourgeois civilization suffers from a lack of myth, of faith,
> of hope. . . . What most clearly and obviously differentiates them in this era
> of the bourgeoisie and the proletariat is myth. The bourgeoisie no longer has
> any myths. It has become incredulous, skeptical, nihilistic. The reborn lib-
> eral myth has aged too much. The proletariat has a myth: the social revolu-
> tion. It moves toward that myth with a passionate and active faith. . . . The
> strength of revolutionaries is not in their science; it is in their faith, in their
> passion, in their will. It is a religious, mystical, spiritual force. It is the force
> of myth. (Mariátegui 2011: 383, 387)

The revolution was therefore an emotional catalyst that activated a people, generating communion and movement and inevitably coloring the epoch. And in contrast to the Sorelian and Nietzschean modulation with which Mariátegui imbued the revolutionary myth, the principles that guided them through their golden nineteenth century—science, progress, reason, and parliamentary democracy—entered into radical crisis along with the bour-geoisie. These icons, which had become entrenched in the reformist and evolutionary socialism of the Second International, now revealed their weak-ness when faced with the power of the event embodied by Red October. According to Mariátegui ([1950] 1994: 496), "All the romantic energies of the Western man, anesthetized by long stretches of comfortable and generous peace, reemerged tempestuous and powerful. . . . The Russian Revolution breathed a warring and mystic spirit into socialist theory."

Without appealing to the phantasmatic imagery of the *Communist Manifesto*, the revolution was for Mariátegui a kind of spirit that roamed about activating and influencing subjects and situations. The nomadism of people and ideas was, for him, one of the most fruitful aspects of modernity. For instance, in a 1929 article in which he criticized the projects that "aimed to reduce the Jews to a nation, a state," he declared: "The Jewish people I love do not speak exclusively Hebrew or Yiddish; it is a polyglot, migrant, supranational people" (Mariátegui [1969] 1994: 1221). The postwar socialism Mariátegui defended, full of vitalist, neoromantic, and even mystical accents (Löwy 2008), acquired the physiognomy of a "religious emotion" (Mariátegui [1950] 1994: 499) and therefore flowed freely about the globe.

But this perspective framed in a heroic and romantic socialism— which, like the rise of fascism it competed with, claimed to pursue the Nietzschean principle of "living dangerously"—expanded, in Mariátegui's restless spirit, into the visualization of myriad cultural phenomena that caught his attention, either because they offered clues to the crisis of civilization under way or because through their innovative facets they had themselves become imbued with an antibourgeois sensibility. Such is the case of Isadora Duncan, whose "adventurous and magnificent" career made her "one of the women whose biographies, whether deciphered or not by Spengler's Germanic formula, the historian of *The Decline of the West* could hardly disregard." In the portrait Mariátegui sketched for his readers in *Variedades*, he recorded both Duncan's "radical rebellion" against established forms of dance (in his opinion no one but she "could have made Rousseau, Whitman and Nietzsche their dance teachers") and "her two years of experience in Bolshevik Russia." Thus, as the vanguards demanded, Mariátegui ([1950] 1994: 593–94) chose to read both "her art and her life" together, concluding that the two paths "had always been a protest against bourgeois taste and reason."

But if in these Mariateguian analyses—composed to the rhythm of the communicational framework that constructed world-renowned scenes and figures—the surrounding presence of this "excitement of our times," encouraged by a revolutionary horizon, cast light on figures of emerging mass culture such as Duncan, it also enabled even more direct connections with social and political contemporary phenomena. What is interesting is that in this process, the guiding light that was the Russian Revolution lost its specificity and became, simply, "revolution." "Two spirits coexist in the modern world, that of revolution and that of decadence," Mariátegui wrote in 1926 in one of the first issues of his magazine *Amauta* (553). In this sense, the Bolshevik event saw the particularities of its origins erased and came to characterize the period as a whole. And if while in its delocalized progression it was reinscribed into unique situations, it never ceased to make its universal strength felt. "The revolutionary tide has not only affected the West," but "the East is also convulsed, restive, stormy," Mariátegui ([1925] 1959: 190) declared at the beginning of the section of *The Contemporary Scene* dedicated to that vast area of the planet. He also stated: "India, China, and contemporary Turkey are living examples of these rebirths. The revolutionary myth has the potential to shake and revive these peoples in collapse" (Mariátegui 2011: 391).

From this perspective, we can see that the anti-particularist force of the revolution is present even in the indigenous question, the topic that has led many to insist that Mariátegui paradigmatically thematizes the irreducibility of American singularities. While it is true that in *Seven Interpretive Essays* he writes that "literary indigenism reflects a state of mind and of conscience in the new Peru" (Mariátegui [1928] 1993: 299), in the same volume he also notes "the consanguinity of the Indian movement with world revolutionary currents" (quoted in Paris 1981: 184). And in an article published in *Amauta* in early 1927, he writes that "indigenism receives its ferment and momentum from the 'worldwide phenomenon.' It is nourished by the 'socialist idea,' not as we have instinctively inherited it from the extinct Inca Empire but as we have learned it from Western civilization, in whose science and technology only utopian romanticism can fail to see the inescapable and magnificent acquisitions of modern man" (quoted in Terán 2008: 182).

Therefore, while a portion of Mariátegui's work (which has been the focus of much attention but constitutes only one area of his mature production) is effectively directed at scrutinizing Peruvian specificities, this approach does not materialize in his work as the defense of Peru *as national difference*. Rather, this is merely one moment in his reflection that is never detached from the global dynamics that contain it and participate in its configuration.[4]

Defense of Marxism

Throughout his career, Mariátegui showed a constant concern with specifying the characteristics and outlines of the "epoch," an omnipresent notion in the economy of his texts. Having decidedly assumed that the Great War and the Russian Revolution represented a historic break giving way to an unprecedented scenario, he repeatedly alluded to the new times that he witnessed and which constituted the inevitable terrain on which he based his reflections. It was not a coincidence that the first magazine with a socialist orientation he founded and directed with his friend César Falcón in 1918 was called *Nuestra época* (*Our Epoch*). From that point on, this reference to an encapsulating period was often repeated. For instance, in the prologue to *The Contemporary Scene*, mentioned above, Mariátegui ([1925] 1959: 11) writes that the texts included "contain the primary elements of a sketch or an interpretative essay on this epoch and its stormy problems"; in the essay dedicated to

Henri Barbusse in the same volume, he states, "The truth of our epoch is the Revolution" (158); and as he indicates in another text from 1925: "What differentiates men of our epoch is not only the doctrine, but above all, sentiment. Two opposing concepts of life, one prewar, one postwar . . . this is the central conflict of the contemporary crisis" (Mariátegui [1950] 1994: 495).

Captivated by an insistent desire to clarify the primary coordinates of his era, Mariátegui was continually preoccupied with classifying the events he witnessed as either emergent or declining, as communicating vitality or sinking behind the horizon (expressed through the verb *tramontar*, an Italianism he used on numerous occasions), as representing dawn or dusk.[5] In line with Sorel's thinking, for Mariátegui war and revolution had distorted the accumulative time that had been consubstantial to the age of faith in progress (Terán 1985: 72). In a fractured epoch, split in two, he was obsessed with detecting the manifestations of the new. Hence his profound interest in the vanguard. For instance, he wrote: "Several phases of ultramodern art coincide with other contemporary phases of the spirit and mentality. . . . Dadaism, in its own ultraist and extremist language, is an attack on the service of art to intelligence. And this movement coincides with the fading of rationalist thinking" (Mariátegui [1950] 1994: 573–74).

But if Dadaism was a testament to the crisis of nineteenth-century bourgeois rationalism, if it was "like black music, like boxing and other current things, a peculiar and spontaneous symptom and the legitimate product of a civilization that is dissolving and decaying," Mariátegui ([1950] 1994: 573) found surrealism (which he explored in several of his texts) even more attractive because "given its antirationalism, it is related to contemporary philosophy and psychology" and also because of "its revolutionary rejection of capitalist thinking and society" (564).

It was within this framework of discernment that Mariátegui felt the need vehemently to excoriate de Man's book *Au-delà du marxisme*, which by 1928 had become in Europe an influential text that, from a reformist-socialist perspective, decreed the demise of the Marxist doctrine. Although the author of *Seven Interpretive Essays* tended to adopt an equally summary position when diagnosing the outdated or anachronistic nature of elements from previous periods, this time he did the opposite: in the substantial series of brief essays inspired by de Man's book, from the projected title conceived to unite them, he assumed a position in "defense of Marxism," understanding this as the task of refuting its supposed unsuitability to the period. For Mariátegui, both the "heroic and creative" socialist era that had begun with the Russian Revolution as well as the ties that Sorel, André Breton, and others had traced between revolutionary movements and "contemporary philosophies" (vitalism, antirationalism, psychoanalysis, etc.) were obvious signs of the plenitude of Marxism, quite distinct from the economistic matrix, blind to the issues of subjectivity, that de Man biasedly presented. On the contrary, Mariátegui ([1934] 2015: 81) made an effort in those texts to show the affinities between Freud and Marx, while at the same time affirming that "Lenin proves to us, with the irrefutable testimony of a revolution, that Marxism is the only means of following and surpassing Marx."

Yet who were the readers Mariátegui had in mind when he spoke out against a book that, having been rapidly translated into several languages, by the late 1920s was at the forefront of the worldwide anti-Marxist controversy? On a few occasions, Mariátegui provided incidental references to the concrete audience he imagined for his texts (whether it was the vanguard of the Peruvian proletariat or the broader and more generic readership of weeklies such as *Mundial* and *Variedades*). But what is interesting about *Defense of Marxism* is that it exemplifies a habitual attitude of his mature writing: that of imagining himself in dialogue with a worldwide audience. In *Cosmopolitan Desires: Global Modernity and World Literature in Latin America*, Mariano Siskind (2014: 6–7) establishes that the contributions of cosmopolitan Latin American intellectuals and writers are constructed on the basis of "an omnipotent fantasy (an imaginary scenario occupying the place of the real, according to Lacan), a strategic, voluntaristic fantasy." Leaving aside his peripheral geopolitical location, the cosmopolitan Latin American subject constructs the fiction of a horizontal and global cultural space in which he inscribes his discourse in deliberate ignorance of his marginal condition. Similar to the cases studied by Siskind—and with a marked voluntaristic emphasis—Mariátegui in his texts acts *as if* the world were a smooth space, *as if* from a decentered corner of the planet such as Lima he could effectively participate in a "global conversation" with the most up-to-date and vanguard aspects of Marxist culture of his time.[6] Of course, he was aware of the inequities and fractures of the political and cultural internationalization he was witnessing, but it should be noted that in his work he focused much more on temporal coordinates than on spatial ones. In other words, Mariátegui was interested much more in the *epochal difference* than in the *geographical-cultural difference* (overestimated by most scholars of his work). Ultimately, this position proved to be enormously productive for the Peruvian intellectual. Far from the habitual and unfruitful position assumed by nationalism and Latin Americanism aimed at protesting and denouncing the inequalities and hierarchies of the world (often mobilized through various forms of cultural anti-imperialism), Mariátegui, through his imaginary dialogue with political and cultural materials from around the world, ended up producing one of the most original and penetrating bodies of work not only in Latin American Marxism but in the entire intellectual history of the continent in the twentieth century.

World Literature and "New Russia"

As mentioned above, Mariátegui's world yearnings were reflected in a vast number of brief articles on distinct cultural objects around the globe. Film, theater, visual arts, and phenomena such as dance formed part of this essayistic repertoire. Within this context, it is undoubtedly literature, to which he dedicated hundreds of brief texts analyzing new developments in the field, that most attracted his interest. However, Mariátegui was not merely a shrewd and informed reviewer and commentator of books. In a more general sense, he was also an active promoter of the global sphere of literary exchanges that has been called "world literature." Coined by Goethe in the nineteenth century and recently reclaimed in the debate on the humanities, the notion of *Weltliteratur* had also been alluded to by Engels and Marx ([1848] 1998: 39) in a well-known passage of the *Communist Manifesto*: "In place of the old local and national seclusion and self-sufficiency, we have intercourse in every direction, universal interdependence of nations. And as in material, so also in intellectual production. The intellectual creations of individual nations become common property. National one-sidedness and narrow-mindedness become more and more impossible, and from the numerous national and local literatures, there arises a world literature."

Mariátegui, who subscribed to Marx and Engels's position on the formation of a world literary network, was himself an intervening factor in the transcultural operations that converted Peru and Latin America into regions actively participating in its dynamics. In addition to offering to his Lima-based readership critical commentary on texts he read in foreign languages, Mariátegui also encouraged the international circulation of books and promoted translation, along with overseeing the production of Spanish-language publishing companies. To cite an example, in his article "Italian Culture" from 1925, he laments: "Among us, Italian books have enjoyed little, almost no circulation." And when they had, it was in unsatisfactory conditions. "We have gotten to know and admire [Gabriele] D'Annunzio through mediocre, even deplorable Spanish translations," he writes. In this essay, in which he proposes "to inspire our scholars and students to direct their attention to

Italian culture," Mariátegui ([1950] 1994: 531–32) praises it for being a window onto other literatures: "In Italy, so much is translated painstakingly and directly from Russian, Norwegian, etc. The most exotic and distant cultures have scholars and translators in Italy. . . . Reading Italian—for reasons explained above—requires delving into the unique and substantial Italian culture, while at the same time approaching other literatures, more quickly and meticulously translated into Italian than into Spanish."

In his mature stage, Mariátegui dedicated essays to a wide variety of figures from world literature, including Waldo Frank, Henri Barbusse, Rabindranath Tagore, Romain Rolland, Giovanni Papini, José Vasconcelos, Paul Morand, Miguel de Unamuno, James Joyce, Tristan Tzara, John Dos Passos, Enrique Gómez Carrillo, Valery Larbaud, and others less well known or remembered, such as the Romanian Panait Istrati and the Spaniard Jorge Manrique. Around 1929, Mariátegui likewise dedicated a series of texts to literature evoking the Great War in a saga that extends from Erich María Remarque to Ernest Glaesser. In this context, just as the Bolshevik Revolution had represented an essential catalyst for expanding the lens with which Mariátegui observed the world, literature for him would be the privileged entry into the exploration of what he designated the "new Russia."

In his aesthetic conception, Mariátegui was far from the orientations that, following his death, would officially be exalted in Russia as so-called socialist realism (Melis 1994). Even in his maturity, he defended the iconoclastic spirit of Dadaism, for instance, in articles such as "Defense of Pure Nonsense" that appeared in his magazine *Amauta*. Similarly, he liked to cite and endorse the socialist vision of Oscar Wilde, "who in the liberation of labor saw the liberation of art" (Mariátegui [1950] 1994: 552). And in his essay "Literary Populism and Capitalist Stabilization," he strongly repudiated the "essentially demagogic" bias of the return to the "naturalist description" he detected in French literature in early 1930, concluding that "on the desk of a revolutionary critic, independent of any hierarchical consideration, a book by Joyce will always be more valuable than one by any neo-Zola" (559–60).

Yet this does not imply for Mariátegui the defense of a literature disconnected from reality. Rather, there is a pedagogical disposition insinuated, albeit indirectly, in the extended series of reviews of texts on revolutionary Russia he wrote in the 1920s: literature vividly communicated not the falsely idyllic face of the Soviet experience but rather the vitality and drama of the collective and individual commitment to the future. Thus to capture the "heroic atmosphere of the revolution," Mariátegui ([1934] 2015: 10) opted for the travel chronicles of the Spaniard Julio Alvarez del Vayo—laden with a "light novelistic element"—and the American John Reed. He also paid particular attention to the fictional portraits of now-forgotten Russian authors such as Kostia Riabtzev, Lidia Seifulina, Leonidas Leonov, and Larisa Reissner, whose works translated into French or Spanish he commented on in successive articles. In short, while stressing that "one of the most distinguished traits of the new Russian literature is its epic," citing Ilya Ehrenburg, Mariátegui ([1950] 1994: 625–26) warns: "Foreigners unfamiliar with the new Russian literature are unfamiliar with the new Russia, because only literature, at least partially or conventionally, can make them understand the magnificent process, closer to geology than to politics, at work in a people of 150 million souls." Ultimately, in that era of cultural and political globalization, literature—capable of activating the imagination of readers—was a powerful means to spread the worldwide revolutionary excitement emerging from within Russia.

By Way of Conclusion: Mariátegui and Cosmopolitan Socialism in Latin America

The heterodox nature of Mariátegui's Marxism has frequently been highlighted. Yet this bias has not often been tied to his cosmopolitan dispositions, connected—as I have sought to demonstrate in this essay—to the way the Russian Revolution oriented him not only toward socialism but also, more generally, toward the inscription of his intellectual praxis in constant contact with the political and cultural materials of an age of accelerated internationalization. Mariátegui was more of a cosmopolitan socialist than an internationalist (even though some of his texts suggest otherwise), and it is partly due to this that he was slow to enter into contact with the Third International and, once he did, resisted integration into its ranks. This inclination not only allowed him to maintain a certain intellectual autonomy that he defended when faced with the rigidification of international communism (which in Latin America was just beginning to develop when Mariátegui died). But in more general terms, his cosmopolitanism also seemed to appease his intuition regarding the way the world revolution could capture the attention and sympathy of a broader public through cultural artifacts such as the press, the arts, and literature. His intellectual praxis can thus be seen as a pedagogy in two ways: by connecting his readers with objects of global culture that could expand their geographic horizon and sensitize them to distant situations in which there were also struggles for the future of the world and by distilling, through these references, socialist and class orientations. In this way, in Mariátegui's intellectual trajectory, socialism and cosmopolitanism interact and reinforce each other.

The lens through which we have reread Mariátegui in this essay, in addition to more accurately revealing his intellectual path, contributes to illuminating the tradition of cosmopolitan socialism in Latin America, a tradition that, although embodied by a minority, has not ceased to occupy an important space in leftist culture on the continent and should necessarily play a significant role in any twenty-first-century socialist project.

—Translated by Rebecca Wolpin

Notes

1   This stance is more notable in some (Flores Galindo [1980] 1994; Aricó 1980; Terán 1985; Franco 1980) than in others (Melis [1967] 1999; Paris 1981). In later critiques of Mariátegui, several of these scholars distanced themselves from this approach (Melis 1994; Terán 2008).

2   With the exception of *The Contemporary Scene* and *Seven Interpretive Essays on Peruvian Reality*, published during Mariátegui's lifetime, the majority of his vast collection of shorter essays originally conceived for the press was published by his children in book form in the 1950s and 1960s. These books were compiled in 1994, for the hundredth anniversary of his birth, in a two-volume edition titled *Mariátegui total* (*Total Mariátegui*; see Mariátegui [1955] 1994).

3   In that section, in an essay titled "The Sentimental Preparation of the Reader Faced with the Sino-Soviet Conflict," Mariátegui ([1969] 1994: 1240) asserted that it was the "vigilant exploration of magazines, the attentive commentaries of independent writers, that can defend the public from the potential intoxication they are condemned to by the trustification of the wire."

4   In the same well-known editorial in *Amauta* in which Mariátegui writes that socialism in Peru should avoid being a "carbon copy or an imitation," we read the following: "The Latin American Revolution will be nothing more and nothing less than a stage, a phase of the world revolution. It will simply and clearly be the socialist revolution." And then: "Socialism is certainly not an Indo-American doctrine. . . . It is a worldwide movement in which none of the countries that move within the orbit of Western civilization are excluded. This civilization drives toward universality with the force and the means that no other civilization possessed. Indo-America can and should have individuality and style in this new world order, but not its own unique culture or fate" (Mariátegui 2011: 128–29).

5   To illustrate these ascendant and descendant elements, Mariátegui often resorts to metaphors related to times of day. In "The Morning Soul," for instance, he writes that "the Europe that does not want to die . . . sighs that dawn may soon come," while at the same time stating that "everyone knows that the Revolution moved the clocks of Soviet Russia forward" (Mariátegui [1950] 1994: 493–94).

6   To cite another example, there is something similar in the way Mariátegui traces the itinerary of the vanguards, especially surrealism. For instance, in "A Balance Sheet on Surrealism," written in 1930 shortly before his death, he discusses the latest developments in the movement on an imagined equal footing with Breton and his followers.

References

Aricó, José, ed. 1980. *Mariátegui y los orígenes del marxismo latinoamericano (Mariátegui and the Origins of Latin American Marxism)*. Mexico City: Cuadernos de Pasado y Presente.

Bernabé, Mónica. 2006. *Vidas de artista: Bohemia y dandismo en Mariátegui, Valdelomar y Eguren (Lima, 1911–1922) (Artist Lives: Bohemia and Dandyism in Mariátegui, Valdelomar, and Eguren [Lima, 1911–1922])*. Rosario, Argentina: Beatriz Viterbo.

Clayton, Michelle. 2009. "Mariátegui y la escena contemporánea" ("Mariátegui and the Contemporary Scene"). In *José Carlos Mariátegui y los estudios latinoamericanos (José Carlos Mariátegui and Latin American Studies)*, edited by Mabel Moraña and Guido Podestá, 231–54. Pittsburgh: IILI.

Engels, Friedrich, and Karl Marx. [1848] 1998. *The Communist Manifesto*. London: Verso.

Flores Galindo, Alberto. [1980] 1994. *La agonía de Mariátegui: La polémica con la Komintern (Mariátegui's Agony: Problems with the Comintern)*. In *Obras completes (Complete Works)*, 2: 367–639. Lima: Sur.

Franco, Carlos. 1980. "Sobre la idea de nación en Mariátegui" ("The Concept of Nation in Mariátegui"). *Socialismo y participación (Socialism and Participation)*, no. 11: 169–90.

Ingenieros, José. [1921] 1990. *Los tiempos nuevos (New Times)*. Buenos Aires: Losada.

López, María Pía. 2016. *José Carlos Mariátegui: Lo propio de un nombre (José Carlos Mariátegui: The Same as a Name)*. Buenos Aires: Ediciones UNGS.

Löwy, Michael. 2008. "Communism and Religion: José Carlos Mariátegui's Revolutionary Mysticism." Translated by Mariana Ortega Breña. *Latin American Perspectives* 35, no. 2: 71–79.

Mariátegui, José Carlos. [1925] 1959. *La escena contemporánea (The Contemporary Scene)*. Lima: Amauta.

Mariátegui, José Carlos. [1928] 1993. *Siete ensayos de interpretación de la realidad peruana (Seven Interpretive Essays on Peruvian Reality)*. Mexico City: Era.

Mariátegui, José Carlos. [1934] 2015. *Defensa del marxismo (Defense of Marxism)*. Santiago, Chile: Universidad de Valparaíso.

Mariátegui, José Carlos. [1950] 1994. *El alma matinal y otras estaciones del hombre de hoy (The Morning Soul and Other Stations of Contemporary Man)*. In *Mariátegui total (Total Mariátegui)*, Vol. 1, edited by Sandro Mariátegui Chiappe, 483–727. Lima: Amauta.

Mariátegui, José Carlos. [1955] 1994. *La novela y la vida (The Novel and Life)*. In *Mariátegui total (Total Mariátegui)*, Vol. 1, edited by Sandro Mariátegui Chiappe, 1351–97. Lima: Amauta.

Mariátegui, José Carlos. [1959] 1994. *Historia de la crisis mundial (History of the World Crisis)*. In *Mariátegui total (Total Mariátegui)*, Vol. 1, edited by Sandro Mariátegui Chiappe, 829–919. Lima: Amauta.

Mariátegui, José Carlos. [1969] 1994. *Figuras y aspectos de la vida mundial (Figures and Aspects of Worldwide Life)*. In *Mariátegui total (Total Mariátegui)*, Vol. 1, edited by Sandro Mariátegui Chiappe, 1021–282. Lima: Amauta.

Mariátegui, José Carlos. [1984] 1994. *Correspondencia (Correspondence)*. In *Mariátegui total (Total Mariátegui)*, Vol. 1, edited by Sandro Mariátegui Chiappe, 1567–2097. Lima: Amauta.

Mariátegui, José Carlos. 1997a. "Notas de la conferencia dictada en Barranca" ("Notes of the Conference Given in Barranca"). *Anuario mariateguiano (Mariateguian Yearly)*, no. 9: 18–21.

Mariátegui, José Carlos. 1997b. "Notas del discurso pronunciado en la inauguración de la Editorial Obrera Claridad" ("Notes of the Speech Delivered at the Inauguration of the Obrera Claridad Publishing Company"). *Anuario mariateguiano (Mariateguian Yearly)*, no. 9: 21.

Mariátegui, José Carlos. 2011. *José Carlos Mariátegui: An Anthology*. Edited and translated by Harry E. Vanden and Marc Becker. New York: Monthly Review.

Mazzeo, Miguel. 2013. *El socialismo enraizado: José Carlos Mariátegui: Vigencia de su concepto de "socialismo práctico" (Deep-Rooted Socialism: José Carlos Mariátegui: The Relevance of His Concept of "Practical Socialism")*. Lima: FCE.

Melis, Antonio. [1967] 1999. "Mariátegui, primer marxista de América" ("Mariátegui, America's First Marxist"). In *Leyendo Mariátegui, 1967–1998 (Reading Mariátegui, 1967–1998)*, 11–33. Lima: Amauta.

Melis, Antonio. 1994. "Elogio del conocimiento literario" ("In Praise of Literary Knowledge"). In *Mariátegui total (Total Mariátegui)*, Vol. 1, edited by Sandro Mariátegui Chiappe, 1355–60. Lima: Amauta.

Paris, Robert. 1981. *La formación ideológica de José Carlos Mariátegui (The Ideological Formation of José Carlos Mariátegui)*. Mexico City: Pasado y Presente.

Ramos, Julio. 1989. *Desencuentros de la modernidad en América Latina: Literatura y política en el siglo XIX (Divergent Modernities in Latin America: Literature and Politics in the Nineteenth Century)*. Mexico City: FCE.

Siskind, Mariano. 2014. *Cosmopolitan Desires: Global Modernity and World Literature in Latin America*. Evanston, IL: Northwestern University Press.

Stein, William W. 1997. *Dance in the Cemetery: José Carlos Mariátegui and the Lima Scandal of 1917*. New York: University Press of America.

Terán, Oscar. 1985. *Discutir Mariátegui (Discuss Mariátegui)*. Puebla, Mexico: Editorial Universidad Autónoma de Puebla.

Terán, Oscar. 2008. "*Amauta*: Vanguardia y revolución" ("*Amauta*: Vanguard and Revolution"). *Prismas: Revista de historia intelectual (Prisms: Journal of Intellectual History)*, no. 12: 173–89.

Kathy E. Ferguson

The Russian Revolution and Anarchist Imaginaries

Anarchists participated in the 1917 revolution in Russia in many different ways. Their stories, with a few exceptions, entail poignant accounts of progress, loss, and (sometimes) renewal. They called for and fought for a social revolution that would abolish hierarchy while giving birth, in historian Paul Avrich's (2005: 3) succinct summary, to "a decentralized society based on the voluntary cooperation of free individuals." In their initial enthusiasm and lingering loyalties, anarchists embraced the value and the possibility that ordinary people can create themselves and their institutions as free and self-governing. This was the moment of progress, when all things seemed possible. Institutions of self-government were set up in cities, military units, and workplaces; literary and artistic creations extended the energies of aesthetic freedom into public life; self-governing militias emerged to fight off counterrevolutionaries. In a plea to Lenin in December 1920, anarchist leader Pyotr Kropotkin (1973: 149) invoked this creative moment as the confirmation that revolutionaries were *"working for the future"* and that "with all its defects, it will produce a change in the direction of *equality* which no efforts to return to the past will eliminate" (italics in original).

The South Atlantic Quarterly 116:4, October 2017
DOI 10.1215/00382876-4234983   © 2017 Duke University Press

The 1917 revolution was a decisive period in a larger transnational revolutionary process. Many radicals had earlier emigrated from Russia to the United States to escape czarist repression following the failed revolution of 1905. Other émigrés had fled poverty and anti-Semitic persecution and found anarchism in their new home. In the United States they established the Union of Russian Workers; the anarchist-syndicalist journal *Golos truda* (*Voice of Labor*); the small but fierce journal *Frayhayt* (*Freedom*), which encouraged protests in the United States against US intervention in Russia in 1917; and many other sites of anarchist struggle. When the February Revolution broke out, many of these radicals returned to Russia, either voluntarily (including *Golos truda* editors William Shatov, Volin [Vsevolod Mikhailovich Eikhenbaum], and Maksim Raevskii) or as a result of mandatory exile (including Emma Goldman, Alexander Berkman, and Mollie Steimer) to take part in the revolution.[1] Kenyon Zimmer (2015: 143) estimates that over eight thousand Russians and "Hebrews" left the United States for Russia in 1917, with another twelve thousand following over the next three years. Looking back at the events of 1917 a decade later, Berkman ([1929] 2003: xii) acknowledged that the denaturalization of existing institutions was the Russian Revolution's greatest contribution: "The cherished superstition that what exists is permanent has been shaken beyond recovery."

New political possibilities brought anarchists into the Russian Revolution, while the elimination of those options, and often of the people themselves, quickly pushed the anarchists back out of it. Raids by the Cheka (the secret police) on anarchists in spring 1917 closed down many clubs, centers, and publications. *Golos truda* was repressed by the new state; with characteristic persistence, the editors created a new anarchist journal, *Vol'nyi golos truda* (*Free Voice of Labor*), which was also repressed by the state, followed by *Trud i volia* (*Labor and Liberty*), which produced six issues before being, predictably, shut down (Avrich 2005: 185, 195). Over the next decade, anarchists who opposed the new centralization of power, as well as those who tried for a time to cooperate with the new regime, were eliminated in an "endless chain of arrests and deportations" (247). This was the moment of loss, when the values of freedom and self-government could only be sustained by turning against the Bolsheviks, even if it meant appearing to ally with reactionary voices for whom any revolution was anathema. The time of loss was devastating, yet it was also productive, as anarchists searched their souls and their histories to invent a different way of making a revolution, a better way, a way that could sustain its anarchism. The time of loss also galvanized a remarkable effort by anarchists to support their colleagues imprisoned by the Bolsheviks and to insist on remembering the prisoners' lives as well as the state's cruel repressions.

The failures of the Bolshevik Revolution stimulated spirited inquiries into how to make and sustain a truly anarchist revolution. Moments of renewal emerged, wherein painful lessons were absorbed and a revitalized revolutionary imaginary came into being. In this essay I look briefly at two of those arenas: First, anarchist successes in the Spanish Revolution of the 1930s provided the practical grounds for a return to a renewed anarchist revolutionary imaginary. Second, anarchist activism on behalf of comrades imprisoned in Russia offered a different sort of practical radicalism, delivering needed letters and supplies to beleaguered prisoners while enacting solidarity across the barriers between public assembly and prison isolation. These legacies continue to emerge and thrive today in, for example, the Occupy movement, the counterglobalization protests, the Zapatista rebellion, the exuberant global networks of anarchist zines, websites, artists, musicians, and filmmakers, and more (Antliff 2004; Adams 2013).

The Promise and Loss of the Russian Revolution

The outbreak of the February Revolution was hailed by anarchists as a truly revolutionary event: the spontaneous overthrow of the hated monarchy created a space for anarchist inventions of a new order in which free individuals organized voluntary, self-governing communities. Labor support for anarchism was strongest among the metalworkers in Petrograd; the bakers, leather workers, printers, and railroad workers in Moscow; the sailors in Kronstadt; and the Ukrainian peasantry who joined Nestor Makhno's rebellions (Avrich 2005: 125). While some anarchists put their hopes in handicrafts cooperatives and agricultural collectives, others invested their energies in factory committees organized by the workers, and still others contributed to a creative outpouring of new art and literature. Russian avant-garde artists constituted a vital hotbed of revolutionary anarchism. Nina Gurianova (2012: 17) documents "remarkable intensity and concentration" in poetry, music, and the visual arts, "an attempt to create a new self-identity and to see the world anew, as if for the first time, as 'other.'" For example, the manifesto of a group called Freedom for Art, which drew fifteen hundred art workers to its March 11, 1917, meeting, saw the February Revolution as its inspiration: "The great Russian Revolution calls us to act. Unite, fight for the freedom of art. Fight for the right of self-determination and autonomy. The Revolution creates freedom. Without freedom there is no art. Only in a free democratic republic is democratic art possible" (quoted in Gurianova 2012: 215).

Russian anarchists inherited a long tradition of what Avrich (2005: 3) calls "native radicalism," along with the powerful legacy of Kropotkin, Mikhail Bakunin, Lev Tolstoy, and others. One of the strongest expressions of intertwined US/Russian anarchist voices was the journal *Golos truda*. Having served as an editor of *Golos truda* in the United States, as well as an International Workers of the World (IWW) organizer, Shatov relocated his printing press to Petrograd to continue the journal (Cornell 2016: 62). Alexander (Sanya) Schapiro, who had left Russia as a child and had been active in anarchist circles in London, also returned to Russia in 1917 to join *Golos truda*. Another returning anarchist was Volin, who came back to Russia from New York to join the editorial team of the anarchist-syndicalist journal. G. P. Maksimov, a former seminarian and agronomist, became a member of the Central Council of Factory Committees as well as *Golos truda*'s "most prolific contributor" (Avrich 2005: 139). *Golos truda* advocated radical reconstruction of the economy through the empowerment of "the intricate network of popular organizations" that arose after the February Revolution, including "soviets of peasants', workers' and soldiers' deputies, industrial unions, factory committees, unions of landless peasants" (*Golos truda* 1973: 70). Their goal was the creation of direct factory democracy through workers', peasants', and soldiers' councils. Publications by anarchist artists included *Anarkhiia* (*Anarchy*) and the *Manifesto of Company 41°*, which aimed "to place the world on a new axis" (quoted in Gurianova 2012: 214). As the writers irreverently declared: "This newspaper [*Manifesto of Company 41°*] will be a haven for happenings in the life of the company as well as a cause of constant trouble. Let's roll up our sleeves" (214). While anarchist artists often called on the legacy of Max Stirner and Nietzsche, and the labor-based anarchists looked more to Bakunin and Kropotkin, they shared enthusiasm for the opportunities for individual freedom, creativity, and self-organization enabled by the revolution.

So long as the anarchists and the Bolsheviks agreed on the basics of revolutionary transformation—"Down with the war! Down with the Provisional Government! Control of the factories to the workers! The land to the peasant!" (Avrich 1973: 16)—an uneasy peace prevailed, but the overthrow of Aleksandr Kerensky's government in October 1917 marked the beginning of the end of their cooperation. The Bolsheviks took over the workers' councils and created the Cheka, whose forces soon killed, wounded, or arrested hundreds of anarchists and other dissenters in raids intensifying in April 1918 and continuing for some years. In April 1921, at the Tenth Congress of the

Russian Communist Party, Lenin declared war on anarchism and syndicalism. Under the accusation of "banditism," anarchists were arrested and imprisoned or executed. Anarchist publications and organizations either closed or went underground, including *Golos truda*, whose editors escaped, were imprisoned, or were sent into exile. *Anarkhiia* was banned in April 1918, while Anarkhiia House and the Poets' Café in Moscow were closed. The Artists' Union, originally an anarcho-syndicalist organization, was taken over by the Bolshevik-controlled Union of Soviet Artists (Gurianova 2012: 250).

Many anarchists fled to Ukraine, including Volin, Shatov, and Schapiro of *Golos truda*, and joined the Nabat, a federation of anarchist organizations affiliated with the popular guerrilla army led by Makhno (Avrich 2005: 204). Makhno's (1973) army fought the German army, then the White army and other counterrevolutionaries, and finally the Red Army, while also appropriating land from landowners and setting up agricultural communes organized along anarchist lines. In an address to "Comrade[s] in the Red Army," the Makhnovists appealed to Bolshevik soldiers to recognize the anarchists as "freedom-loving revolutionary insurgents" rather than "bandits and counterrevolutionaries," as the Bolshevik authorities claimed ("Manifestos of the Makhnovist Movement" 2005: 304, 303). In the end, the Makhnovists were defeated by the Red Army and Makhno himself was exiled to Western Europe. Avrich (1973: 26) concludes, "The downfall of Makhno marked the beginning of the end of Russian anarchism." On February 8, 1921, the anarchist movement was dealt another blow when the internationally admired anarchist Kropotkin died. Tens of thousands of supporters walked in Kropotkin's funeral procession, including anarchists who were let out of prison to attend the event, under the proviso that they return afterward. To the great surprise of their captors, they did (Goldman [1931] 1970: 869).

Two weeks later the sailors of Kronstadt naval base, earlier praised by Leon Trotsky as "the pride and glory of the revolution," rebelled against the Bolsheviks and embraced their own free soviet to govern themselves (Avrich 1970: 88). The demand of the Kronstadt soldiers, sailors, and workers—"All power to soviets and not to parties"—clearly announced their loyalty to "Soviet power and democracy" and not Bolshevik rule (Getzler 1983: vii). Avrich (1970: 58) remarks that "Kronstadt's residents displayed a real talent for spontaneous self-organization." Historian Israel Getzler (1983: viii) concurs, concluding that they "creat[ed] virtually from scratch a rich and impressive political and social culture, a Russian echo of the Paris Commune." In short order, the Red Army crushed the rebellion in a bloody assault. The Kronstadt massacre marked another turning point in anarchist participation in the Russian Revolution. Remaining anarchist bookstores, printing presses, art galleries, and clubs were closed. Anarchists continued to be arrested, imprisoned, and executed. In an introductory essay in Gregory Petrovich Maximoff's book *The Guillotine at Work*, veteran activist Sam Dolgoff (2013: 13) observed, "The backbone of the growing anarchist movement was broken." Many anarchists who had maintained a working relationship with the Bolsheviks until that point, including Goldman and Berkman, concluded that the revolution was dead and the Bolsheviks had killed it. In "The Bolshevik Myth," published in 1925, Berkman (in Avrich 1973: 163) wrote of the anguish he felt while listening to the battle at Kronstadt in which thousands of sailors and workers died: "My heart is numb with despair. Something has died within me." Goldman ([1931] 1970: 881), too, was paralyzed with disappointment; in her autobiography she recalled, "My voice seemed to have left me, for I could not utter a sound." After escaping Russia, Berkman and Goldman regained their revolutionary capacities, and in publications and speeches they contested those on the left who were "carried away by the Bolshevik glamour" (963). With others, Berkman and Goldman (1922) documented the Bolshevik state's campaign against anarchists to audiences often unwilling to face the disappointment.

When Goldman and Berkman left Russia, they were haunted by the revolution's failure, yet it was the lost possibilities of the Russian Revolution that spurred their later and more productive thinking about revolution. They always maintained that revolution required *"a fundamental transvaluation of values"* (Goldman [1922] 1970: 258–59; italics in original), but they turned their attention toward the practical issues of organization in ways that, prior to the Russian disaster, anarchists typically neglected. Looking back at the Russian Revolution in 1922, Goldman wrote in *My Disillusionment in Russia*: "The anarchists, the future unbiased historian will admit, have played a very important role in the Russian Revolution—a role far more significant and fruitful than their comparatively small number would have led one to expect. Yet honesty and sincerity compel me to state that their work would have been of infinitely greater practical value had they been better organized and equipped to guide the released energies of the people toward the reorganization of life on a libertarian foundation" (251–52). It was this capacity for ongoing practical organization that Goldman found two decades later in Spain.

A Better Revolution

Debates over the direction anarchism should take after the Russian Revolution occupied anarchists around the world for many decades. Factional disputes across the Left took their toll. As Goldman ([1931] 1970: 963) succinctly lamented, "They were all at each other's throats over the question of Russia." One faction, led by respected Russian exiles including Petr Arshinov and Makhno, published "The Organizational Platform of the General Union of Anarchists," which responded to the Bolshevik victory by calling for "greater theoretical unity and organizational discipline" (Cornell 2016: 107). Andrew Cornell notes the predictable response: "Unsurprisingly, antiorganizationalists denounced 'The Platform' as a deviation from anarchist principles, one that bordered on submission to Leninism" (107).

In the United States, Communist Party efforts to gain power in some unions met with anarchist resistance. In the International Ladies' Garment Workers' Union (ILGWU), for example, Rose Pesota and others allied with union moderates against Communists, a strategy that brought some support to anarchist projects while pushing anarchists uncomfortably toward a centrist position (81). Splits between anarchist-syndicalists and Communists in the IWW further weakened that union, which had already been decimated by the postwar repression called the "Red Scare" (82).

Goldman and Berkman forged a more interesting path. Rather than focus on what anarchists should do, they focused on what revolutions actually do and what role anarchists could play in popular rebellions. Emphasizing the importance of preparation, Goldman and Berkman asked how people could become prepared to create new order *while* dismantling the old. In Cornell's otherwise solid assessment of twentieth-century anarchism, *Unruly Equality*, he overstates the common criticism leveled at anarchists for dwelling on exposing Bolshevik repression rather than "refreshing their own [theories]" (144). While internecine conflict took a toll, Cornell's remarks neglect the necessary connection between critique and creativity (Antliff 2001: 207–8): Goldman's *My Disillusionment in Russia*, Berkman's "The Bolshevik Myth," and other reflections on the failed Russian Revolution subsequently provided material for reinventing revolution. Further, the bitter denunciations of treacherous alliances with the Communist Party in Russia were again tragically relevant a few years later in Spain.

In Berkman's last book, *What Is Anarchism?*, he digests the painful lessons of the Russian Revolution and anticipates a different and better revolution. Berkman ([1929] 2003: xiii) writes, "The lessons of the Russian Revolution in particular call for a new approach to various important problems, chief among them the character and activities of the social revolution."[2] Goldman concurred. On June 7, 1935, she wrote to Albert de Jong that this book was "the plainest and simplest modern exposé of our ideas" (Goldman

1990: reel 34). Beginning with Pierre-Joseph Proudhon's maxim "Property is theft," Berkman gently, conversationally, walks his reader through the basics of revolutionary anarchism. He starts with the presumption that everyone wants pretty much the same things out of life: "health, liberty, and well-being" (Berkman [1929] 2003: 2). Because we live in a system of private ownership and profit making, those who create wealth through their labor are being robbed by those who do not. Law and government protect the interests of the owning class, while employing some members of the working class to control the rest. Schools, media, and churches perpetuate the idea that this grave injustice is natural, inevitable, and right. Capitalism produces wars of conquest and profit; it produces crimes of desperation and greed. However, there is a general tendency toward justice in people, since "by nature and habit we are social beings" (42). It is precisely this spirit of justice and rebellion that capitalism and the state try to kill.

These conditions can be changed, however, if working people withhold their obedience from the government and their labor from employers. Working people cannot change the state by utilizing the methods of the state, because, as Berkman writes, "the means you use to attain your object soon themselves become your object" (92). To develop a society without inequality, people must begin to live as equals. To foster freedom, people must care for their own freedom as well as the freedom of others. People's capacity to be creative will lead them toward the work they can best do, and their desire to be useful to their fellows will motivate their contributions. To struggle against power, people must govern themselves: "It is *power* which corrupts. The consciousness that you possess power is itself the worst poison that corrodes the finest metal of man" (95; italics in original). A social revolution will be necessary, but rebellion against the ruling class and the state is only one step; the people must be prepared, both philosophically and materially, to step forward in the moments of upheaval and to reconstruct their own production, "to take over things for the general benefit . . . to reorganize conditions for the public welfare" (184). Berkman is at his most eloquent when he tells his reader how to prepare:

> If your object is to secure liberty, you must learn to do without authority and compulsion. If you intend to live in peace and harmony with your fellow men, you and they should cultivate brotherhood and respect for each other. If you want to work together with them for your mutual benefit, you must practice cooperation. The social revolution means much more than the reorganization of conditions only: it means the establishment of new human

values and social relationships, a changed attitude of man to man, as of one free and independent to his equal; it means a different spirit in individual and collective life, and that spirit cannot be born overnight. It is a spirit to be cultivated, to be nurtured and reared, as the most delicate flower is, for indeed it is the flower of a new and beautiful existence. (185)

Anarchism, in other words, requires practice. Workplaces can become sites where workers learn how to organize their labor, to integrate mental and manual work, and to manage themselves. Production and trade can be organized on the basis of ability and need. Decision making can be decentralized, and localities can strive for self-sufficiency. People are not "naturally good," as anarchists' opponents often caricature anarchists' views, but they have the capacity for great idealism, and it is the job of anarchists to "exemplify and cultivate this spirit and instill it in others" (222). For Goldman and Berkman, the way people live their lives is a political act, both creating an example of liberated space within the larger oppressive society and building a bridge to a future transformation.

Goldman ([1937] 2003: ix, x) wrote in her preface to the 1937 edition of *What Is Anarchism?* that Berkman's book was intended as a "primer of Anarchism," as well as a "new orientation of revolutionary tactics called forth by the experience of the Russian Revolution." "The old style, the old generalizations, etc., will not do," Berkman wrote to Goldman on February 24, 1927. "We must show clearly what we want and how we are going to reach it" (in Goldman 1990: reel 17). A romantic belief in the magic power of revolution had utterly failed in the nascent Union of Soviet Socialist Republics (USSR), because the needed "economic and social preparation," the "will to constructive work," was insufficient in Russia—although it blossomed in Spain after Berkman's death (Goldman [1937] 2003: x).

Goldman's passionate advocacy of the Confederación Nacional del Trabajo–Federación Anarquista Ibérica (CNT-FAI), the main anarchist organization during the Spanish Revolution and Civil War, was grounded in her enormous respect for the anarchists' concrete accomplishments in reorganizing their society. Goldman made three trips to revolutionary Spain, visiting flourishing agricultural and industrial cooperatives in Catalonia, including fifty-two villages in regions controlled by the anarchists (Dolgoff 1974; Ealham 2010). Goldman (Porter 1983: 231) wrote to her old friend Tom Bell that their comrades in Spain won her consistent support, despite significant disagreements, because "they have made the first halting steps towards the beginning of a new social structure." In her radio address of September 23, 1936,

Goldman praised the Barcelona anarchists for preserving the means of production that they collectivized, eschewing the temptation to revenge: "I was told that the workers felt they had produced the wealth and that it would have been nothing short of stupidity to destroy anything that can now be made accessible to all who labor" (216). In contrast to the shortsighted invocations of revenge against employers that some anarchists called for in 1917 (Avrich 2005: 126), Spanish anarchists focused on what comes next. The redirection of revolutionary rage into constructive efforts to reorganize production was, for Goldman, the epitome of anarchist political accomplishment. The ability of ordinary workers and peasants to create and run anarchist collectives was the historical evidence Goldman held up to the world to show that a different, better way of living was possible. In revolutionary Spain, Goldman found the needed historical circumstances for successful anarchist work: a spirit and practice of collective life that took hold across several generations, preparing people to step in when the circumstances opened up. To her friend Evelyn Scott, she wrote that a revolutionary sensibility is both parent and child of political struggle: "Those still capable of independent thinking will now be compelled to see that Revolution does not express [only] the overthrow of institutions, necessary as that may be, but also the inner growth as well of conscious intelligent understanding for the individual and collective life" (Porter 1983: 245).

Goldman was well aware of the irony of her position: her cherished ideal of anarchism was widely held to be destructive, criminal, entirely negative, opposed to everything, embracing nothing. In her final public speech in London on March 24, 1939, she argued that it was the Spanish anarchists' ability to create workable alternative institutions that provoked opposition from all sides:

> I was amazed at the tremendous constructive work that the Spanish workers achieved side by side with their struggle, with the loss of life, with hunger, with all sorts of things against them; and that is what was feared the most. Don't you see, don't you realise, to demonstrate that Anarchists, who are decried by all sorts of people, working men, liberals, labour people, the capitalist class, as criminals who go about with bombs in their hands or pockets, and with knives and with poison, and who can only be appeased if they destroy the children of the capitalists and hang the priests on the nearest lamp-post—that such Anarchists, hated by everyone, condemned by everyone, attacked by everyone, were able to show a new line of procedure in revolutionary struggle—what greater crime or offence? And that is why it was necessary to do everything possible in order to destroy that marvellous beginning. (276)

The successes in Spain, even though eventually defeated by the combined forces of well-supplied communist and fascist armies, continue to inspire anarchist politics today.

Prison Activism

A second arena of creative, enduring anarchist organizing in response to the Russian Revolution addresses the tragic circumstances of political prisoners. For the ascendant Bolsheviks, the anarchists were usefully ambiguous figures because they could be pulled back and forth across the shifting, treacherous line separating allies from enemies. Anarchists operated as liminal figures, both defining and obscuring the porous boundary between revolutionaries and criminals.[3] For the Bolsheviks, anarchists were allies when the task at hand was fighting antirevolutionary forces and enemies when the fight shifted to consolidating state and Communist Party power: they worked as figures who both marked and disguised the boundary between politics and crime, between revolutionaries and "bandits." So anarchists' own insistence on blurring the boundary, on noticing the rebellions within prisons as well as the criminality within states, was an effort to reverse the moral weight of Bolshevik judgment. As the lengthy quotation above from Goldman's last speech in London indicates, anarchists insisted on remembering and contesting the conditions of making knowledge about them. In their defiant politics of mourning political prisoners, anarchists kept alive their sense of what could have been.

Political prisoners were recognized as such in Russia in earlier times: after the failed 1905 revolution, Boris Yelensky reports, "politicals" were separated from the rest of the prison population, were allowed to elect representatives who negotiated with the prison administration, and received outside aid. They created an attenuated but still real public space within prison walls (Yelensky 1958: 10–14). Prior to World War I, the Anarchist Red Cross already existed to send "money and letters of support to anarchists imprisoned in Russia" (Cornell 2016: 26). Recording the work of the Anarchist Red Cross (later called the Black Cross) after 1917, Yelensky (1958: 21) laments that no one had foreseen that the czar's brutality was "like child's play" compared to the Bolsheviks, yet the struggle to recognize (and in the process help to create) political resistance within prison continued.

The campaigns on behalf of political prisoners took many forms. Anarchists allowed to leave Russia immediately organized committees to aid their imprisoned comrades. Goldman, Berkman, and Schapiro approached

European syndicalists to appeal to Lenin on behalf of imprisoned anarchists, who were sometimes released providing they left Russia. Once released into exile, Volin, Maksimov, Yelensky, Steimer, and Senya Fleshin joined the efforts to publicize and advocate for their comrades. These well-known anarchists attempted to mobilize international pressure against the regime while providing material aid to every imprisoned anarchist they could reach. The relief groups included the Joint Committee for the Defense of the Revolutionists Imprisoned in Russia (Berlin 1923–26), the Relief Fund of the International Working Men's Association for Anarchists and Anarcho-Syndicalists Imprisoned or Exiled in Russia (Berlin and Paris, 1926–32), and the Alexander Berkman Aid Fund (Chicago, 1921–198?).

Berkman led nearly a decade and a half of relief work for anarchists imprisoned by the Soviet government. After Kronstadt, anarchists were arrested and sent to concentration camps in the north, to ominous places called "political isolators," which were "veritable coffin[s] in which the political [were] buried alive" (Alexander Berkman Social Club 2010: 11); to prisons in the Urals; or to penal colonies in Siberia (Avrich 2005: 235). Political prisoners endured severe conditions of cold, illness, starvation, solitary confinement, and forced labor. Paul Avrich and Karen Avrich (2011: 322) report that "the files accumulated by these advocacy groups bulged with letters and dossiers of incarcerated anarchists, their names followed by such grim annotations as 'beaten in Butyrki,' 'repeated hunger strikes,' 'killed in prison,' 'shot by Kiev Cheka,' 'beaten for resisting forced feeding,' and 'fate unknown.'" Reflecting on the aid groups' dogged persistence, the Alexander Berkman Social Club (2010: x) writes: "A whole generation of militants had been executed, starved to death, or driven to suicide. All those voices had been stilled. Those in Russian prisoner support observed the creation of a systematic state of terror far beyond the wildest nightmares of any anarchist."

The anarchists in the prison support movement did more, though, than observe or lament the terror—it organized against it. The organizing required was extensive—protest meetings, endless fund-raising, writing and publishing bulletins, writing letters, and sending packages—and took a great deal of energy and resources from this crowd of aging anarchists, but they deemed it essential. Aid organizations resumed the cultural activities that had sustained anarchist groups in the past: concerts, dances, plays, speaking tours, mail-order book services, and the ubiquitous journals, including *Free Society, Road to Freedom,* and the *Bulletin of the Joint Committee for the Defense of Revolutionists Imprisoned in Russia,* published in several languages. In 1925, with the help of civil libertarian Roger Baldwin and other prominent intellectuals, the International Committee for Political Prisoners published *Letters from Russian Prisons*, injecting both the prisoners' words and the work of the aid groups into broader circulation.

The successes of the prisoner aid groups were enabled by the personal transnational connections between anarchists who were held by the state and those who were not. "Anarchism was a transnational movement," writes Zimmer (2015: 111), "comprised of overlapping networks, loosely defined by region, language, and ideology, which in turn overlapped with a wide variety of other revolutionary causes." They were connected by shared participation in international organizations and congresses, by the vigorous global circulation of their publications, and by their interpersonal, familial, community, and workplace links. Direct personal communication was particularly effective at making prisoners' voices audible, Zimmer explains, because "anarchists belonging to one particular network were typically . . . only one or two removes from any other node within this web of connections" (112). In the ILGWU, for example, anarchists prevailed in their effort to censure the USSR over political prisoners because anarchists in the union had direct personal communication with their imprisoned comrades (Cornell 2016: 90). At the anarchist colony Stelton, "letters from friends and relatives began to arrive, carrying news of the growing centralization of power and the repression of anarchists and other Left dissidents," and were read "aloud at public meetings" by "community leaders" (98).

The aid groups attempted to track the whereabouts and conditions of anarchists and other radicals taken into custody and to provide money, clothes, food, books, and moral support to every prisoner allowed to receive mail (102). The prisoners reported that the letters and packages were "a godsend," a "breath of fresh air in this stifling atmosphere" (Avrich 2005: 235). Avrich concludes, "Only the letters from their families and comrades kept alive a flicker of hope" (234). Yet, important as personal support for imprisoned comrades and calls to condemn Bolshevik oppression were to the anarchist movement, the prison networks served another political function: they created a form of solidarity in which those whose lives were intended to be lost to public sight were able to claim a tenuous public presence. "The prison," political philosopher Judith Butler (2015: 173) surmises, "remains the limit case of the public sphere, marking the power of the state to control who can pass into the public and who must pass out of it." The capacity to assemble for political ends is "haunted by the possibility of imprisonment" (173); the anarchists tried to reverse this specter, making prison a place that is haunted by the possibility of free public assembly. The anarchists who were released from prison for one day to attend Kropotkin's massive funeral gathering, to assemble with thousands of other radicals, are a poignant example of the shadow of imprisonment within assembly and assembly within imprisonment. Released with the proviso that they return to prison after the funeral, the anarchists did so not out of loyalty to the Bolsheviks or to the rule of law but to their own past and future rebellions. They reassembled themselves in the prison, as they had in the street, to assert their power to appear in public and to create an alternate public by the act of appearing. In this regard, I find Cornell's (2016: 93) analysis of the prisoner aid movement to be problematic; he argues, "Prisoner defense work threatened to overtake other movement-building responsibilities in the 1920s." My argument is that prisoner aid work was a key aspect of anarchists' movement-building responsibilities, not a distraction from them. Prisoner aid groups such as the Anarchist Black Cross and others, which still work with political prisoners in the United States and elsewhere (287), continue the constitutive political work of politicizing and publicizing the porous boundary between publics and prisons.

Calling themselves the Alexander Berkman Social Club (2010: x), the editors of a 2010 collection of Berkman's journals regarding imprisoned revolutionaries give in their introduction two reasons for collecting and republishing the works: First, "to name names; to, at least, bring these people back from the darkness of the Bolshevik pit. To shed a little light on the struggle of our comrades and keep their names alive even in our small circles." Second, "to commemorate those who, in the most trying of personal and economic circumstances, refused to forget their comrades in Russia." These radicals, especially the indefatigable Berkman, "were a tiny voice, but they never stopped shouting."

What goes into this "shouting"? How do anarchists produce the rememberings that they need? Reflecting on the relation of memory to power, Nietzsche talks about a double forgetting. Power, he suggests, does its most nefarious work when we forget twice: we forget, then we forget that we forgot. We cushion ourselves from recovering or reinventing those memories with the second forgetting, which erases not just the content of the memory but the possibility of there being such a memory at all. Anarchists' determined recirculation of imprisoned voices works to flip that insight around, creating a double remembering: the aid groups remember, and we can remember that they remember, creating a circuit of memory and using their recollected voices to hold on to our capacity for cultivating politically needed memories. The letters poke and prod their readers; they keep calling for attention. The idea is not only to remember something that might otherwise be forgotten but to intervene in the conditions of possibility regarding remembering, to remember that others remember. In that second remembering, audiences may launch an incipient process: to hold on not only to the content of these particular recollections but also to a larger process of creative recollecting. The prisoner aid groups' determined, ongoing circulation of imprisoned anarchists' names and words constructs a needed form of double remembering. The anarchist aid groups are inviting listeners to resist the process of erasure, to remember that others remember, that it is possible to remember, that we must struggle to keep remembering.

Conclusion: What Do Anarchists Want?

Anarchists are frequently criticized during moments of political upheaval because they announce no reform agenda, issue no demands. Instead, they create compressed versions of the world they want, via occupations, guerrilla movements, schools, art projects, journals, unions, puppet theaters, houses of the people, encampments, collective gardens, and more. While anarchist organizing in the Russian Revolution was summarily dispatched, many anarchists cultivated those lessons and applied them in Spain and elsewhere. Contemporary advocacy on behalf of political prisoners continues past activist projects (Antliff 2004: 163–67). In our time, we see the Occupy encampments, the Zapatista movement, the women's encampments for a future of peace and justice, Native American's protests against the Dakota Access pipeline, and many other expressions of an essentially anarchist idea of working for a new world by creating the conditions it requires. Stories of successful prefigurative events resonate within anarchism and its sister movements. They mobilize traces of previous actions to gesture toward those yet to come. They are events in an active, ongoing sense—not just things that happen but invitations to make new things happen. The anarchist imaginary that was articulated during the early days of the 1917 revolution, and then repressed, reemerges with new strength and fresh insights in revolutionary settings today and in the future.

Notes

Portions of this discussion are taken from Kathy E. Ferguson, *Emma Goldman: Political Thinking in the Streets* (Lanham, MD: Rowman and Littlefield, 2011), 139–40, 293–300.

1   Goldman and Berkman were exiled to the Soviet Union after serving two-year prison terms for opposing conscription. Steimer was sent into exile as part of the resolution of her conviction under the Sedition Act.

2   *What Is Anarchism?* has a confusing publication history. It was also published as *Now and After: The ABC of Communist Anarchism* and other titles. See Barry Pateman's (2003: vii) introduction to *What Is Anarchism?*

3   I am indebted to Lisa Lowe's (2015: 25) discussion of the way that the shifting figure of the "coolie" worked in British colonial imaginaries: the "coolie" served "to both define and to obscure" the boundary between slave and wage labor.

References

Adams, Jason. 2013. *Occupy Time: Technoculture, Immediacy, and Resistance after Occupy Wall Street.* New York: Palgrave Macmillan.

Alexander Berkman Social Club. 2010. *The Tragic Procession: Alexander Berkman and Russian Prisoner Aid.* London: Kate Sharpley Library.

Antliff, Allan. 2001. *Anarchist Modernism: Art, Politics, and the First American Avant-Garde.* Chicago: University of Chicago Press.

Antliff, Allan, ed. 2004. *Only a Beginning: An Anarchist Anthology.* Vancouver, BC: Arsenal Pulp.

Avrich, Paul. 1970. *Kronstadt 1921.* Princeton, NJ: Princeton University Press.

Avrich, Paul, ed. 1973. *The Anarchists in the Russian Revolution.* Ithaca, NY: Cornell University Press.

Avrich, Paul. 2005. *The Russian Anarchists.* Oakland, CA: AK Press.

Avrich, Paul, and Karen Avrich. 2011. *Sasha and Emma: The Anarchist Odyssey of Alexander Berkman and Emma Goldman.* Cambridge, MA: Harvard University Press.

Berkman, Alexander. [1929] 2003. *What Is Anarchism?* Oakland, CA: AK Press. Originally published by Vanguard.

Berkman, Alexander. 1973. "The Bolshevik Myth." In Avrich, *Anarchists in the Russian Revolution*, 163–64.

Berkman, Alexander, and Emma Goldman. 1922. "Bolsheviks Shooting Anarchists." *Freedom*, January 7, 4.

Butler, Judith. 2015. *Notes toward a Performative Theory of Assembly.* Cambridge, MA: Harvard University Press.

Cornell, Andrew. 2016. *Unruly Equality: U.S. Anarchism in the Twentieth Century.* Berkeley: University of California Press.

Dolgoff, Sam, ed. 1974. *The Anarchist Collectives: Workers' Self-Management in the Spanish Revolution, 1936–1939.* New York: Free Life Editions.

Dolgoff, Sam. 2013. "Gregory Petrovich Maximoff." In *The Leninist Counter-Revolution*, vol. 1 of *The Guillotine at Work*, by Gregory Petrovich Maximoff, 11–16. East Sussex, UK: ChristieBooks.

Ealham, Chris. 2010. *Anarchism and the City: Revolution and Counter-Revolution in Barcelona, 1898–1937.* Oakland, CA: AK Press.

Getzler, Israel. 1983. *Kronstadt 1917–1921: The Fate of a Soviet Democracy.* Cambridge: Cambridge University Press.

Goldman, Emma. [1922] 1970. *My Disillusionment in Russia.* New York: Apollo Editions.

Goldman, Emma. [1931] 1970. *Living My Life.* Vol. 2. Mineola, NY: Dover.

Goldman, Emma. [1937] 2003. Preface to Berkman, *What Is Anarchism?*, ix–xi.

Goldman, Emma. 1990. *The Emma Goldman Papers Project: A Microfilm Edition.* Edited by Candace Falk with Ronald J. Zboray et al. Alexandria, VA: Chadwyck-Healey.

Golos truda. 1973. "Declaration of the Petrograd Union of Anarcho-Syndicalist Propaganda." In Avrich, *Anarchists in the Russian Revolution,* 68–72.

Gurianova, Nina. 2012. *The Aesthetics of Anarchy: Art and Ideology in the Early Russian Avant-Garde.* Berkeley: University of California Press.

International Committee for Political Prisoners. 1925. *Letters from Russian Prisons.* New York: Albert and Charles Boni.

Kropotkin, Pyotr. 1973. "Two Letters to Lenin." In Avrich, *Anarchists in the Russian Revolution,* 146–49.

Lowe, Lisa. 2015. *The Intimacies of Four Continents.* Durham, NC: Duke University Press.

Makhno, Nestor. 1973. "Agricultural Communes." In Avrich, *Anarchists in the Russian Revolution,* 128–33.

"Manifestos of the Makhnovist Movement." 2005. In *Anarchism: A Documentary History of Libertarian Ideas,* edited by Robert Graham, 1: 300–304. Montreal: Black Rose Books.

Pateman, Barry. 2003. Introduction to Berkman, *What Is Anarchism?,* iii–viii.

Porter, David. 1983. *Vision on Fire: Emma Goldman on the Spanish Revolution.* Edinburgh, UK: AK Press.

Yelensky, Boris. 1958. *In the Struggle for Equality: The History of the Anarchist Red Cross.* Edited by Matthew Hart. Chicago: Alexander Berkman Aid Fund. www.abcf.net/la/pdfs/layelensky.pdf.

Zimmer, Kenyon. 2015. *Immigrants against the State: Yiddish and Italian Anarchism in America.* Urbana: University of Illinois Press.

Enzo Traverso

Historicizing Communism:
A Twentieth-Century Chameleon

Throughout the twentieth century, the legacy of
the October Revolution was torn between two
antipodal interpretations. The rise to power of the
Russian Bolsheviks appeared, on the one hand, as
the announcement of a global socialist transformation and, on the other hand, as the event that
set the stage for an epoch of totalitarianism. In
1927 Sergei Eisenstein shot *October*, a film that
shaped the imagination of several generations in
depicting the revolution as an epic mass uprising.
The historiographical equivalent of this work of
art was Leon Trotsky's *History of the Russian Revolution* ([1932] 2008), both a chronological and an
analytical reconstruction of this event, in which
the empathetic, colorful narration of the witness
merged with the conceptual insight of the Marxist
thinker, like an astonishing fusion of the styles of
Jules Michelet and Karl Marx. Isaac Deutscher, in
a chapter of his biography of the head of the Red
Army titled "The Revolutionary as Historian,"
summarizes Trotsky's method of history writing
by comparing it with Thomas Carlyle's capacity to
grasp the emotions of oppressed people suddenly
transformed into political actors, but Deutscher
([1954] 2003: 189) emphasizes that the Bolshevik
thinker was able to combine this "imaginative

The South Atlantic Quarterly 116:4, October 2017
DOI 10.1215/00382876-4234994 © 2017 Duke University Press

élan" with "crystalline clarity." The result is a book written with both passion and thought. For a century, and across the world, most of the Left—far beyond the official communist movements—perceived the October Revolution in a similar way: both as the iconic image of utopian aspirations and as the irrefutable evidence of a teleological vision positing socialism as the natural end of history.

The antipodal interpretation depicted the Bolsheviks as the embodiment of the totalitarian potentialities of modernity. After the consolidation of the Union of Soviet Socialist Republics (USSR) in the second half of the 1920s, the initial descriptions of a herd of baboons jumping over a field of ruins and skulls—according to Winston Churchill's prose—was abandoned, but communism continued to be depicted as a dangerous pathology of modern societies. For many conservative thinkers, from Isaiah Berlin to Martin Malia, from Karl Popper to Richard Pipes, it was a sort of "ideocracy," the inevitable outcome of the coercive transformation of society according to an abstract and authoritarian model (see Traverso 2015: 77–88). According to this right-wing wisdom, the will to create a community of equals engenders a society of slaves. François Furet (1981: 12), for his part, rejected the communist "passion" and its ideology and connected them to the original madness of revolution itself, establishing a linear trajectory from the Jacobin Terror to the Soviet Gulag: "Today, the Gulag is leading to a rethinking of the Terror precisely because the two undertakings are seen as identical."

The most radical versions of these opposed interpretations—official communism and Cold War anticommunism—also converge insofar as, for both of them, the Communist Party was a kind of demiurgic historical force. As Claudio S. Ingerflom (2000: 121) ironically observes, most Cold Warrior scholars defended "the anti-Bolshevik version of a 'bolshevized' history." As in the Bolshevik version, ideology indisputably dominated the landscape and the party appeared as its trustful instrument, even if now the road to paradise had become the road to hell. Twenty-five years after the end of the USSR and real existing socialism, only the first variant of this symmetrical representation has disappeared; the second one still exists, holds a strong—even if no longer hegemonic—position in scholarship, and deeply shapes the public uses of the past, from media vulgarizations to memory policies.

Historicizing the communist experience, therefore, means overcoming this dichotomy between two narratives—one idyllic and the other horrific—which are also fundamentally alike. Several decades after its exhaustion, the communist experience does not need to be defended, idealized, or demonized; it deserves to be critically understood as a whole, as a dialectical totality shaped by internal tensions and contradictions, presenting multiple dimensions in a vast spectrum of colors going from redemptive élans to totalitarian violence, from participatory democracy and collective deliberation to blind oppression and mass extermination, from the most utopian imagination to the most bureaucratic domination, sometimes shifting from one to the other in a short span of time. In 1991 Edgar Morin (1991: 7), writing a new preface to the autobiographical account of his rupture with the French Communist Party, proposed a definition of Stalinism that captures at the same time the complexity and the contradictory character of the communist experience: it was, he wrote, "the monstrous step of a gigantic adventure for changing the world." Inevitably, this nightmarish moment shadowed the rest—in fact, it shadowed the entire twentieth century—but this adventure had begun earlier and continued after the fall of real socialism. Thus historicizing communism means inscribing it into this "gigantic adventure," as old as capitalism itself. Communism was a chameleon that could not be isolated as an insular experience or separated from its forerunners and inheritors.

Communism came out of the October Revolution, which was a *process*, even if it did not reproduce Edward Gibbon's evolutionary vision of the Roman Empire: origins, rise, and fall. Neither its emergence nor its conclusion was inevitable, despite its historical premises, and many of its turns resulted from unexpected circumstances. Far from being linear, its trajectory was fractured, shaped by breaks and bifurcations. It includes insurgencies from below and radical changes "from above," leaps and Thermidorian regressions that a retrospective view could inscribe into a single historical sequence. Lenin and Stalin were not alike, Sheila Fitzpatrick (1994: 3) emphasizes, but belong to the same process: "Napoleon's revolutionary wars can be included in our general concept of the French Revolution, even if we do not regard them as an embodiment of the spirit of 1789; and a similar approach seems legitimate in the case of the Russian Revolution." In Fitzpatrick's book, the Russian Revolution runs from February 1917 until the Great Purges of 1936–38. Believing in a possible "regeneration" of its original spirit, Deutscher extended the process through the de-Stalinization of 1956. Today we can easily recognize that his diagnosis was wrong, but his perception of an ongoing movement was shared by millions of people across the world. The binary vision of a revolutionary Bolshevism opposed to a Stalinist counterrevolution allows distinguishing between emancipatory insurgency and totalitarian violence but hides the connections that unite them and risks becoming as sterile as the conservative interpretation of a substantial continuity from Lenin to Mikhail Gorbachev grounded on the ideological bases of the USSR.

Understanding communism as a global historical experience requires distinguishing between movements and regimes—as Renzo De Felice (1977) recommended for interpreting Italian fascism—without separating them: not only did movements shift into regimes, but the latter kept a symbiotic link with the former, orienting their projects and actions. The Bolshevik party before 1917, composed mostly of exiled and pariah intellectuals, seems a different universe from the gigantic bureaucratic apparatus that led the USSR in the following decades. They are two different worlds, but many threads connect them. This concerns not the history of Russian Bolshevism exclusively but rather the history of communism as a whole, at least during its first decades. Whereas in the USSR Stalin decided to eliminate the Bolshevik old guard and beyond (half a million of estimated executions in the second half of the 1930s and the 1940s), Communists led resistance movements against fascism in Western Europe and organized one of the most epic revolutionary experiences of the twentieth century with the "Long March" across China (1934–35). Many communist leaders, from Palmiro Togliatti to Otto Braun, from Georgi Dimitrov and Manabendra Nath Roy to Ho Chi Minh, lived or were instructed in Moscow.

Like many other "isms" of our political and philosophical lexicon, *communism* is an ambiguous word. Historically understood, it is neither an ideal type nor really a concept, but rather a metaphor for multiple events and experiences. Its ambiguity does not lie exclusively in the discrepancy that separates the communist idea—elaborated by many utopian thinkers up through Marx—from its historical embodiments. It lies in the extreme diversity of its expressions. Not only were Russian, Chinese, and Italian communism different, but also in the long run many communist movements deeply changed, despite keeping their leaders and their ideological references. Considered as a whole, communism appears rather as a mosaic of communisms. Sketching its "anatomy," one can distinguish at least four broad forms of communism, interrelated and not necessarily opposed to one another, but different enough to be recognized on their own: communism as *revolution*, communism as *regime*, communism as *anticolonialism*, and, finally, communism as a variant of *social democracy*. The October Revolution was their common matrix. This does not mean that all of them had a Russian origin, insofar as Bolshevism itself was the product of a global historical process. But it does mean that all forms of twentieth-century communism were related to the Russian Revolution, the great historical turn in which they recognized a departure and an epiphany.

The Process of Revolution

Revolution is a process, Fitzpatrick explained, but the vision of communism as revolution focuses mostly on its inaugural moment and emphasizes its disruptive character. Revolution is the moment in which, recalling Deutscher's words, human beings make their own history; it is the transitional, ephemeral, magical moment in which the oppressed become historical subjects, turn upside down the old social and political order, and try to replace it with a new one. Revolution is a suspension of historical time, when the linearity of a "homogeneous and empty" time is violently broken, opening new horizons and projecting society into a future to be invented. To quote an image suggested by Walter Benjamin (1999: 463), one could compare this disruptive moment to "the process of splitting the atom" that suddenly "liberates the enormous energies of history." We could call it the Eisensteinian stage of communism: *October* is not a historical reconstitution of the Russian Revolution; it is a masterpiece that captures its emancipatory élan. Revolution deals with power relations, tactics and strategy, movements and leaderships, and the art of insurrection, but it also concerns aspirations, rage, resentment, happiness, commonality, utopias, and memory. In short, it is a moment in which politics is suddenly flooded with feelings and emotions. It is a practice of the common exactly antipodal to the model of a society of isolated individuals acting as competitors posited by classical liberalism. In such historical circumstances, the leaders are pushed forward and oriented by these new forms of collective agency. They simply record and formalize the decisions of a constituent power rising from below. Trotsky, in his autobiography, vividly mentions this feature of any revolutionary process, describing the thrilling atmosphere of his speeches at the Modern Circus of Petrograd in 1917. The crowd penetrated his subconscious and spoke through his voice: "No speaker, no matter how exhausted, could resist the electric tension of that impassioned human throng. . . . On such occasions I felt as if I were listening to the speaker from the outside, trying to keep pace with his ideas, afraid that, like a somnambulist, he might fall off the edge of the roof at the sound of my conscious reasoning" (Trotsky [1929] 2007: 315).

It is important to remember the mood of the Russian Revolution because it powerfully contributed to creating an iconic image that survived the misfortunes of the USSR and shadowed the entire twentieth century. Its aura attracted millions of human beings across the world and remained relatively preserved even when the aura of the communist regimes completely fell apart. In the 1960s and 1970s, it fueled a new wave of political radicalization that, more than simply claiming its autonomy from the USSR and its allies, perceived them as enemies.

The Russian Revolution came out of the Great War. It was a product of the collapse of the "long nineteenth century," the age of the "hundred years peace," to speak with Karl Polanyi ([1944] 1971: 5), and the symbiotic link between war and revolution shaped the entire trajectory of twentieth-century communism. Emerging from the Franco-Prussian War of 1870, the Paris Commune had been a forerunner of militarized politics, as many Bolshevik thinkers often emphasized, but the October Revolution extended it to an incomparably larger scale: the National Guard was not the Red Army, and the twenty districts of the French capital simply cannot be compared with the czarist empire. The First World War transformed Bolshevism itself, which changed many of its features: several canonical works of the communist tradition such as Lenin's 1918 *The Proletarian Revolution and the Renegade Kautsky* or Trotsky's 1920 *Terrorism and Communism* simply could not be imagined before 1914. Just as 1789 introduced a new concept of revolution—defined no longer as an astronomical rotation but rather as a social and political break—October 1917 reframed it in military terms: crisis of the old order, mass mobilization, dualism of power, armed insurrection, proletarian dictatorship, civil war, and violent clash with counterrevolution. Lenin's 1917 *State and Revolution* formalized Bolshevism as both an ideology (an interpretation of Marx's ideas) and a whole of strategic precepts distinguishing it from social democratic reformism, a politics belonging to the exhausted age of nineteenth-century capitalism. Bolshevism came out of a time of brutalization of culture and politics, in which war irrupted into politics, changing its language and its practices. It was a product of the anthropological transformation that, speaking with George L. Mosse (1990), shaped the old continent at the end of the Great War. This genetic code of Bolshevism was visible everywhere, from texts to languages, from iconography to songs, from symbols to rituals. It outlasted the Second World War and remained extremely pregnant in the rebellious movements of the 1970s, whose slogans and liturgies obsessively emphasized the idea of a violent clash against the state. Bolshevism created a military paradigm of revolution that deeply shaped the history of communisms throughout the planet. The European Resistance, as well as the socialist outbreaks in China, Korea, Vietnam, and Cuba, reproduced a similar symbiotic link between war and revolution. Therefore, the international communist movement was conceived as a revolutionary army formed by millions of combatants, and this had inevitable consequences in terms of organization, authoritarianism, discipline, task repartition, and, last but not least, gender hierarchies. In a movement of warriors, female leaders could only be exceptions. Even Antonio Gramsci, who tried to put into question this Bolshevik paradigm for the revolution in the West, did not avoid a military theoretical framework in which he distinguished between "war of movement" and "war of position."

The Communist Regime

The communist regime institutionalized this military dimension of revolution. It destroyed the creative, anarchistic, self-emancipatory spirit of 1917, freezing and emptying the forms and practices of democracy invented during a year of social and political effervescence, but at the same time inscribed itself into the revolutionary process. The shift of the revolution toward the Soviet regime passed through different steps: the civil war (1918–21), the collectivization of agriculture (1930–33), and the political purges of the Moscow Trials (1936–38). Dissolving the constituent assembly, in December 1917, the Bolsheviks affirmed the superiority of Soviet democracy, but by the end of the civil war the latter was dying. During this atrocious and bloody conflict, the USSR introduced censorship, suppressed political pluralism until finally abolishing any fraction within the Communist Party itself, militarized labor and created the first camps of forced labor, instituted a new political secret police (Cheka), and coercively Sovietized nations whose right of self-determination had previously been affirmed. In March 1921, the violent repression of Kronstadt symbolized the end of soviet democracy and the USSR emerged from the civil war as a single-party dictatorship. Ten years later, the collectivization of agriculture brutally ended the peasant revolution and invented new forms of totalitarian violence and bureaucratically centralized modernization of the country. In the second half of the 1930s, the political purges physically eliminated the vestiges of revolutionary Bolshevism and disciplined the entire society by establishing the rule of terror. For two decades, the USSR was a gigantic system of concentration camps. Between the collectivization and the Moscow Trials, the cultural revolution that had spread after 1917 was brutally smashed; the aesthetic avant-garde was brought to heel, and socialist realism became the official Soviet doctrine in literature and the arts, while Russian nationalism was restored in all non-Russian republics of the USSR. Stalinism resulted from these transformations.

Since the mid-1930s, the USSR roughly corresponded to the classical definition of totalitarianism elaborated a few years later by many conservative political thinkers: a correlation of official ideology, charismatic leadership, single-party dictatorship, suppression of state of law and political pluralism, monopoly of all communication means through state propaganda, social and political terror organized by a system of concentration camps, and suppression of free-market capitalism by a centralized economy. This description, currently used to point out the similarities between communism and fascism, is not wrong but extremely superficial. One can skip the enormous differences that separated the communist and fascist ideologies, as well as the social and economic content of their political systems—this is another debate—but it remains that such a classical definition of totalitarianism does not grasp the internal dynamic of the Soviet regime. It is simply unable to inscribe it into the historical process of the Russian Revolution. It depicts the USSR as a static, monolithic system, whereas the advent of Stalinism meant a deep and prolonged transformation of society and culture.

Similarly unsatisfactory is the definition of Stalinism as bureaucratic counterrevolution or a "betrayed" revolution. Stalinism certainly signified a radical departure from any idea of democracy and self-emancipation, but it was not, properly speaking, a *counterrevolution*. The comparison with the Napoleonic Empire is pertinent insofar as Stalinism consciously linked the transformations engendered by the Russian Revolution to both the Enlightenment and the tradition of Russian empire, but Stalinism was not the restoration of the Old Regime, neither politically nor economically, nor even culturally. Stalinism belonged to the process of the Russian Revolution, Stephen Kotkin suggests, because its project was the building of a new civilization. Bolshevism, he emphasizes, "must be seen not merely as a set of institutions, a group of personalities, or an ideology but as a cluster of powerful symbols and attitudes, a language and new forms of speech, new ways of behaving in public and private, even new styles of dress—in short, as an ongoing experience through which it was possible to imagine and strive to bring about a new civilization called socialism" (Kotkin 1995: 14). In the wake of Bolshevism, he continues, "Stalinism was not just a political system, let alone the rule of an individual. It was a set of values, a social identity, a way of life" (23). Far from restoring the power of the old aristocracy, Stalinism created a completely new economic, managerial, scientific, and intellectual elite, recruited from the lower classes of Soviet societies—notably the peasantry—and educated by the new communist institutions. This is the key for explaining why Stalinism had benefited from a social consensus, in spite of terror and mass deportations. According to Boris Groys, even in the aesthetic field Stalinism unfolded, despite its totalitarian forms, the creative élan of revolution. Therefore, it would be wrong to reduce socialist realism to a simple form of neoclassicism. Like the avant-garde, he suggests: "Stalinist culture continues to be oriented toward the future; it is prospective rather than mimetic, a visualization of the collective dream of the new world and the new humanity rather than the product of an individual artist's temperament; it does not retire to the museum, but aspires to exert an active influence upon life. In brief, it cannot simply be regarded as 'regressive' or pre-avant-garde" (Groys 2011: 113).

Interpreting Stalinism as a step in the process of the Russian Revolution does not mean sketching a linear track. The first wave of terror—pertinently comparable to the Jacobin Terror of 1794—took place during a civil war, when the existence of the USSR itself was threatened by an international coalition. The brutality of the White counterrevolution, the extreme violence of its propaganda and of its practices—pogroms and massacres—pushed the Bolshevik power to establish a pitiless dictatorship. Stalin initiated the second and third waves of terror during the 1930s—collectivization and the purges—in a pacified country whose borders had been internationally recognized and whose political power had been menaced neither by external nor by internal forces. Of course, the rise to power of Hitler in Germany clearly signaled the possibility of a new war in the medium term, but the massive, blind, and irrational character of Stalin's violence significantly weakened the USSR instead of reinforcing and equipping it to face such dangers. Stalinism was a "revolution from above," a paradoxical mixture of modernization and social regression, whose final result was mass deportation, a system of concentration camps, a whole of trials exhuming the fantasies of Inquisition, and a wave of mass execution that decapitated the state, the party, and the army. In rural areas, Stalinism meant, according to Nikolay Bukharin, the leader of the "right-wing" Bolshevik opposition, the return to "military feudal exploitation" of the peasantry with catastrophic economic effects (see Werth 1997: 162). Thus Eric Hobsbawm's (1996: 390) apologetic vision of Stalin as a dictator adapted to the historical conditions of a peasantry whose mentality recalled that of the Western plebs of the eleventh century seems highly debatable. At the same moment in which the kulaks starved in Ukraine, the Soviet regime was transforming tens of thousands of peasants into technicians and engineers. In short, Soviet totalitarianism merged modernism and barbarism; it was a peculiar, frightening, totalitarian Promethean trend. In the wake of Deutscher, Arno J. Mayer (2000: 607) defines it as "an uneven and unstable amalgam of monumental achievements and monstrous crimes." Of course, any left scholar or activist could easily share Victor Serge's ([1946] 2012: 326) assessment on the moral, philosophical, and political line that radically separated Stalinism from authentic socialism, insofar as Stalin's USSR had become "an absolute, castocratic totalitarian State, drunk with its own power, for which man does not count," but this does not change the fact, perfectly recognized by Serge himself, that this Red totalitarianism pursued and unfolded in a historical process started by the October Revolution (326). Avoiding any teleological approach, one could observe that this result was neither historically ineluctable nor coherently inscribed into a Marxist ideological pattern. The origins of Stalinism, nevertheless, cannot simply be imputed, as radical functionalism suggests, to the historical circumstances of war and the social backwardness of a gigantic country with an absolutist past, a country in which building socialism inevitably required reproducing the gruesomeness of "primitive capital accumulation." Bolshevik ideology played a role during the Russian Civil War in this metamorphosis from an emancipatory democratic élan to a ruthless, totalitarian dictatorship. Its normative vision of violence as the "midwife of history" and its culpable indifference to the juridical framework of a revolutionary state, historically transitional and doomed to extinction, certainly favored the birth of an authoritarian, single-party regime. Multiple threads run from revolution to Stalinism, as well as from the USSR to the communist movements acting across the world. Stalinism was both a totalitarian regime and, for some decades, the hegemonic current of the Left on an international scale.

The World October Made

The October Revolution laid the premises of decolonization. Because of its intermediary position between Europe and Asia, with a gigantic territory extending to both continents, inhabited by a variety of national, religious, and ethnic communities, the USSR became the locus of a new crossroads between the West and the colonial world. Bolshevism was able to speak to the proletarian classes of the industrialized countries and to the colonized people of the South as well. One needs to go back more than a century earlier, with the symbiotic link between the French and the Haitian Revolution, to find a historical event with a similar global impact. During the nineteenth century, anticolonialism was almost nonexistent in the West, with the notable exception of the anarchist movement, whose activists and ideas widely circulated between Southern and Eastern Europe, Latin America, and different Asian countries. After Marx's death, socialism based its hopes and expectations on the growing strength of the industrial working class, mostly white and male, and concentrated in the developed capitalist countries of the

West. All mass socialist parties included powerful currents defending the "civilizing mission" of Europe throughout the world. The extreme violence of colonialism could be vigorously denounced—as after the extermination of the Herero in German Namibia in 1904—without putting into question the historical right of the European empires to rule Asia and Africa. The socialist parties—particularly those located in the biggest empires—postponed colonial liberation after the socialist transformation of Europe and the United States. When the colonial question was debated at the congresses of the Second International—in Amsterdam in 1904 and in Stuttgart three years later—the definition of the colonized people as "inferior races" had been criticized, but nobody contested the legitimacy of its advocates within the socialist parties, where they were well represented.

The Bolshevik Revolution was a radical break with such a tradition. The second congress of the Communist International, held in Moscow in June 1920, approved a programmatic document calling for colonial revolutions against imperialism; its goal was both the creation of communist parties in the colonial world and a clear departure from the ambiguities of the old social democracy. A couple of months later, the Bolsheviks organized the Congress of the Peoples of the East in Baku, Azerbaijan, which convened almost three thousand delegates from most Asian countries and which ended with a spirited speech by Grigory Zinovyev appealing for a jihad against imperialism (see Broué 1997: 181–82). Gathering intellectuals involved in the first embryonic communist movements, leaders of trade unions and peasant associations, as well as representatives of several emerging nationalist currents, this meeting had a strong impact that hid its ambiguities and internal contradictions, embodied by the presence of both Armenian Socialists and Turkish Nationalists—four years after the Anatolian genocide—and even some Chinese Nationalists who, just five years later, would violently smash a communist uprising in Canton. The conflicting relationships between communism and nationalism would become clarified in the following decades, but the October Revolution was the inaugural moment of global anticolonialism, insofar as it recognized the colonized peoples as political subjects and historical actors. Roughly speaking, the October Revolution put an end to more than a century of "silencing the past," a time in which the Haitian Revolution had been removed from both historiography and the historical consciousness of the West insofar as it was simply inconceivable according to its epistemological categories. For Michel-Rolph Trouillot (1995: 82), the overthrow of colonial rule and slaves' self-emancipation that took place in Saint-Domingue from 1791 to 1804 challenged "the ontological and political assumptions" of Western cultures, until putting into question the "conceptual frame of reference" of its most radical political currents. Its impact on the elaboration of an idea of universalism inherited from the Enlightenment was as influential as it was hidden, unconscious, and finally unthinkable. As a result, the Haitian Revolution was completely removed from the intellectual landscape of the Left. October 1917 reintroduced it. C. L. R. James's *The Black Jacobins* ([1938] 1989: ix), the history of the transformation of the slaves "into a people able to organize themselves and defeat the most powerful European nations of their day," was published in 1938, but the "conceptual frame" of this *suppression* was broken in 1917. Beginning in the 1920s, anticolonialism suddenly shifted from the realm of historical possibility to the field of political strategy and military organization. The proclamation of the People's Republic of China in Beijing in 1949 was the result of a process that, from the Canton uprising of 1925 to the Long March and the anti-Japanese struggle, found one of its necessary premises in the Bolshevik Revolution.

Of course, this historical turn—both political and epistemological—had multiple dimensions. On the left, it meant the reconfiguration of the relationship between race and class, extending the conception of political agency to the colonized peoples. This change took place within the theoretical framework of Marxism and shaped the entire trajectory of twentieth-century communism as a new stage of radical Enlightenment: communism merged humanism, anticolonialism, and universalism. On the right, it meant the racialization of Bolshevism itself. Since the Russian Civil War and the revolutionary uprisings in Central Europe, from Berlin to Budapest, nationalist propaganda had begun to depict the Bolsheviks as savages, as the embodiment of a dangerous form of "Asiatic barbarism" that threatened the West. Under the Weimar Republic, pan-Germanism assimilated the Slavonic peoples to inferior races and depicted the Bolsheviks as the leaders of a gigantic revolt of slaves. Racist stereotypes—from the Asiatic origins of Lenin to the myth of a Chinese Cheka—saturated anticommunist literature. In the following decade, National Socialism completed this picture by describing Bolshevism as the coalition of a nonwhite subhumanity led by a revolutionary Jewish intelligentsia. In a famous speech delivered in Dusseldorf in 1932 before an audience of German industrialists, Hitler presented the USSR as a major threat to the "white race" and Western civilization. For several decades, colonialism, anti-Semitism, and anticommunism have been essential dimensions of the political culture of Western conservatism, in a wide spectrum merging multiple currents and running from Churchill to Hitler.

This alliance between communism and anticolonialism experienced several moments of crisis and tension, related to both ideological conflicts and the imperatives of the USSR's foreign policies. In the 1930s, the antifascist turn of the French Communist Party (Parti Communiste Français, or PCF) took place as a peculiar symbiosis of Stalinism and national republicanism, which inscribed the Russian Revolution into the national tradition of Jacobinism and socialist internationalism into its universal civilizing mission. As a consequence, anticolonialism was put aside. At the end of the Second World War, the PCF participated in a coalition government that violently repressed anticolonial revolts in Algeria in 1945 and Madagascar in 1947, and in the following decade it supported the prime minister, Guy Mollet, at the beginning of the Algerian War (see Moneta 1971). In India, the communist movement was marginalized during the Second World War because of its choice of suspending the anticolonial struggle and supporting the British Empire in a military alliance with the USSR against the Axis powers. If these examples clearly show the contradictions of communist anticolonialism, they do not change the historical role played by the USSR as a rear base for many anticolonial revolutions. The entire process of decolonization took place in the context of the Cold War, within the relations of force established by the existence of the USSR. In many cases, anticolonial communism transcended the borders of Stalinism, the USSR, and China, as proved by the guerrilla movements in Latin America after the Cuban Revolution. The wave of neo-imperial wars that have swept the Middle East since the collapse of the USSR shows, even if in a purely negative form, the organic connection that related communism and decolonization. Retrospectively, the latter appears as a historical experience in which the two dimensions of communism previously mentioned—emancipation and authoritarianism, revolution and dictatorial power—permanently merged. In most cases, anticolonial struggles were conceived and organized as military campaigns carried on by liberation armies, and the political regimes they established were, since the beginning, one-party dictatorships. Some colonial revolutions experienced successively two different moments: first, the euphoric, exalting, joyful, often ephemeral moment of emancipation when the old rulers fall down and the ruled become free men and women and, second, the dark, overwhelming moment of oppression, when human beings lose any decisional power and are once again enslaved and transformed into a reified, consumable stuff. In Cambodia, at the end of a ferocious war, the military dimension of the anticolonial revolution completely suffocated its emancipatory impulsion, and the conquest of power by the Red Khmers immediately resulted in establishing a genocidal power. The happiness of insurgent Havana on the first of January 1959 and the terror of the Cambodian killing fields are the dialectical poles of communism as anticolonialism.

A Social Democratic Communism

The fourth dimension of twentieth-century communism is social democratic, that is, its capacity, in certain countries and periods, to play the role traditionally fulfilled by social democracy. This happened in some Western countries, mostly in the postwar decades, thanks to a lot of circumstances related to the international context, the foreign policy of the USSR, and the absence or weakness of classic social democratic parties, as well as in some countries born from decolonization. The most significant examples of this peculiar phenomenon are located in the United States, at the time of the New Deal; in postwar France and Italy; and in India (Kerala and West Bengal). Of course, social democratic communism was geographically and chronologically more circumscribed than the other communisms, but it did exist nonetheless. To a certain extent, the rebirth of social democracy itself after 1945 was a by-product of the October Revolution, which had changed the balance of power on a global scale and compelled capitalism to a significant transformation, adopting a "human face."

This oxymoronic definition does not ignore the links that French, Italian, or Indian communism had with revolutions, Stalinism, and decolonization; their capacity to lead insurgent movements, notably during the Resistance against the Nazi occupation; or their organic connections with Moscow for several decades, insofar as their first open criticism of the USSR's foreign policy took place only in the 1960s, first with the Sino-Soviet split and then with the invasion of Czechoslovakia by Soviet tanks. Even their internal structure and organization was, at least until the end of the 1970s, much more Stalinist than social democratic, as were their culture, theoretical references, and political imagination. In spite of these clearly recognizable, never denied features, these parties played a typical social democratic role: reforming capitalism, containing social inequalities, and getting accessible health care, education, and leisure to the largest number of people, in short, improving the living conditions of the laboring classes and giving them political representation. Their goal was not the abolition of capitalism but rather a global, social reformation within the framework of capitalism itself. Their politics fundamentally corresponded to the theoretical "revision" of classical Marxism proposed by Edward Bernstein in 1899 in his famous work *The*

Preconditions of Socialism, which envisaged a gradual transformation of capitalism and an evolutionary road to socialism, even if no communist party ever recognized this connection. Their doctrinal armory still remained strong and compelling, even if they were building Western liberal democracies. In Italy, however, the Communist Party tried to conceptualize its strategic orientation by inscribing it into the canonical tradition. The publication of Gramsci's *Prison Notebooks* in 1948–51, with his reflections on hegemony, national culture, historical bloc, Machiavelli, and the differences between the state in Russia and the West, was instrumental in legitimizing this social democratic turn (and sterilizing at the same time the reception of Gramsci's work [see Anderson 2016]). The last attempt to give a theoretical ground to this kind of reformism was, in the mid-1970s, the idea of Eurocommunism, which some intellectuals elaborated by connecting it to the tradition of Austro-Marxism, embodied in the first half of the twentieth century by thinkers such as Otto Bauer, Karl Renner, and Rudolf Hilferding (see Magri 2011). With very few exceptions—notably Santiago Carrillo, the author of *"Eurocommunism" and the State* (1978), who led the Communist Youth during the Spanish Civil War and later lived in exile in Moscow—most representatives of this current abandoned any reference to communism after 1989.

Of course, one of the peculiar features of social democratic communism was its exclusion from political power, except for a couple of years between the end of World War II and the breakout of the Cold War. Unlike the British Labor Party, the German Social Democratic Party, or the Scandinavian social democracies, it could not claim the paternity of the welfare state. In the United States, the Communist Party was one of the left pillars of the New Deal, along with the trade unions, but it never entered Franklin Roosevelt's administration. It experienced not power but only the purges of McCarthyism. In France and Italy, the communist parties were strongly influential in the birth of postwar social policies simply because of their conditioning strength outside of the governments. The realm of their social reformism was "municipal socialism," in the cities they led as hegemonic strongholds, such as in Bologna or the Parisian "Red Belt" (*banlieue rouge*). In a much bigger country such as India, the communist governments of Kerala and West Bengal could be considered equivalent forms of "local," postcolonial welfare states. The experience of social democratic communism had two necessary premises: on the one hand, it was a by-product of the Russian Revolution itself, a reformation of capitalism threatened by the communist alternative; on the other hand, it was inscribed into a cycle of economic growth allowed by postwar reconstruction. It exhausted its trajectory in the 1980s, when the fall of the USSR strongly favored the advent of a new wave of neoliberal capitalism. The time of both communism and social democracy was over.

Excluded from central power, the communist parties tended to act as "counter-societies" in which the entire existence of their members was reshaped, from their workday (where there were communist cells) to their cultural practices and imagination (Kriegel 1968). Communists had their own newspapers and magazines, publishing houses, movies, and music, their own leisure activities, and their own rituals. Communism was a kind of anthropological microcosm that enveloped their daily life. As many testimonies emphasized, the Communist Party was at the same time a church, that is, a community of faith, an army with a hierarchy and discipline, and a school, with educational purposes. Coming in was experienced as a conversion, and exiting was impossible without apostasy and excommunication. Thus social democratic communism did not escape from the legacy of both communism-revolution and communism-regime: the revolution conceived according to a military paradigm and the regime built as a monolithic system of power. The logic of the Cold War reinforced this pattern. Depicting the communist movements in the West as foreign bodies and fifth columns inside liberal democracy, anticommunism reinforced their tendency to act as counter-societies, monolithic and impermeable to any external influence. Intellectuals and artists were mostly "fellow travelers," insofar as their party membership would have been lethal for their creation.

In 1989 the fall of communism closed this stage, as epic as it was tragic, as exciting as it was monstrous, of the human "gigantic adventure for changing the world." The time of decolonization and welfare state was over. The collapse of communism as regime, nevertheless, took with it communism as revolution. Instead of liberating new forces, the end of Stalinism engendered a widespread awareness of the historical defeat of the revolutions of the twentieth century: the shipwreck of real socialism engulfed also the communist utopia. The revolutions of the twenty-first century are compelled to reinvent themselves, to distance themselves far from the previous patterns. They will create new models, new ideas, and a new utopian imagination. This reconstruction is not an easy task, insofar as the fall of communism left the world without alternatives to capitalism. This created a new mental landscape. A new generation grew up in a neoliberal world in which capitalism has become a "natural," almost ontological form of human life. The Left rediscovered a whole of revolutionary traditions that had been suppressed or marginalized throughout a century, first of all anarchism, and recognized a plurality of political subjects previously ignored or relegated to a secondary position. The experiences of the "alterglobalization" movements, the Arab revolutions, Occupy Wall Street, the Spanish Indignados, Syriza, and the French Nuit Debout, are steps in the process of the invention of a new "communism," discontinuous, nourished by memory, but at the same time severed from the twentieth-century history and deprived of a usable legacy.

Born as an attempt at taking heaven by storm, twentieth-century communism became, like and against fascism, an expression of the dialectic of the Enlightenment. Were not the Soviet-style industrial cities, five-year plans, agricultural collectivization, spacecraft, gulags converted into factories, nuclear weapons, and ecological catastrophes different forms of the triumph of instrumental reason? Was not communism the frightening face of a Promethean dream, of an idea of Progress that had erased and destroyed any experience of self-emancipation? Was not Stalinism a storm "piling wreckage on wreckage" and which millions of people mistakenly called "Progress" (Benjamin [1940] 1968: 257)? Fascism merged a whole of conservative values inherited from the counter-Enlightenment with a modern cult of science, technology, and mechanical strength. Stalinism combined a similar cult of technical modernity with a radical, authoritarian form of Enlightenment: socialism transformed into a "cold utopia." A new, global Left will not succeed without "working through" this historical experience. Extracting the emancipatory core of communism from this field of ruins is not an abstract, merely intellectual operation; it shall need new battles, new constellations in which suddenly the past will reemerge and "memory flash up." Attempts at critically historicizing communism are necessary but certainly not enough.

References

Anderson, Perry. 2016. "The Heirs of Gramsci." *New Left Review*, no. 100: 71–97.

Benjamin, Walter. [1940] 1968. "Theses on the Philosophy of History." In *Illuminations*, edited by Hannah Arendt, translated by Harry Zohn, 253–64. New York: Schocken Books.

Benjamin, Walter. 1999. *The Arcades Project*. Translated by Howard Eiland and Kevin McLaughlin. Cambridge, MA: Belknap Press of Harvard University Press.

Broué, Pierre. 1997. *Histoire de l'Internationale communiste, 1919–1943* (*History of the Communist International, 1919–1943*). Paris: Fayard.

Carrillo, Santiago. 1978. *"Eurocommunism" and the State*. London: Lawrence and Wishart.

De Felice, Renzo. 1977. *Interpretations of Fascism*. Translated by Brenda Huff Everett. Cambridge, MA: Harvard University Press.

Deutscher, Isaac. [1954] 2003. *The Prophet Outcast: Trotsky, 1929–1940*. London: Verso.

Fitzpatrick, Sheila. 1994. *The Russian Revolution*. New York: Oxford University Press.

Furet, François. 1981. *Interpreting the French Revolution*. Translated by Elborg Forster. New York: Cambridge University Press.

Groys, Boris. 2011. *The Total Art of Stalinism: Avant-Garde, Aesthetic Dictatorship, and Beyond.* London: Verso.

Hobsbawm, Eric. 1996. *The Age of Extremes: A History of the World, 1914–1991.* New York: Vintage Books.

Ingerflom, Claudio S. 2000. "De la Russie à l'URSS" ("From Russia to the USSR"). In *Le siècle des communismes* (*The Century of Communisms*), edited by Michel Dreyfus et al., 113–22. Paris: Editions de l'Atelier.

James, C. L. R. [1938] 1989. *The Black Jacobins: Toussaint L'Ouverture and the Santo Domingo Revolution.* New York: Vintage Books.

Kotkin, Stephen. 1995. *Magnetic Mountain: Stalinism as a Civilization.* Berkeley: University of California Press.

Kriegel, Annie. 1968. *Les communistes français: Essai d'ethnographie politique* (*French Communists: A Political Ethnography Essay*). Paris: Seuil.

Magri, Lucio. 2011. *The Tailor of Ulm: Communism in the Twentieth Century.* Translated by Patrick Camiller. London: Verso.

Mayer, Arno J. 2000. *The Furies: Violence and Terror in the French and Russian Revolutions.* Princeton, NJ: Princeton University Press.

Moneta, Jakob. 1971. *Le PCF et la question coloniale, 1920–1965* (*The PCF and the Colonial Question, 1920–1965*). Paris: Maspero.

Morin, Edgar. 1991. *Autocritique* (*Self-Criticism*). Paris: Seuil.

Mosse, George L. 1990. *Fallen Soldiers: Reshaping the Memory of the World Wars.* New York: Oxford University Press.

Polanyi, Karl. [1944] 1971. *The Great Transformation: The Political and Economic Origins of Our Time.* Boston: Beacon.

Serge, Victor. [1946] 2012. *Memoirs of a Revolutionary.* Translated by Peter Sedgwick. New York: New York Review of Books.

Traverso, Enzo. 2015. *Il totalitarismo: Storia di un dibattito* (*Totalitarianism: History of a Debate*). Verona: Ombre Corte.

Trotsky, Leon. [1929] 2007. *My Life: An Attempt at an Autobiography.* New York: Dover.

Trotsky, Leon. [1932] 2008. *History of the Russian Revolution.* Translated by Max Eastman. Chicago: Haymarket Books.

Trouillot, Michel-Rolph. 1995. *Silencing the Past: Power and the Production of History.* Boston: Beacon.

Werth, Nicolas. 1997. "Un état contre son peuple: Violence, répression, terreurs en Union soviétique" ("A State against Its People: Violence, Repression, Terror in the Soviet Union"). In *Le livre noir du communisme: Crimes, terreur, répression* (*The Black Book of Communism: Crimes, Terror, Repression*), edited by Stéphane Courtois et al., 43–295. Paris: Robert Laffont.

Michael Hardt

Red Love

A true revolutionary, Che Guevara (2003: 225) declares, must be guided by strong feelings of love. Alexandra Kollontai, Bolshevik revolutionary and minister in the first Soviet government, would ultimately agree, but the first task is to critique and destroy the forms of love that now predominate. In line with feminists such as Mary Wollstonecraft a century before her and Shulamith Firestone decades after, Kollontai recognizes that love—particularly heteronormative romantic love and family love—serves as a trap for women and a structure that guarantees their subordination.[1] The dominant forms of love in contemporary society, furthermore, are socially limiting and politically harmful, for men and women alike. The root of the problem, Kollontai claims, is what I call property love, that is, the fact that we regard our bonds to each other in terms of ownership and property relations.[2] The distinctive feature of Kollontai's position, then, is that the critique of love is inherently a property question and thus that overcoming property love requires not only equality—equal property, for instance—but also a radical social transformation, an explicitly anticapitalist project. Only once property love is abolished can we begin to invent a new love, a revolutionary love, a red love.[3]

The South Atlantic Quarterly 116:4, October 2017
DOI 10.1215/00382876-4235005   © 2017 Michael Hardt

During the first decade after the October Revolution, a period of intense cultural, artistic, social, and political experimentation, several intellectuals explored how deeply property relations are insinuated into every aspect of social life, well beyond the economic sphere. And they sought, by unearthing and eradicating property relations from all corners of society, to imagine how a new society could be built. In effect, they experimented with and extended Marx and Engels's (2008: 18) claim that "the theory of the Communists may be summed up in a single sentence: Abolition of private property." In this regard, Kollontai's analysis of property love in the couple and the family is parallel, for instance, to Evgeny Pashukanis's (2002) critique of law and the state, developed in the same years.[4] Pashukanis argued that modern juridical and constitutional concepts are based ultimately on property and commodity relations. Abolishing property relations, then, he reasoned, would necessarily undermine state sovereignty and require a complete reformulation of the basis of normativity and law (see Amendola, this issue). Just as for Pashukanis the abolition of private property in communist society directly implies the withering of the state, for Kollontai it entails the withering of the bourgeois couple and family.

It might be tempting to read Kollontai and Pashukanis in a traditional structure-superstructure framework, assuming, in other words, that elements or characteristics of the economic base of society are primary and reflected, secondarily, in the ideological and cultural spheres. But property, in their arguments, is not merely an economic category: it is from the beginning a logic and a mode of relation that spans all realms of life. One cannot simply aim for the abolition of property in the economic relations, then, and assume that other social realms will follow suit. Instead, the struggles against property relations must proceed in parallel in all social domains. And in each social domain one must invent an alternative. What is a subject not defined by its possessions? What is a legal relation not founded on property? And what can love be when free of the logic of possession and ownership?[5]

Property Love

The logic that binds the modern couple, Kollontai asserts, is based ultimately on property relations. In pursuing this critical claim, she is certainly concerned, as are many other feminists, with the gendered right to ownership and inheritance of material wealth, but her argument stresses more strongly a different insight: that we regard our bonds to each other in terms of property and possession. In capitalist society even romantic love is a property relation. "You are mine" and "I am yours" are emblematic of the pledge of love as property. Consider, Kollontai explains, the experience of two people who, soon after falling in love and forming a couple, exert rights over the other's relationships, including even those relationships begun before they knew each other. It would be regarded as lack of trust or, really, a breach of property rights to refuse to share any experience past or present, any friendship, past lover, or family relationship. The mistake of many women in particular, she explains, is the belief to have found the person with whom "we could blend our soul" (Kollontai 1971: 8). Everyone keeps some secrets and insists on some independent friendships, but those are the exception because the social norm, the regulative ideal of romantic love, requires that when you enter into a couple you give yourself over and expect the other to do the same in return.

Property love was not always the norm, at least not in the same way and to the same extent. In premodern European society, Kollontai claims, men took possession of women's bodies and women were obliged to be faithful to men physically (economically and sexually), but women's minds and souls were to a large extent their own. In bourgeois society, however, she continues, the love-property relation shifts and deepens: "It is the bourgeoisie who have carefully tended and fostered the ideal of absolute possession of the 'contracted partner's' emotional as well as physical 'I,' thus extending the concept of property rights to include the right to the other person's whole spiritual and emotional world" (Kollontai 1977d: 242). In addition to the inequality and the subordination of women created by bourgeois property rights in the couple and the family, then, the possession of the other—the fact that love requires you to give all of yourself as property—adds another layer of unfreedom.

It may seem incongruous to claim that modern love is a property relation since the standard historical account maintains that modernity freed love from property, doing away with arranged marriages, primogeniture inheritance laws, and, eventually, legal structures that designate women as the property of fathers and husbands. Although most life decisions must be made with regard to property interests, according to this view, there is at least one realm in life, the intimate sphere of the couple and the family, where decisions are made on the basis of love. Modern novels are full of narratives, for instance, in which choosing a partner against the pressures of property interests—Rochester chose Jane Eyre, after all—demonstrates the triumph and autonomy of love in the intimate sphere. The realm of love, the thinking goes, is the one place free of property, a space of the common where we share money and goods. Kollontai's argument, in contrast, is that even when legal designations of property are not involved today, we still conceive our intimate bonds according to the logic of property relations, as a form of ownership and possession. Kollontai, in this sense, gives new meaning to Marx's (1974: 351) claim that private property has made us so stupid that we can only think of something as ours when we own it.

One consequence of love being configured as a property relation is to make the couple a "complete" and thus isolated unit. By the logic of property love, Kollontai reasons, since you have a right only to what is yours, bonds with all those outside the couple must be subordinated. "I am yours" thus goes together with "you are everything to me." Indeed, complementarity and wholeness are standard clichés of romantic love: the two lovers are missing puzzle pieces who complete each other and together form a whole. Freud (1959: 72) reports this standard view of the couple as a kind of scientific fact: "The more they are in love, the more completely they suffice for each other." For Kollontai, however, the complementarity and the resulting isolation of the couple is neither natural nor desirable. Such complementarity negates freedom inside the couple. Insofar as you exist for the other, oriented to your other half, you become a limited and partial person. "The individualistic property morality of the present day is beginning to seem very obviously paralysing and oppressive" (Kollontai 1977d: 240). All the existing and potential aspects of yourself that do not function as complement to the other—all the pieces that do not fit in the couple puzzle—must be set aside or subordinated.

Kollontai is more concerned, however, with the external restrictions of the "complete" couple. "The ideal of the bourgeoisie was the married couple, where the partners complemented each other so completely that they had no need of contact with society" (Kollontai 1977e: 230). Since the two suffice for each other, the couple severs or fails to establish social ties. (How often have you had a friend disappear after falling in love, ensconced in a "complete" couple, only later to reappear again to renew your friendship once the couple breaks up?) The couple, in effect, fulfills the bourgeois ideal of the sovereign individual, internally unified and self-sufficient, acting according to extended egotism, an egotism masquerading as altruism, making decisions according to what is best for the two. As Nietzsche (1973: 72), an unlikely ally of Kollontai, writes, "Love of one is a barbarism: since it is practiced at the expense of all others." Couple love, like property love in general, discourages and even prohibits caring for and forming bonds with what is not yours.

The Glass of Water Theory

Kollontai's challenge to the antisocial couple bound by property relations inevitably raises a series of straw man arguments and panic reactions regarding sex. If the two are not bound by mutual ownership in property love, according to such fears, then anything goes, raising the specter of "free love" and polyamory. We need to reduce the focus on sex, however, to appreciate Kollontai's argument about love.

In the early 1920s, Soviet revolutionaries debated the glass of water theory of sex, a theory widely attributed to Kollontai.[6] Having sex, the theory goes, should be no more complicated or problematic than drinking a glass of water. The glass of water theory, however, simple as it is, proved difficult for many to understand. Whereas, perhaps predictably, the metaphor generated for many a heightened focus on sex—along with titillation and panic regarding casual sex and multiple sex partners as well as disapproval for violating traditional morality—it was intended, to the contrary, to sideline such excited discussions. Since having sex, like drinking water, is a normal bodily function, it should be neither subject to moral injunction and social control nor the object of political celebration.

The glass of water theory would likely be equally misunderstood today, since it does not conform easily to established political positions regarding sex, especially those we have inherited from the "sex wars" of the 1980s. The theory certainly does not fit, for example, with either what came to be cast as sex-negative positions (which arose in part to highlight the damages accrued to women in and by pornography and the sex industries) or sex-positive ones (that advocate, in contrast, sexual freedom and the liberatory character of nonnormative sex practices). Whereas both sex-negative and sex-positive positions agree that sex is important politically and socially, the glass of water theory maintains it is not.

The glass of water theory proves so difficult to grasp in part due to its paradoxical rhetorical strategy: it brings something to light in order to diminish its significance. Its intended function is thus subtractive. In its rhetorical strategy, the glass of water theory resonates with the social interventions of the ancient Cynics, such as, for example, their reported practice of masturbating in public. No one should be scandalized, they argued, by our satisfying a bodily need that is of the same order as satiating thirst or hunger. If only it were as easy, Diogenes of Sinope allegedly declared, to banish hunger by simply rubbing my belly! Diogenes's point is obviously not to concentrate political or philosophical attention on masturbation, to celebrate it, or to create an onanist cult. On the contrary, the point is subtractive: to release us from pre-occupations about sex so that we can direct our attention elsewhere.[7] That is the function of the glass of water theory: stop being distracted by sex so as to focus on the important social and political issues.

This raises, however, another obstacle to understanding the glass of water theory today: that it could appear to assert that sex is personal and thus not political, running counter to the important second-wave feminist slogan. Furthermore, it could mask the sexual dangers women face, including unwanted pregnancy, rape, and other forms of sexual violence. I understand the glass of water theory, however, as positioning sex as political but imagining it in a society of freedom, where sexual violence, unwanted pregnancy, and the constraints of normativity and moralisms are a thing of the past. In effect, the theory is a demand for that utopian future, in which having sex can become no more complicated than drinking a glass of water.

Although likely not responsible for the idea, Kollontai is a good representative of the glass of water theory. She was regarded by others and indeed presented herself as embodying the new liberated woman. The characters in her novels, such as *Red Love*, experiment freely with various amorous arrangements. And in her life, too, she reports treating sex openly and without moralisms. "I make no secret of my love experiences," she explains in her autobiography; "when once love came, I have my relations to the man" (Kollontai 1971: 5). By demystifying sex, she sought to counter the moralism, prohibitions, and shame associated with sexual activity in traditional Russian society, which served as weapons for the domination of women. And she lamented that asceticism regarding sex, often mixed with traditional moralism, remained widespread even among Soviet revolutionaries: "My theses, my sexual and moral views, were bitterly fought by many Party comrades of both sexes" (43).

Lenin is one who was puzzled and a bit disturbed by all the discussions of the glass of water theory. "Of course," Lenin admits, in conversation with Clara Zetkin (1934: 49), "thirst must be satisfied. But will the normal man in normal circumstances lie down in the gutter and drink out of a puddle, or out of a glass with a rim greasy from many lips?" The first sentence shows that Lenin, even if he thinks he is disagreeing, understands correctly the primary point of the glass of water theory: sex, like thirst, is a normal bodily function and thus should be stripped of the traditional meanings and values attached to it. But then he seems to take the metaphor too literally and betrays traditional male fears of "polluted" women. The idea of women having multiple partners and casual sex elicits a kind of panic in Lenin. But if one can filter out Lenin's fear of female sexuality, then perhaps his question can be understood as simply an extension of the initial point. Stripping sex of moralism does not imply having sex indiscriminately, indifferently, Lenin seems to suggest. Instead, sexual activity, like drinking water, should be treated in terms of care of the self—take care of your body and meet its needs. Maybe food, then, would be a better metaphor than water for Lenin. Nutritionists may offer general guidelines for a healthy diet, but one has to discover the needs of one's own body in balance with pleasure: discover what sex, how, how often, and with whom, agrees with you and pursue that, avoiding what harms you. No model of healthy sex can be prescribed for all, in other words, but neither is it a matter of indifference. Communism is no asceticism, Lenin adds, to make sure that Zetkin does not misunderstand him: healthy sex, along with sports and other activities, is part of a joyful life (50).[8]

Lenin is clear, however—and this too, I would argue, is in line with the spirit of the glass of water theory—that these questions about sex are not the most significant social and political issues. "But the social aspect is most important of all," he continues. "Drinking water is of course an individual affair" (Zetkin 1934: 49). Lenin may still be taking the metaphor too literally: sexual activity, after all, is not like drinking water in all its aspects. But the substance of Lenin's point—that the social aspect is most important—is, in fact, very close to Kollontai's primary concerns.[9] "It is time to recognize openly," she writes, "that love is not only a powerful natural factor, a biological force, but also a social factor. Essentially love is a profoundly social emotion" (Kollontai 1977b: 278). Sexual relations alone, inevitably, regardless of how many sexual partners one has, remain asocial in Kollontai's terms because sex itself is too narrow a basis to carry the multiplicity of bonds that love must generate and sustain. The important question for Kollontai is how to create a variety of lasting, social bonds (involving sexual relations or not) that are not constituted by property relations. Only in that way can we begin to explore the social significance and political possibilities of a new love.

The Antisocial Family

The nature of property love in the couple is repeated in the family, creating what Michèle Barrett and Mary McIntosh (1982) call the antisocial family. Like the couple, according to Kollontai, the family becomes in capitalist society an isolated unit more completely closed on itself. The regulative ideal requires that you devote your love most to your kin, and then to others in concentric waves extending outward from the family. The resulting assumption that family members love each other most and thus should have the most right and responsibility is inscribed in a series of legal structures and customary practices. (Hospital nurses are trained to stop you at the loved one's sickroom door: "Are you family?") Kollontai (1977c: 262) cites the fact that Aspasia, the mistress of Pericles, "was respected by her contemporaries far more than the colourless wives of the breeding apparatus" as evidence of bonds outside the family in other societies, ties that have been lost or weakened today.

The antisocial and possessive nature of the family and its extended egotism are even more pronounced in decisions regarding children. Kollontai (1977a: 259) laments and mocks the typical proprietary attitude of parents: "These are my children, I owe them all my maternal solicitude and affection; those are your children, they are no concern of mine and I don't care if they go hungry and cold—I have no time for other children." Ownership, as the ideologues of private property will tell you, comes with responsibility: you are obliged to care for what is yours. And, consequently, tending to the property of others—in this case caring for their children—is not only not required but also would be a violation of property rights, just as if you were to decide to paint over the hideous color of your neighbor's house. As much as property love requires you to care for what is yours, it discourages or even prohibits you from caring for what is not.

Property love in the couple and the family is parallel to (and often bleeds into) identitarian love on the political terrain. Limiting love to what is "yours" is another face of the love of the same. Love in the couple may seem on the surface to be aimed at someone different, but once the two are conceived as complementary and the couple is a "complete" whole, then two collapses back into one. The family too, with the proprietary conception of my children and my spouse, is a unit of identitarian attachment. Property breeds love of the same.

Here, yet again, arise straw man arguments. Destroying the antisocial family—and, moreover, destroying the property-based love on which it rests—does not mean stripping children away from their parents to be raised collectively. Nor does separating love from property, no longer loving only what is yours, mean loving all indifferently. One could certainly interpret as indifference Kollontai's (1977a: 259) mandate, after critiquing parents who act in the interest of only their own children, that "the worker-mother must learn not to differentiate between yours and mine." Such statements, however, have to be read together with her encouragement to develop many and varied bonds of love and friendship. The point is that the couple and the family should not be the limits of your love. Loving other children, caring for them, and making social decisions with their welfare in mind need not prevent you from loving your own. "Caring, sharing, and loving would be more widespread," Barrett and McIntosh (1982: 80) argue, "if the family did not claim them for its own." You can construct lasting bonds of various types with those close and far. Challenging property-based love, then, requires breaching the boundaries of the couple and the family, nurturing and developing modes of social love based not on sameness but on difference, and inventing social institutions that allow and encourage us to love and care for others in the widest possible frame, developing a wide variety of social bonds.

Kollontai (1977a: 258) claims—with a mix of description, prescription, and hope—that the family, as an antisocial institution of gender subordination and property bonds, began to be undermined in capitalist society and will further wither away in communist society. The withering and eventual abolition of the family are steps toward the equality and freedom of women, releasing them from the isolation and burden of domestic labor and subordination of familial gender hierarchies. In capitalist society, she explains, the family was initially an economic necessity as a unit of both production and reproduction. The production component has already been all but destroyed by capitalist development: the domestic industries, such as spinning yarn and making clothing at home, were rendered obsolete by processes of commodification and the creation of new markets for capitalist goods. "The family no longer produces; it only consumes" (254). In communist society, she predicts, the economic bases of the sexual division of labor in the family will be weakened, women will no longer be responsible for unpaid domestic labor, and reproductive labor in the home will be socialized: she envisions restaurants and canteens providing food for all; child rearing will be socialized; and the fatigue of domestic tasks, such as washing and cleaning, will be reduced with industrial appliances (255).

Kollontai, particularly in her role as minister of social welfare, took some practical steps to hasten the withering of the family in the Soviet Union. She participated, for instance, in drafting the 1917 law on marriage, which gave women the right to seek divorce and receive alimony. For the Eighth Party Congress in 1919, Kollontai prepared an amendment to affirm in explicit terms the withering away of the family, but Lenin, although sympathetic to her aims, claimed that it was not yet the right time. "We have in fact," he is reported to have responded, "to save the family."[10] As minister she proposed a series of institutional women's health initiatives, such as having the state take over maternity hospitals and the provision of prenatal care. These proposals, however, were met with great resistance, even among the most forward-thinking Soviets. "My efforts to nationalize maternity and infant care set off a new wave of insane attacks against me," she writes, and detractors claimed that she was trying to "nationalize women" (Kollontai 1971: 38).

Kollontai's efforts to destroy the antisocial family were thwarted. "The failure of the Russian Revolution to achieve the classless society," Firestone (1970: 190) reflected a half century later, "is traceable to its half-hearted attempts to eliminate the family and sexual repression." Her project to root out property relations from love, however, remains as relevant today.

Tragedy of the Commons

The fear (or thrill) that the critique of the couple and the family necessarily leads to "free love" and polyamory betrays a poverty of imagination and, specifically, a failure to conceive bonds outside the model of property love. This is the "tragedy of the commons" in the realm of love. The classic argument against the commons, articulated by Garrett Hardin (1968), asserts that wealth and resources, such as land, can only be properly managed when they are owned (as private or public property). No one is responsible for what is common, the argument goes, and thus shared resources, such as grazing land or fishing waters, are inevitably overused and ruined because they are not managed. Ownership, in other words, either private or public, carries with it the power and obligation to manage resources efficiently—and it is the only social structure that does so.

In the same way, if love were to be separated from property relations, if I were not yours and you not mine, a parallel argument goes, there would be no mechanism to manage our bonds to each other and assure their longevity. Fidelity, in other words, is *the* problem for bourgeois love. And property is the solution: the only way the other will remain true to me is to be mine. Without possessing each other, our unmanaged desires run wild and we are constantly in danger of drifting off with others. If there is no property, as Ivan Karamazov might say, everything is permitted. Hence free love, meaning indiscriminate sexual partnering and no durable bonds.

Kollontai insists that we need to stop thinking of those we love in terms of ownership. "A jealous and proprietary attitude to the person loved," she argues, "must be replaced by a comradely understanding of the other and an acceptance of his or her freedom" (Kollontai 1977e: 231). Here again, however, the threat of "free love" and unrestrained promiscuity rears its head. Does freedom in love mean that "anything goes" and no bonds are maintained? If you are not tied to your partner by the chain of property relations, will you have sex with anyone at any time (and then ask your partner for "comradely understanding")? It certainly can seem that way to a proprietary mentality, that is, if one believes that property is the only guarantee of intimate and social bonds. When Kollontai exhorts us to recognize the freedom of loved ones, then, that does not mean to let them go and break bonds with them. It means to escape from the prison of property and create a more generous conception of love, with more social and expansive bonds.

Kollontai's position is parallel to the most intelligent refutations of the "tragedy of the commons" arguments. She does not fall into the trap prepared by the "tragedy" argument. Some critics of property accept that property is the sole means to manage what we share and thus reject all management, assuming that the good for society can spontaneously be achieved, without any management. The better response is that private property and the state are not the only options: alternative, nonproperty means of management are available. The common must be managed, and so too the bonds of love must be the object of social and political reasoning.[11] "Love is not in the least a 'private' matter," Kollontai (1977b: 279) writes, "concerning only the two loving persons." The couple and the family are always socially regulated, through laws that define the legal couple, for example, and sexual divisions of labor founded on property relations. We are suffering today, in other words, what Pierre Dardot and Christian Laval (2014: 14) call "the tragedy of the non-common." Kollontai argues, however, that we must get beyond the bourgeois belief that property is the only force that can form lasting bonds at both the intimate and the social levels. Her focus instead is to discover a logic by which social and intimate bonds are or can be nourished and managed outside the confines of property relations.

Winged Eros

Sex, in Kollontai's view, need not always be accompanied by love. During the revolutionary struggle, for example, she explains in a speech to Soviet youth (1977b: 277), revolutionaries had little intellectual and emotional energy for anything but combat: sex without intimate bonds, which she calls "unwinged Eros," became the rule since there was no time for the relationships and commitments of love. In the early 1920s, however, with the emergency period passed, she exhorted Soviet youth to invent a new love, a winged Eros. This is not a moralistic caution to young people that sex without love is an empty experience, but rather an attack on property relations. Kollontai's winged Eros, as Barbara Evans Clements (1979: 227) explains, is "eroticism with the possessiveness removed, it [is] the attraction of equals that enhance[s] the harmony of the group rather than isolating the couple in self-absorption." Winged Eros configures a love beyond property, regardless of whether sex is involved.

Like Barrett and McIntosh writing more than half a century later, Kollontai does not advocate the reform of the family or even the invention of alternative family forms, households, kinship networks, or the like. Like Kollontai, Barrett and McIntosh do not see this argument, however, leading toward a society characterized by indifference that lacks strong, lasting attachments—on the contrary. "What is needed," they write, "is not to build up an alternative to the family—new forms of household that would fulfil all the needs that families are supposed to fulfil today—but to make family less necessary, by building up all sorts of other ways of meeting people's needs" (Barrett and McIntosh 1982: 159). The most important consequence of the abolition of the family is to increase our power to relate to and be connected with others. The effect, specifically, will be to open experimentation with a wide variety of social bonds.

Kollontai thus envisions a social love defined by multiplicity along two axes: a love of many in many ways. On the first axis, beyond the bounds of those who are yours—the couple, the family, the identity, the people—she urges us to develop bonds with a wide range of people, developing forms of love-comradeship and love-solidarity. "The 'sympathetic ties' between all the members of the new society" will have to grow and be strengthened (Kollontai 1977b: 290). The qualities and intensities of these diverse attachments, obviously, will not be the same. On the second axis, then, one must develop "many and varied bonds of love and friendship" (Kollontai 1977e: 231). No bond, no matter how much in love you are, suffices entirely, and you do not complement the loved one in such a way that forms a complete whole. Winged Eros, Kollontai (1977b: 288) says, has "many forms and facets." One must assume that the duration of these bonds will also vary: you will remain attached to some people all your life, and with others it is better to break completely after a short period. Kollontai does not go very far in delineating the character of this new love, but she does give a solid foundation: freed from property love and the love of the same it fosters, a new, social love will have to explore and proliferate multiplicities.

To extend Kollontai's initial thoughts about a new love and bring these questions closer to the concerns of our time, we can look to Michel Foucault's similar affirmation of multiple social bonds. Like Kollontai, he warns that resting political hopes on sex and sexual revolution is misplaced. Foucault's view, too, disrupts the conventional opposition between sex-positive and sex-negative positions. He thinks it a mistake to attribute much political significance to sex itself and, certainly, to hope for a sexual revolution. An image of homosexuality centered on sex acts, he argues, even when these acts are deemed to transgress the norms of society or nature, does not really even unsettle dominant society.

Instead, what really has the power to threaten the social structure—and, more importantly, ground and animate new social relations—is an alternative form of life, and specifically a mode of love characterized by multiple bonds. Focusing on homosexual sex, in fact, he explains, distracts from or eclipses the really transformative social potential:

> It cancels everything that can be disturbing in affection, tenderness, friendship, fidelity, camaraderie, and companionship, things that a rather sanitized society [une société un peu ratissée] cannot allow a place for without fearing that new alliances are formed and unforeseen lines of force are forged. I think that is what makes homosexuality "troubling": the homosexual mode of life, much more than the sex act itself. Imagining a sex act that does not conform to law or nature is not what disturbs people. But that individuals begin to love each other—that's the problem. (Foucault 1994: 164; my translation)[12]

By looking beyond sex—both the prohibitions and the affirmations of homosexual sex—Foucault can reveal three levels of transformative potential. At the first level, or base, are the different bonds that he tries to capture with his catalog: affection, tenderness, friendship, and so forth. As for Kollontai, key for him is the multiplicity along two axes: that we form many kinds of bonds with many different people. These affects and attachments have the power to trouble dominant society because they open to a second level, in which they compose new social assemblages and new modes of life. Whereas nonnormative sex acts can be accommodated or tolerated within dominant society—contained as a subset, a minority—the composition of a new mode of life seeps into the dominant order, permeates it, and thus threatens to transform it from within. The repertoire of multiple affects and attachments of the new mode of life creates a pole of attraction for homosexual and heterosexual communities alike. The third level, finally, is the invention of a new love, a social form of love capacious enough to include the many different kinds of bonds with different people. Such a new love has the potential not only to disturb dominant structures but also to transform them. In the homosexual mode of life Foucault glimpses the potential of a winged Eros.[13]

The social aspect, for Foucault as for Lenin and Kollontai, is what is really important. Only once we demystify and desacralize sex—sweeping away prohibitions and moralisms—can we begin to transform love and realize its social potential as a new form of life composed of multiple bonds, relationships, and modes of attachment. That is the horizon of a new love that could, fulfilling Guevara's dictum, provide a guide for revolutionaries.

Notes

1 For an excellent presentation of feminist arguments against romantic love, repurposed in the critique of "love your work" management discourses, see Weeks, forthcoming.

2 Firestone's diagnosis is parallel to Kollontai's, although she focuses on unequal power rather than property relations. "Thus it is not the process of love itself that is at fault, but its *political*, i.e. unequal *power* context: the who, why, when, and where of it is what makes it now such a holocaust" (Firestone 1970: 119).

3 For a reading of Kollontai on love that points in a different direction from mine, see Ebert 1999.

4 I have found no evidence that Kollontai and Pashukanis knew each other or even that they were familiar with each other's work, although Soviet intellectual circles of the 1920s were small. The correspondences between their critiques of property relations are testament, instead, to the wide questioning of property in early Soviet society.

5 Although the originality and intellectual coherence of her writings gained Kollontai respect among Soviet intellectuals, the political positions suggested by her work were opposed by those in power. Kollontai was sidelined from central government circles and sent to Norway as ambassador (a kind of gentle exile) after her support for the Workers' Opposition, a 1922 political proposition to decentralize power away from the state (1977f). Kollontai's views on the family and the couple did not win much favor either, as indicated by Lenin's opposition to her amendment affirming the withering away of the family. "My theses," she writes, "my sexual and moral views, were bitterly fought by many Party comrades of both sexes" (Kollontai 1971: 43). That view lasted for decades in official Soviet circles. The collection of her writings published in the Soviet Union in the 1970s contains none of her essays on love, the couple, and the family. Instead, the editor notes in the introduction that, as a person of inquiring mind, Kollontai was "liable to error": her error, specifically, was to criticize the family and make claims that could be misconstrued to imply, the editor continues, "immorality, promiscuity or loose living" (Dazhina [1972] 1984: 13).

6 The glass of water theory probably derives from August Bebel's 1879 *Woman under Socialism*, a book Kollontai, Lenin, and many other Soviet figures had read carefully. The exact formulation "glass of water" does not appear in the book, but Bebel ([1879] 1904: 79–81, 343) does explain that sex is a natural and healthy human need comparable to eating, drinking, and sleeping. There is no record of Kollontai having used the glass of water formulation, although the general idea runs throughout her writings. "According to the most famous legend," writes Iring Fetscher (1971: 111), "Alexandra Kollontai is supposed to have declared that sexual contacts were matters as simple and as unproblematic as drinking a glass of water." On Kollontai's reading Bebel, see Porter 1980 and Renault 2017.

7   Michel Foucault (2009: 158) is intrigued by Diogenes's reported masturbation in pub-
     lic and its subtractive function, which he describes as "a mode of life that has a reduc-
     tive function with respect to conventions and beliefs" (translation mine).

8   In my view, Srećko Horvat (2015: 87–88) misinterprets Lenin's reference to sport in his
     response to Zetkin as an antisex position, exhorting us to do sports instead of have sex,
     to sublimate desire. I think it is clear, instead, that Lenin's comparison between sex and
     sports simply puts sex on the same level with other healthy bodily activities. It is true
     that Lenin, insisting that "the revolution demands concentration," pronounces against
     "orgiastic conditions" (Zetkin 1934: 50), but I read this as a panic reaction to an imag-
     ined "free love." Judith Stora-Sandor goes further than Horvat and, since she under-
     stands Kollontai's work (incorrectly in my view) primarily in terms of sexual revolution,
     interprets Lenin's response as evidence of his reactionary position. "It is not a matter
     here of lodging an accusation against Lenin. We simply want here to signal that with
     regard to sexuality the most eminent Marxists of the age show themselves to be com-
     pletely reactionary" (Stora-Sandor 1971: 46; translation mine).

9   Horvat (2015: 101–2) rightly poses the proximity of Lenin and Kollontai in this regard:
     "In fact, Lenin and the most radical reformers of love relationships (Kollontai, Clara
     Zetkin, etc.) during the early October Revolution had much more in common than they
     themselves were aware of."

10   Lenin's comment, reported by Anna Itkina on page 208 of her 1964 biography of Kol-
     lontai, is quoted in Porter 1980: 337. This response—agreement in principle but the
     time is not right—is also Lenin's basic position regarding the Workers' Opposition.

11   See Elinor Ostrom's (1990) critique of Hardin.

12   I am indebted to Lauren Berlant for conversations about this text.

13   For a similar argument about the disruptive powers of happiness, see Foucault 2011:
     392–93.

References

Barrett, Michèle, and Mary McIntosh. 1982. *The Anti-Social Family*. London: Verso.

Bebel, August. [1879] 1904. *Woman under Socialism*. Translated by Daniel De Leon. New
     York: New York Labor News Company.

Clements, Barbara Evans. 1979. *Bolshevik Feminist: The Life of Aleksandra Kollontai*. Bloom-
     ington: Indiana University Press.

Dardot, Pierre, and Christian Laval. 2014. *Commun: Essai sur la révolution au XXIe siècle*
     (*Common: An Essay on Revolution in the Twenty-First Century*). Paris: La Découverte.

Dazhina, I. M. [1972] 1984. "An Impassioned Opponent of War and Champion of Peace and
     Female Emancipation." In *Alexandra Kollontai: Selected Articles and Speeches*, edited
     by I. M. Dazhina, 5–15. Moscow: Progress Publishers.

Ebert, Teresa L. 1999. "Alexandra Kollontai and Red Love." *Against the Current*, no. 81. www
     .solidarity-us.org/node/1724.

Fetscher, Iring. 1971. Afterword to Kollontai, *Autobiography*, 105–35.

Firestone, Shulamith. 1970. *The Dialectic of Sex: The Case for Feminist Revolution*. New York:
     William Morrow.

Foucault, Michel. 1994. "De l'amitié comme mode de vie" ("Friendship as a Way of Life"). In
     Dits et écrits, 1954–1988 (*Essential Writings, 1954–1988*), 4:163–67. Paris: Gallimard.

Foucault, Michel. 2009. *"Le courage de la vérité": Le gouvernement de soi et des autres II; Cours au Collège de France, 1984 ("The Courage of the Truth": The Government of Self and Others II; Lectures at the Collège de France, 1984).* Edited by Frédéric Gros. Paris: Gallimard/Seuil.

Foucault, Michael. 2011. "The Gay Science." Translated by Nicolae Morar and Daniel Smith. *Critical Inquiry* 37, no. 3: 385–403.

Freud, Sigmund. 1959. *Group Psychology and the Analysis of the Ego.* Translated by James Strachey. New York: Norton.

Guevara, Che. 2003. "Socialism and Man in Cuba." In *Che Guevara Reader,* edited by David Deutschmann, 212–28. Melbourne: Ocean Press.

Hardin, Garrett. 1968. "The Tragedy of the Commons." *Science* 162, no. 3859: 1243–48.

Horvat, Srećko. 2015. *The Radicality of Love.* Cambridge, UK: Polity.

Kollontai, Alexandra. 1971. *The Autobiography of a Sexually Emancipated Communist Woman.* Edited by Iring Fetscher, translated by Salvador Attansio. New York: Herder and Herder.

Kollontai, Alexandra. 1977a. "Communism and the Family." In *Selected Writings of Alexandra Kollontai,* translated and edited by Alix Holt, 250–60. London: Allison and Busby.

Kollontai, Alexandra. 1977b. "Make Way for Winged Eros: A Letter to Working Youth." In Kollontai, *Selected Writings,* 276–92.

Kollontai, Alexandra. 1977c. "Prostitution and Ways of Fighting It." In Kollontai, *Selected Writings,* 261–75.

Kollontai, Alexandra. 1977d. "Sexual Relations and the Class Struggle." In Kollontai, *Selected Writings,* 237–49.

Kollontai, Alexandra. 1977e. "Theses on Communist Morality in the Sphere of Marital Relations." In Kollontai, *Selected Writings,* 225–31.

Kollontai, Alexandra. 1977f. "The Workers' Opposition." In Kollontai, *Selected Writings,* 159–200.

Marx, Karl 1974. "Economic and Philosophical Manuscripts," 279–400. In *Early Writings.* London: Penguin.

Marx, Karl, and Friedrich Engels. 2008. *The Communist Manifesto.* New York: Oxford University Press.

Nietzsche, Friedrich. 1973. *Beyond Good and Evil.* Translated by R. J. Hollingdale. London: Penguin.

Ostrom, Elinor. 1990. *Governing the Commons: The Evolution of Institutions for Collective Action.* Cambridge: Cambridge University Press.

Pashukanis, Evgeny. 2002. *The General Theory of Law and Marxism,* translated by Barbara Enhorn. New Brunswick, NJ: Transaction.

Porter, Cathy. 1980. *Alexandra Kollontai: The Lonely Struggle of the Woman Who Defied Lenin.* New York: Dial.

Renault, Matthieu. 2017. "Alexandra Kollontaï et le dépérissement de la famille . . . ou les deux verres d'eau de Lénine" ("Alexandra Kollontai and the Withering of the Family . . . or the Two Glasses of Water of Lenin"), 63–87. In *Pour un féminisme de la totalité,* edited by Félix Boggio Éwanjé-Épée. Paris: Éditions Amsterdam.

Stora-Sandor, Judith. 1971. Introduction to *Alexandra Kollontai: Marxisme et révolution sexuelle* (*Alexandra Kollontai: Marxism and Sexual Revolution*), 9–47. Paris: Maspero.

Weeks, Kathi. Forthcoming. "Down with Love: Feminist Critique and the New Ideologies of Work." *Women's Studies Quarterly.*

Zetkin, Clara. 1934. *Reminiscences of Lenin.* New York: International Publishers.

John MacKay

Did the Revolution Happen?
Some Reflections on Early Soviet Cinema

In memory of Hannah Frank

One of the difficulties we have in conceptualizing the 1917 Russian Revolution today (as compared with a few decades ago) springs from our increased awareness of the multipronged character of the "revolution" itself: so multipronged, indeed, that an argument could be made for speaking only about "revolutions," exclusively in the plural. The year saw not only the fall of Europe's oldest autocracy and the Bolshevik takeover but also (among other things) the emergence of proletarian self-rule in the form of the soviets, the stirrings of national independence movements in the former empire, and, perhaps most important, the onset of the spontaneous seizure in midyear of virtually all arable land by the (mainly) Russian peasantry, an epochal process completed by 1919 that not only occurred independently of the guidance of any political party or faction but also set many of the terms for both the post–civil war New Economic Policy (NEP) and the cataclysmic confrontation between the Soviet regime and its rural and nomad populations at the end of the 1920s (Wade 2017: 282).

The South Atlantic Quarterly 116:4, October 2017
DOI 10.1215/00382876-4235016   © 2017 Duke University Press

To be sure, the majority of the disparate protagonists were united by the conviction that the old order had been superseded and would not return. The "old order," however, signified different things for different groups: for radicalized proletarians, the exclusion of working people from political life; for the peasantry, gentry ownership of land; for various nationalities, their subjugated place within the former empire. These varying relationships to the revolution can in no way be folded into one another, whatever determinations they might share—indeed, they demarcate vast terrains of imminent conflict far more than any common "revolutionary" front—and in some ways they offer a forecast of the contradictions of later revolutionary conjunctures as well.

It follows that the term *Russian Revolution* might pose referential conundrums, and not only because of the multitude of meanings those events of 1917–18—or should we say 1914–21? (Holquist 2002)—had for people in Russia and abroad. We tend to think of the Russian Revolution, and particularly its October culmination, as, above all, the sudden opening of a radical political horizon, however evaluated: the emergence, in the far from classically capitalist Russian Empire, of a real possibility of communism, on which the Bolsheviks were prepared to act (and acted). Yet it is in no way clear that this meaning captures what those who witnessed and participated in those events, however distantly, actually thought and experienced.

They certainly knew they were living through, and (if they survived) had lived through, tumultuous times, involving much more than Nicholas II's abdication, the fall of the provisional government, or the dissolution of the constituent assembly. The Russian Empire saw 5 million war casualties between 1914 and 1917 alone, more than any other combatant nation, and 6 million people made refugees by war prior to February 1917. Soviet Russia saw another million dead either in combat or by falling victim to terror during the civil war, millions more perishing during the same conflict due to disease or starvation, at least another million gone through flight or exile, 5 million dying in the famine of 1921, millions of children made homeless or orphaned, and, concomitantly, nearly total economic and infrastructural collapse across the country. The old world had plainly been overturned: no one had any doubt about *that*. But had the *revolution*—thought of as that inaugural but definitive passage toward communism, toward radical democratic control over production, distribution, and valuation in all spheres of life—actually *happened*?

In one sense, of course, the answer under the Bolshevik regime had to be a resounding yes, although there were plenty of seasoned and thoughtful revolutionaries who disagreed, right from November 1917. That the regime was "communist"—or "proletarian" or "Soviet," to name other adjectives that varyingly persisted within the same semantic field—meant, among other things, that the revolution had indeed occurred. The revolution was characterized as a punctual event and specifically the overturning of the old order by the proletariat at the end of 1917 (filmmaker Dziga Vertov called it "the reef of the Revolution"; Vertov 1984: 12). Rituals were installed to mark the time: revolutionary reenactments and other festivals celebrated November 7 starting in 1918 (Geldern 1993: 93–134), commemorations of various kinds continue to be staged in Russia even today, and workers enjoyed a "revolutionary" day off right through 2004.

Peripeteias in Early Soviet Film

The revolutionary turning point became one of the great narrative tropes of Soviet film, and aficionados will immediately recall some of these peripeteias, often motivated on the plot level by indignation at gross injustice and usually spreading rapidly out from one exemplary agent to a larger group allegorizing the class or mass as such. Hannah Arendt (1990) suggested that one of the main ways the Bolshevik revolutionaries went astray was in their singular focus on the alleviation of material poverty, at the expense of liberating the people's political capacities, but in the films at least—think of Sergei Eisenstein's buff sailors in his 1925 *Battleship Potemkin*, enraged at being fed maggots but apparently thriving on bread, water, and salt—it is more typically offense at indignity that provokes revolt, as filmmakers strum the strings of an affective interval harmonizing the dissonances of privation and heightened consciousness that (for Marx) typify proletarian being (Balibar 2011). Grigory Vakulinchuk's galvanizing cry of "Brothers!" in *Potemkin* remains the most famous example—recall how Chris Marker employs it as a kind of blasting cap at the outset of his revolutionary conspectus *A Grin without a Cat* (figure 1)—but we can also think of the mind-boggling, comicheroic fusion of revolutionary army with "Mongol horde" at the end of Vsevolod Pudovkin's 1928 masterpiece *Storm over Asia*, among numerous other instances.

Vertov, the great antagonist of narrative fiction, for his part, overwhelmingly allegorizes revolutionary transition by means of visual and sonic contrast, rather than the affective and moral travails of exemplary protagonists. Stylistically, Vertov's performances of the transition score are thus considerably more *piano* than those of his contemporaries, his ear-splitting more-revolutionary-than-thou public rhetoric notwithstanding. My favorite instance is the extraordinary opening sequence of his 1928 *The Eleventh*

Figure 1. From Chris Marker, *A Grin without a Cat* (*Le fond de l'air est rouge*; 1977, rereleased 1993). The intertitle, taken from Sergei Eisenstein's 1925 film *Battleship Potemkin*, reads "Brothers!"

Year, a film mainly about the early stages of the building of the famous Dnieper Hydroelectric Station near Zaporizhzhya, Ukraine. In poker-faced travelogue style, we get a brief intertitle-laden tour of the most famous large rocks in the Dnieper River—"Catherine's Armchair," the "Bogatyr [Russian folk hero]" rock, and the "Crag of Love"—culminating in a shot of the ossified bones of a "2,000-year-old Scythian." These particular named crags were doubtless selected for self-reflexive reasons—as analogues of the kind of ossified cinematic romance and historical drama that Vertov's cinema promised to overcome, much the way (as contemporary promotional propaganda endlessly affirmed) the revolutionary state would remove the actual stone, making the river's energies available for use.

The prologue is succeeded by a remarkable, prolonged full-screen image of the river surface, no longer rapids but still trembling with undulations (figure 2). This image is out of keeping with what has preceded it—it is mere water, rather than a conventional "historical site" with a name—and marks an unnoticeable transition to the rest of the mainly intertitle-less first reel with its depictions of the "storming" of the Dnieper and the reduction of the obstructing rocks to rubble. Only retroactively do we realize that the bare

Figure 2. From *The Eleventh Year* (Dziga Vertov, 1928). *Source*: Yale University Film Archive

river surface was an interruption, a noiseless rejection of the genre of travelogue with its dependence on existing conventions (here *nonfictional* conventions) of differentiating important from unimportant sites. Standard frameworks for interpreting the images are allowed to drift away, and *The Eleventh Year* becomes a film about the elements (including the human element) and their movements as such—leading, ultimately, to the collective creation of a new history and new conventions out of those raw energies, inscribed on that tabula rasa. (To be sure, for most of the film, the agent directing those energies is obscured: only at the end do we find it represented, again indirectly, in the shape of the Kremlin walls.)

Of course, from one perspective, this kind of restraint defeats the very purpose of representing the revolutionary transition, which is to make it visible and well-nigh palpable: a change we can believe in, whether as a condensation of past history or as an affirmation of future possibility. Indeed, from 1918 forward, the overwhelming majority of supporters of revolutionary art advocated a practice that was narrative, mimetic, and centered on dramatic

peripeteias. I think in particular of the influential 1918 *Revolution and Theater* by Platon Kerzhentsev (1918: 40–41), where the author insists that the
basis of Soviet cinema would be (alongside nationalization) new scripts and
new films, especially those with mass participants (D. W. Griffith's 1915 *The
Birth of a Nation* is named as a possible model); those focused on "social
struggle" in the past (Spartacus, peasant uprisings, and so on); and biopics
about great revolutionaries from Alexander Radishchev to Sofia Perovskaia,
Georgi Plekhanov, and Marx and Engels. Much Soviet revolutionary film,
including by its greatest fictional practitioners, indeed came to be constructed around the transformative Event, whose most sophisticated film-
theoretical conceptualization is to be found in Eisenstein's musings on
ecstatic transition (*ex-stasis*) as a kind of universal motor of movement
stretching all the way from the mollusks of the Precambrian to the revolutionary present. (His rival Vertov's fussy montage subtleties were famously
too impalpable and inward-directed for Eisenstein.)

Needless to say, there is nothing specifically revolutionary about narrative peripeteias, as the word's Aristotelian provenance should remind us;
there is, however, something very *Hollywood* about them, cinematically
considered. Many scholars have pointed out the centrality of productivist
ideology—the insistence that (in one historian's words) "maximising economic output should be the first priority of the revolution," prompted not
least by a permanent anxiety about possible internal revolt and external military attack (Read 2013: 170)—across Soviet history from the 1920s onward. I
would not be the first observer to identify the well-known "Americanism" of
the early Soviet filmmakers as another instance of the general Soviet preoccupation with US technological achievement (Buck-Morss 2000: 107–10,
157–72), in this case with the *affective* power to micro-organize the dramatic
scene into intense moments of crisis, overturn, and resolution through the
resources of (among other things) continuity editing.

Yet the Soviet filmmakers wished to turn this power to different ends,
and were thought by many to have done so already—from a most unpropi-
tious starting point, as I have stressed—by the end of the 1920s in the major
works of Eisenstein, Pudovkin, Vertov, Alexander Dovzhenko, and others.
The poet, playwright, theorist, and future victim of Stalinist terror Sergei
Tretyakov saw *The Birth of a Nation* in 1924 in China, twenty-five years
before that country's revolution and just before *Potemkin* startled the world
with its unprecedented appropriation and redeployment of cinematic devices
for revolutionary ends. The 1916 film *Intolerance*, which had an overwhelming impact on the fledgling Soviet filmmakers after its first Moscow screen-

ing in 1919, was certainly the Griffith work that most influenced Eisenstein, but Tretyakov (1925: 141) presciently regarded the earlier *Birth of a Nation* (see figure 3) as a kind of accumulator and refiner of techniques that would ultimately be used against everything Griffith's hymn to the Klan stood for:

> It's difficult to conceive of a film more deliberately constructed, more vile, more pogrom promoting, but also more skillfully saturated with emotion than [*The Birth of a Nation*].

> The much-loved Mrs. Beecher Stowe has been replaced by the predacious whoop of the pogromists of chauvinist imperialism: "Beat him, the black beast!"[1]

> This American *War and Peace* shows that the Negro question is to contemporary America what the Jewish question was to czarist Russia.

> But . . . I, CONSIDERING THIS FILM AS A WORK OF ADVANCED CINEMATIC TECHNIQUE, AND CONSIDERING ITS AGITATIONAL EFFECT, WOULD LIKE TO SIMPLY NOTE HOW DEFTLY, PRECISELY, AND DELIBERATELY AMERICAN CAPITALISM PLAYS ITS MELODIES, SEIZING ON THE FULL RANGE OF MOODS, TASTES, DISPOSITIONS, AND SYMPATHIES OF THE AMERICAN PHILISTINE. And we have to learn from this technical skill in agitation and effect SO THAT, IN RESPONSE TO *THE BIRTH OF A NATION*, THE SOVIET LAND MIGHT ANSWER NOT WITH THE KIND OF FILM-FUDGE WE PRODUCE NOW BUT WITH COUNTER FILMS TWICE AS SKILLFUL AND POWERFUL, THAT WOULD HELP PREPARE THE EXPLOSION WHOSE NAME WILL BE—*THE DEATH OF NATIONS*. (Tretyakov's emphases in capital letters)

Revolutionizing "Everyday Life" and the Tensions of "Progress"

Lenin famously despised any notion of a new proletarian or "revolutionary" art, but certainly believed that the dissemination of culture, including art (via education), would and should have culturally revolutionizing effects on "everyday life"—my translation of that untranslatable word *byt*—something about which his comrade Leon Trotsky in particular wrote a great deal in the early 1920s. The revolution as "turning point" was seen, particularly during the NEP period (1921–28), as the enabling precondition for the socialist economic and cultural revolution to come, even if these two meanings of the revolutionary *punctum*, overturn and condition of possibility, were occasionally thought to be in tension. We find a good example of this anxiety in

Figure 3. From D. W. Griffith, *The Birth of a Nation*, 1915

Trotsky's witty 1923 remark that the Russian proletariat was able so swiftly to do away with bourgeois power precisely because it had received virtually no inhibiting cultural inheritance from the bourgeoisie. (The founder and first commander in chief of the Red Army, Trotsky probably knew what he was talking about in this respect.) This meant, Trotsky (1923: 12–13) insisted, that the proletariat now had to acquire "culture," including everything from literacy to hygiene to punctuality at the workplace, on a new, socialist basis.

And indeed, "culture" was the leitmotif of revolution's second dominant meaning during this period, a meaning with a wholly different temporal implication. The revolutionizing of "everyday life" implied a drawn-out, if not interminable, process of progressive change (involving property relations, hygiene, education, sexual mores, and much, much more), whose representation became a concern of the state cinema institutions no later than 1923 (Sovnarkom RSFSR 1923: 20–24). Needless to say, representing *byt* and its mutations is a considerably trickier matter than embellishing the conventional interval of "transition" with new chord changes, not least because doing so seems an inherently *documentary* task, an ongoing confrontation with a world full of inertias, unevenness, and antagonism. Yet the Soviets did manage to produce remarkable cinematic investigations and evaluations of those mutations, whether in nonfiction (Vertov's *Stride, Soviet* from 1926 would be exemplary in this case) or fiction, often inflected toward comedy (Abram Room's *Bed and Sofa* from the following year would be the classic instance).

These representations of everyday life were never meant to be dispassionate or disinterested, but rather were intended to be diagnostic (a "pulse-taking of the time," to use another Vertovian metaphor) and to function to varying degrees as propaganda (i.e., an extended *lesson* about the current state of society) and as agitation (a prompt to get up and do something). Soviet forms of social self-reflection, which, to be sure, could be severely hemmed in by censorship and regime paranoia, were nearly always inflected by two distinct imperatives—industrialization (economics), on the one hand, and the "building of socialism" (culture), on the other—that were entwined from the start and never fully disentangled. Indeed, each was taken to be the precondition of the other, even as both were thought to be moving inexorably in a "progressive" historical direction, blown forward by the wind of the revolution.

Politically speaking, it is my own sense—and here I concur with positions recently articulated by Immanuel Wallerstein (1992) and Étienne Balibar (2016: 63–69)—that the crisis of political imagination and narrowing of political horizons that so many speak of as characteristic of our own time afflict less the notion of "revolution" than this larger category of "historical progress" as such, which Socialists such as the Bolsheviks had inherited (as Wallerstein shows) from post–French Revolution liberalism and which came to characterize all modern political ideologies, including conservative ones. The waning of this progressivist horizon, far more fundamentally than any dispersal of "revolutionary dreams," makes the watching of Soviet revolutionary films an alternately melancholy and (unintentionally) comic experience, simply because those films delineated more insistently than any others that horizon, which was also (it turns out) our own.

The Alternative Possibilities of Production

As I have indicated, productivism became the privileged expression for, or vulgarization of, history's forward motion during the early Soviet period and was an ideology shared by all filmmakers of the time, not least the futurist and machine-obsessed Vertov. The neologism *Vertov*—his given name was David Kaufman—derives from the Russian verb meaning "to rotate or turn," and we are probably not wrong to see the proliferation of spinning and turning mechanisms in Vertov's films (and especially in his most personal film, *Man with a Movie Camera* from 1929) as a kind of autobiographical signature, like Bach's B-A-C-H or Dmitry Shostakovich's D-S-C-H motif, whereby he ties his own identity to that of the machine.[2] (On the other hand, of course, the motif of rotation inscribes a larger historical-political idea into an apparently personal name: "revolution," no less.) For a host of reasons I do not need to list here, not least ecological ones, we are unable to share this enthusiasm today, even if Vertov's films retain the uncanny power to rekindle it momentarily (as do certain Hollywood blockbusters); whatever way forward we find (if we do), it will not repeat the productivist trajectory. Can we, however, find somewhat different attitudes toward production in Vertov, more usable notions of collective creation and creativity? I would like to suggest a couple of possibilities.

The first is a certain countervailing celebration, not of industry, but of DIY handiwork. For the entire lifetime of the Union of Soviet Socialist Republics, and not least in the film industry (Tcherneva 2014), anxieties about the persistence within production of much-loathed "artisanal practices" (*kustarnichestvo*) seem to have coexisted, perhaps inevitably, with a certain admiration for and even enthusiasm about creative "work-around" tactics that became enormously important within industry, including the film industry. Due to a lack of editing equipment in the state film studio, Vertov ended up having to edit some issues of *Kino-Nedelia* (*Film-Week*), the first Soviet newsreel, on a minuscule old Pathé montage table in the apartment of his friends, the veteran father-and-son cameramen team of Grigorii Lemberg and Aleksandr Lemberg (1968: 43). (The displacement to the Lembergs' kitchen gave the fledgling filmmaker the chance to chat directly with both *père* and *fils* about montage and cinematography while he was at work.) Vertov himself recounted in 1929 how, in the absence of any knowledge of animation equipment, the artist and later cameraman Ivan Beliakov quickly drew the figures for one of the earliest Soviet cartoons on a huge piece of paper spread across the floor, which Mikhail Kaufman, Vertov's brother, had to film while suspended from the studio ceiling like some proto–abstract expressionist. Nowadays, Vertov (2008: 172–73) grumbled, the youngsters are too lazy even to "rotate the crank on an animation stand [or] turn on its motor" with their feet.

Mikhail Kaufman (1976: 72) early on became especially renowned for his inventiveness, and by 1923 the room in which he lived had become (in his words) "something like a branch of the studio": "[In the early years] due to lack of materials, I would have to construct any technical and optical instruments we'd come up with from whatever was available, even cardboard and tin cans. . . . My room . . . turned into an experimental laboratory and our own peculiar club." Kaufman's first movie camera was a broken old Pathé he pulled out of a warehouse and repaired; he spliced together bits of unused film left behind by other cameramen to use for his first shots. Vertov openly reveled in Kaufman's abilities, and even after they split professionally and (for a while) personally in 1928, he would find occasion, in his ever more frequent historical reminiscences, to praise Kaufman's resourcefulness back in the good/bad old days, as here in early 1929: "We resolved to work in any conditions, bad or good, to shoot on lousy, partially exposed film, paying no attention to what they did in the lab, almost without equipment, and finding ways to use empty condensed milk cans. Kaufman was crazy about that milk, and from them all sorts of things were made: a lamp for making enlargements, an iris diaphragm" (Vertov 2008: 172).

There arose a small-scale cult of resourcefulness, physical prowess, and initiative among nonfiction cameramen and their fans—yes, they had a few fans—and Kaufman developed (and promoted) a lasting reputation as among the most fearless and inventive, solidified to be sure through his starring role as the "man with the movie camera" in Vertov's eponymous 1929 film. A newsreel cameraman from a different generation, Evgenij Akkuratov (b. 1927), told me of his surprise when he saw Kaufman, with whom he worked briefly in a provincial city in the 1950s, pick up a long-abandoned, crank-driven, silent-era Debrie camera sitting on a dusty shelf in the local film studio—Kaufman's more modern camera had broken down—and get the relic working almost immediately. Kaufman's handyman reputation persisted, in other words, in part because the problems themselves did.

Though typical "how we paid our dues" tales in a sense, stories such as Akkuratov's and Vertov's could also be regarded as profoundly embarrassing from a "progressivist" point of view. Why would a truly adequate, modern film studio need a spontaneously constituted one-room "branch" that made vitally necessary equipment out of discarded condensed milk cans? Better evidence of backwardness vis-à-vis the capitalist opponent, about whose endless supply of new and improved cinema technology the Soviets knew a great deal, is hardly required. Yet in another sense, this *kustarnichestvo*, or artisanship, expressed a persistent, never entirely devalued *democracy* of talent and skill, a tacit extolling of the capacity of human beings—with male human beings featured most prominently: the gendered character of this DIY heroism should not escape our notice—to produce new and useful things with their hands and minds out of the materials and even the detritus fluxing and refluxing out of the capitalist world. (*Man with a Movie Camera* is, of course, the greatest and most concrete cinematic expression of this ideology.) On the other side would stand the dominant, basically productivist position, the one whose name could be spoken aloud (and on behalf of which *Man with a Movie Camera* also testifies): specifically, that the power of the global class enemy could be effectively confronted only by a still greater concentration of technological and intellectual resources, along a single front.[3]

Perhaps the most extraordinary expression of the Vertovian privileging of the artisanal appears in some hitherto unpublished remarks he made at a meeting of his *kinok* (Kino-Eye) group in 1923, when he offers part of the motivation for his and the group's implacable (and ultimately fateful) opposition to the very principle of the script:

> [For us] the author and the director, the film composer, are the same person: the *kinok*.
>
> This is how things have worked up until now. A writer writes a story. A director stages the story. The writer and the director visualize the production differently and imprecisely. This imprecision is then made worse by the imprecisions of the set designer and then finally detached from any original source by the individuality of the cameraman and the caprices of the actor. This cheerful, nervous mess is what's been called "shooting a picture." (Vertov 1923: 6–7)

Indeed—except that the "cheerful, nervous mess" described here conforms almost perfectly to what would emerge, and in Hollywood had already emerged, as the dominant *industrial* model for film production, overwhelmingly centered on the script as the core element around which everything from budget to casting to set design to costuming would be organized. By contrast, Vertov is proposing, via his exclusion of the script—this section of his talk is titled "Death to the Script"—an anti- or counter-industrial production practice, one that would have involved a different, far less preset kind of collective work by professionals and nonprofessionals, had it been realized. (No wonder avantgarde filmmakers love Vertov so much!) In the end, he wound up being fired from the State Committee for Cinematography (Sovkino) studio in Moscow at the beginning of 1927 for refusing to provide a script for the film he was then working on (the first version of *Man with a Movie Camera*), and his main creative labors during his last twenty years would be devoted to scripts for documentary films, almost none of them produced.

My other example comes from the film that landed him in the greatest trouble precisely because of its scriptlessness: *One Sixth of the World* from

1926, his grandiose, eccentric, overstuffed, money-losing, Walt Whitman-inspired film-poem about the NEP economy (and made at the behest of the state organization for external trade). Extravagantly wordy in its final form, *One Sixth of the World* grew its poetic exoskeleton—complete with long lists and direct second-person address—only late in the production, after Mikhail Kaufman suggested that Vertov (who was drowning in footage) compose a libretto in the style of the much-revered Whitman as a structuring device. In one crucial section of the film's second part, in which various national members of the Soviet polity are directly addressed (as "you"), images of the industrial proletariat in factory workplaces ("you, who overturned the power of capital in October") are given momentary visual privilege, in part through a spectacular use of superimposition differentiating them from other addressees. They are then engulfed, however, in a long Whitman-inspired syntagmatic chain that places the proletarians on one level with a woman "washing clothes with [her] feet," a baby "sucking [its] mother's breast," a boy "playing with a trapped Arctic fox," and even the audience "sitting in this movie theater," all represented as mutual "owners of the Soviet land" and (eventually) as "building socialism," both on the basis of their engagement in these unremarkable actions and by virtue of being addressed by the film.

These democratic rhetorical gestures infuriated some of the film's early audiences, who quite correctly divined that the film was refusing to strongly distinguish the proletariat from peasant women "sewing during evening gatherings" or Yupik people "eating raw reindeer meat." Even more scandalously (though evidently less noticed), a caricatured foreign bourgeoisie, set brusquely apart from the Soviet world in the first part of *One Sixth of the World*, turns out eventually to be participating in the "building of socialism" anyway through its consumption of Soviet products. The Soviet economy, supposedly characterized by different class relations than its Western counterpart, thereby emerges, perhaps inadvertently, as part of some larger economy incorporating both socialist and capitalist systems.

Filming the NEP

NEP was rooted in a conception of social and historical difference, specifically (in Lenin's [(1922) 1965] terms) the difference between the "new economy" and the "peasant economy," the size of which gap historians continue to argue about. In my view, the question of (social, economic, cultural) *difference and nondifference* powerfully conditioned early Soviet film practice as well, not only on the level of content—that is, as an occasion for ideological construction and

Figure 4. From Dziga Vertov, *One Sixth of the World*, 1926. "You, sitting in this movie theater" looking at "you, washing sheep in the ocean surf." *Source*: Yale University Film Archive

messaging directly influenced by the regime's own policies and practices— but also in relation to cinematic form, and to *montage* and strategies of *audience address* in particular, as *One Sixth of the World* demonstrates (figure 4).

Conceptualizations of montage in the Soviet 1920s were most often carried out, in good film-theoretical fashion, via metaphor rather than argument. Most important by far were the famous productivist metaphors of goal-directed engineering and construction deployed by all the rival filmmakers/theorists, alongside more idiosyncratic tropes deriving from the Marxist chrestomathy (Eisenstein and class conflict) or from other arts or sciences (Vertov's intervals, thought of as an inheritance from music or mathematics). I think it worth entertaining the idea that the NEP-era concern with (primarily economic) linkage—Lenin's famous "alliance," or *smychka*, thematically present everywhere in Vertov's works at least through *One Sixth of the World*, indubitably *the* film about the NEP economy—provided a kind of ideological framework for his reflections on and practice of montage, one that overlapped obliquely, and doubtless not entirely coherently, with his futurist preoccupation with free, formal combination. "THE WORKER IN A MACHINE FACTORY must see the coal miner who provides the factory with the necessary fuel: coal. THE COAL MINER must see the peasant who produces the grain [the miner] needs" (Vertov 2008: 97). For what are the salient elements that enter into a given procedure of linking, and how linkable are they? Which intervals, to use that favorite Vertovian metaphor, separate them in time and space? And what would successful linkage amount to, and who would do it (and how)?

Not only of city and country or peasant and proletariat—those agents for whom "the revolution" meant such different things—but of man and woman, nomad and farmer, young and old, settled and homeless, literate and illiterate, north and south, east and west, Russian and Uzbek, Uzbek and Chechen, Chechen and Yakut, Yakut and German, one-sixth of the world and the other five-sixths? And so on, and so on—leaving aside duos that were taken to be unharmonious a priori like priest and commissar, tradesman and worker, or rich peasant and poor peasant. (And let's not even start on trios, quartets, quintets, and orchestras—though we are, of course, talking here about the largest of large ensembles.)

In these senses—in filmmakers' proposal and discovery of new ways to materially create and their new thinking about connection in an immense and changing terrain of radical difference—the revolution most emphatically *did* happen, if in a way that more celebrated peripeteias might obscure. It was a paradoxical happening to be sure, inasmuch as its achievement, read in the light of the most radical applications of cinematic montage, was a breaking-down of the ideology of *the present* as such, exposing time itself as an ongoing creation of the demos, rather than as some historicist conveyor belt external to collective praxis. Montage—the object of ferocious attack from the 1930s onward—was succeeded in the Soviet Union by discourses and institutions devoted precisely to the sustaining of a reified present, different in content but not in form from our own. Nothing could be more important now than undoing the present's self-evident status; and the Russian Revolution, not least as an event unachieved, furnished us with some of the tools for doing that.

Notes

Unless otherwise noted, all translations are mine.

1   For more on the importance of Stowe to pre- and postrevolutionary Russian culture, see MacKay 2013.

2   These are "musical cryptograms," in which names are rendered into music, forming a motif or melody. In German musical notation, the B flat is written as *B* and the B natural as *H*. In D-S-C-H, the *S*, or *Es*, is E flat.

3   To be sure, both of these positions—the antagonism toward the bureaucratic/technocratic and the stress on centralization and organization—emerge out of the fateful dialectics of the Leninist intellectual ferment. For a superb tracing out of this dynamic and its aporias, see Burbank 1995.

References

Arendt, Hannah. 1990. *On Revolution.* London: Penguin Books.

Balibar, Étienne. 2011. "Le moment messianique de Marx" ("The Messianic Moment in Marx"). In *Citoyen sujet et autres essais d'anthropologie philosophique (Citizen Subject and Other Essays in Philosophical Anthropology)*, 243–64. Paris: Presses Universitaires de France.

Balibar, Étienne. 2016. *Violence and Civility: On the Limits of Political Philosophy.* Translated by G. M. Goshgarian. New York: Columbia University Press.

Buck-Morss, Susan. 2000. *Dreamworld and Catastrophe: The Passing of Mass Utopia in East and West.* Cambridge, MA: MIT Press.

Burbank, Jane. 1995. "Lenin and the Law in Revolutionary Russia." *Slavic Review* 51, no. 1 (1995): 23–44.

Geldern, James von. 1993. *Bolshevik Festivals, 1917–1920.* Berkeley: University of California Press.

Holquist, Peter. 2002. *Making War, Forging Revolution: Russia's Continuum of Crisis, 1914–1921.* Cambridge, MA: Harvard University Press.

Kaufman, Mikhail. 1976. "Poet neigrovogo" ("Poet of the Nonacted"). In *Dziga Vertov v vospominaniiakh sovremennikov (Dziga Vertov as Remembered by His Contemporaries)*, ed. E. I. Vertova-Svilova and A. L. Vinogradova, 70–79. Moscow: Iskusstvo.

Kerzhentsev, Platon. 1918. *Revoliutsiia i teatr (Revolution and Theater).* Moscow: Dennitsa.

Lemberg, Aleksandr. 1968. "Dziga Vertov prikhodit v kino" ("Dziga Vertov Comes to Cinema"). *Iz istorii kino (From the History of Cinema)*, no. 7 (1968): 39–50.

Lenin, Vladimir. [1922] 1965. "Eleventh Congress of the R.C.P.(B.), March 27–April 2, 1922." In *Collected Works*, vol. 33, translated by David Skvirsky and George Hanna, 237–42. Moscow: Progress Publishers.

MacKay, John. 2013. *True Songs of Freedom: Uncle Tom's Cabin in Russian Culture and Society.* Madison: University of Wisconsin Press.

Read, Christopher. 2013. *War and Revolution in Russia, 1914–22: The Collapse of Tsarism and the Establishment of Soviet Power.* Basingstoke: Palgrave Macmillan.

Sovnarkom RSFSR (Council of People's Commissars of the Russian Soviet Federated Socialist Republic). 1923. "Working plan for Goskino for 1923–24." State Archive of the Russian Federation (GARF), Moscow, Archive 2313, list 6, file 304.

Tcherneva, Irina. 2014. "Le cinéma de non-fiction en URSS: Création, production et diffusion (1948–1968)" ("Nonfiction Cinema in the USSR: Creation, Production, and Distribution [1948–1968]"). PhD diss., École des Hautes Études en Sciences Sociales.

Tretyakov, Sergei. 1925. "Kino-ustanovka: Pekinskie pis'ma." In *Al'manakh Proletkul'ta (Proletkult Almanac)*, 137–42. Moscow: Proletkul't.

Trotsky, Leon. 1923. *Voprosy byta: Epokha "kul'turnichestva" i ee zadachi (Questions of Everyday Life: The Epoch of "Cultural Work" and Its Tasks).* 2nd ed. Moscow: Krasnaia Nov'.

Vertov, Dziga. 1923. ["Smert' stsenariiu" ("Death to the Script").] Russian State Archive of Literature and Art (RGALI), Moscow, Archive 2091 [Dziga Vertov], list 2, file 390.

Vertov, Dziga. 1984. *Kino-Eye: The Writings of Dziga Vertov*. Edited by Annette Michelson. Translated by Kevin O'Brien. Berkeley: University of California Press.

Vertov, Dziga. 2008. *Stat'i i vystupleniia* (*Writings and Speeches*). Edited by D. V. Kruzhkova and S. M. Ishevskaia. Moscow: Eizenshtein-Tsentr.

Wade, Rex A. 2017. *The Russian Revolution, 1917*. 3rd ed. Cambridge: Cambridge University Press.

Wallerstein, Immanuel. 1992. "Trois idéologies ou une seule? La problématique de la modernité" ("Three Ideologies or One? The Problematic of Modernity"). *Genèses* (*Genesis*), no. 9: 7–24.

Artemy Magun

Spontaneity and Revolution

Revolutionary events rarely introduce irreversible material changes. Both the French Revolution and, on a much larger timescale, the Russian Revolution later led to restorations that annulled the most significant of their achievements. However, they open up and leave for posterity their grandiose dilemmas, irreversibly setting in the past some burning points of attention. In the case of the French Revolution, such dilemmas were nationalism and universalism, freedom and dictatorship, political friendship/enmity and human rights. In the case of the Russian Revolution, which inherited these same questions, one additional unresolvable issue became *spontaneity and consciousness.*

Rosa Luxemburg famously engaged in a debate with Lenin, in 1904, defending "spontaneity" of the masses versus what she thought was Lenin's ([1902] 1961) authoritarian and repressive bias in his *What Is to Be Done?*

> The *initiative* and conscious leadership of social democratic organizations played an extremely insignificant role [in the recent mass strikes]. This arose, however, not so much from the inadequate preparedness of these special organizations for their role (although this point may

The South Atlantic Quarterly 116:4, October 2017
DOI 10.1215/00382876-4235027　© 2017 Duke University Press

have had considerable influence) and still less from the absence at that time of an all-powerful central authority in the spirit of Lenin's plan. On the contrary, such an authority would very probably only have increased the indecision of the individual party committees and provoked a split between the tempestuous mass and temporizing social democracy. . . . The main features of the social democratic tactic of struggle are on the whole not "invented": on the contrary, they are the consequence of a continuing series of great creative acts of experimental, often of spontaneous, class struggle. Here too the unconscious precedes the conscious, the logic of the objective historical process precedes the subjective logic of its agents. (Luxemburg 2004a: 255)

Later, after the success of the Russian Revolution in 1918, Luxemburg (2004b) actually praised Lenin and thought that his actions allowed for a synthesis of spontaneity and organization. The subsequent interpretation of revolution in the Soviet historiography contrasted the capacity of Bolsheviks to organize and lead with the anarchic spontaneity of unconscious revolutionaries (Clark 2000), even though neither Lenin nor the Soviet ideologists had ever denied the importance of organic, spontaneous self-organization of masses. One has to distinguish the idea of spontaneous automatic protest, which would, according to Lenin, fall into the trap of immediate economic interests, and the gut feeling, the "class instinct" of the workers, which Lenin praised (Krylova 2003) and associated not with immediacy but, on the contrary, with the large-scale logic of history, which is hard to pin down objectively. Lenin ([1902] 1961: 374) calls such advanced spontaneity "consciousness in an *embryonic form*," thus pointing to a latent dialectic of spontaneity and a need of its elaboration.

Recently, after the fall of the Soviet Union, new liberal historiography rejected the Soviet mythical narrative about Bolsheviks having planned and directed the entire Russian Revolution and emphasized, instead, the complexity and spontaneity of the events.[1] Luxemburg was right after all, it would then seem. A close, rational, empirical, and detailed analysis of this rich history predictably shows an interweaving of many simultaneous motives and actors. The empiricist optic of contemporary social science, what Georges Sorel (1999: 116) used to call "la petite science" (small science), privileges spontaneity almost "spontaneously."

The issue of spontaneity is of particular political importance today, in the period of numerous revolutionary and protest movements across the world. The claim of spontaneity contributes, prima facie, to the legitimacy of these movements, since it denies an existence of a narrow conspiracy or of a dogmatism of ideological elites, pointing instead to a drive to change that would rise "from below." However, spontaneity of political action is not something we can take for granted either as fact or as value. Therefore, it is worth looking back at the 1900s and 1910s.

First of all, the debate between Luxemburg and Lenin is complicated by a discrepancy in the meanings of Russian and German (then English) terminology. The word translated as "spontaneity," a philosophical term of Kantian descent, is in Russian *stikhiynost'*, which can literally be rendered as "elementality."

Spontaneity is originally a legal term that thematizes a subject's responsibility and, next, an ethical notion that refers to the intrinsic causation of actions by autonomous free will. *Elementality* is, in contrast, an ontological metaphor that signifies the chaotic amorphous physical forces of matter. But the root also connotes *elements* of which an orderly structure can be composed.

As Lars Lih (2005: 620) rightly notes in his detailed analysis of the Lenin-Luxemburg debate, "'Spontaneity' seems like a plausible translation of *stikhiinost'* because both words revolve around *lack of control*—but *stikhiinost'* connotes the self's lack of control over the world, while spontaneity connotes the world's lack of control over the self." Notably, *elementality* has an *objective* physical connotation, and *spontaneity* refers to subjectivity. In this sense, the "stikhiynoe" movement is a movement that can view itself as a physical, corporeal phenomenon among others, which is so important in the case of recent urban demonstrations, while *spontaneity* is more about somewhat impulsive freedom and lack of external orders.

This tension looks even stronger if we put it in relation to Hannah Arendt's *On Revolution* ([1963] 1990). This book famously denounces Marxism but praises the very form of revolution. It was increasingly influential in the late twentieth century as it strove to rehabilitate revolution in the context of the Cold War and privileged it as a form of political freedom in modernity, at the price of purifying it of concrete ideological or socioeconomic content. Starting in the late 1970s, the United States actually accepted a pro-revolution agenda in its policy, and the anticommunist revolutions of 1989–91 seemed to be a triumph of Arendt's bet on emancipatory events.

Arendt's book is contradictory on the question of spontaneity. First, Arendt bitterly criticizes it. She argues that Jacobins made an error by comparing the revolution to a "revolutionary torrent," thus *naturalizing* their driving forces and displacing agency on nature rather than taking political responsibility. This, she thinks, explains their discourse of necessity and the escalation of violence (8, 209). However, by the end of the book Arendt seems to unconsciously reverse her own argument, because it appears that the only heritage of revolution is the "spontaneously" and ephemerally emerging councils (255, 281).

Arendt's preoccupation with councils and the accent on spontaneity in their regard stems from her longtime sympathy and identification with Luxemburg. She supports Luxemburg probably without knowing that Lenin's argument was from the very start about "elementality," not spontaneity per se, while Luxemburg read him in Russian and must have had the same Russian word in mind. Interestingly, Luxemburg herself does not distinguish between the elemental and instantaneous meanings of spontaneity the way Arendt does. She writes with sympathy of spontaneity as the organic energy of masses and approvingly uses metaphors such as *revolutionary tide*. Her persistent use of organic metaphors suggests not just familiarity with the Russian meaning of *stikhiynost'* but, equally, knowledge of the new meaning of spontaneity. Indeed, by that time, the word *spontaneity* refers to the work of not only Immanuel Kant but also Henri Bergson (who uses it too). Luxemburg's (2004b: 287) understanding of spontaneity reminds us much of élan vital, for instance:

> The party of Lenin was thus the only one in Russia which grasped the true interest of the revolution in that first period. It was the element that drove the revolution forward, and, thus it was the only party which really carried on a socialist policy. . . .
>
> . . . Either the revolution must advance at a rapid, stormy and resolute tempo, break down all barriers with an iron hand and place its goals ever farther ahead, or it is quite soon thrown backward behind its feeble point of departure and suppressed by counter-revolution. To stand still, to mark time on one spot, to be contented with the first goal it happens to reach, is never possible in revolution. (287)

In the Wake of the Russian Revolution: Spontaneity and Legitimacy

In the Russian Revolution of 1917, spontaneity (*stikhiynost'*) was not just the issue of the energy of masses against "economism," as it had been played out between Lenin and Luxemburg. It was also the issue of *legitimacy*. Below we will see why.

The issue of spontaneity has been discussed predominantly with regard to the February Revolution, which started the irreversible process. It was already Leon Trotsky (1959: 130–47) who, in *The Russian Revolution*, raised this issue and derided the theory according to which this revolution was "spontaneous." "Spontaneousness," he wrote, "acquires an almost mystic character" (138). While in fact, "to the question, Who led the February revolution? we can then answer definitely enough: Conscious and tempered workers educated for the most part by the party of Lenin" (147). Trotsky attributes the theory of spontaneity to liberal moderates such as Pavel Milyukov and opposes to them a testimony of former state attorney (*prokuror*) Sergey Zavadsky, who wrote: "After all, what does the word 'spontaneously' mean? . . . Spontaneous conception is still more out of place in sociology than in natural science. Owing to the fact that none of the revolutionary leaders with a name was able to hang his label on the movement, it becomes not impersonal but merely nameless" (143). Note the idea of "sociology" that so drastically contrasts with the contemporary scientific ideology.

Michael Melancon, in his fine study from 2000, shows how a myth of spontaneity was later developed in both Soviet and Western historiography around the revolution of February 1917. The key actors of the events, socialist revolutionaries and right Socialists (Mensheviks), almost unanimously claimed that events took them "by surprise," that no one expected them. But, shows Melancon (2000), the police accounts show just the opposite. They describe an energetic organizational effort on the part of the Socialists in the month preceding the uprising and warn the government that an insurrection may occur around Women's Day, which is when it actually took place. This and the indirect evidence from the memoirs show that, whereas the women's march, the workers joining it, and raising of the bread issue may have been spontaneous, all the rest, including the crucial mobilization of soldiers and the creation of new power structures, was the result of active propaganda by Socialists (in person and through leaflets) and seems to have been part of a premeditated plan.

Why would Socialists deny their role and exaggerate the irrationality of the events? Melancon explains this mostly by the close arrival of the Bolsheviks in power. Bolsheviks were not active in the February events and projected their passivity on others, while other Socialists would later, after October, be afraid to admit their involvement in the "bourgeois" revolution. But I would add that, for Socialists, spontaneity (*stikhiynost'*), even when taken in the negative sense of *unpredictability*, was a sign of spontaneity in the positive sense, that is, of the organic nature of the revolution and the popular base of the new government (which, as we know, consisted in part of liberal politicians and attempted some unpopular policies). The contrast with the police perspective is telling here. For the police, the revolution (as probably any revolution) was a conspiracy of a few and was thus illegitimate and dangerous. Facts were rather on the police side, even though the revolutionary side relied on *nonfacts* (their lack of anticipation), which are hard to disprove. Similarly, Lenin, in 1917, categorically denied his involvement in the July uprising in Petrograd for which the Bolsheviks were outlawed. He claimed that this was a spontaneous, "stikhiynoe" uprising, in which the Bolsheviks only joined, unwillingly, after it started (Lenin [1917] 1964). Lenin, who was proverbially skeptical about purely spontaneous movements, did not think that the July uprising made sense and waited for an occasion to organize something more planned. The provisional government, on its part, held him not simply for a conspirator but, moreover, for a German agent, because he got some support from the enemy country on his way to Russia. I return to this important international aspect below, but here it is just additional proof of the *importance* of being spontaneous.

In social psychology, there is an empirically observed tendency for subjects to explain their behavior by accidental elements of situation and the behavior of others, through their internal dispositions. It is called the "fundamental attribution error" (Ross 1977). While this tendency is not absolute and depends on the level of reflection and on the subjective attitude to the actors and acts in question, it nevertheless helps to elucidate the political phenomena we are describing. Revolutionaries (if they are not the Bolsheviks after October 1917) tend to see and justify their agency as forced by either the circumstances or the elemental movement of the masses, while the police and the conservative government attribute them to a conspiracy and search for particular perpetrators, in order to efficiently neutralize them. The former think metaphysically and believe in the "people," in the "elements," and in the "event," while the latter think positively and search for tangible individuals and rational plans. At the same time, the former soberly trust the phenomena, while the latter tend toward mystical conspiracy theories, so that their very positive rationalism becomes irrational on another level. But both perspectives, seriously speaking, are partial and unilateral.

This vulnerability of the "spontaneity" argument is discernible also in theoretical writings. It is important that Arendt makes her aforementioned plea for spontaneity in the midst of the Cold War. Notably, her immediate inspiration is the Hungarian Revolution of 1956, on which she wrote a long article two years later (Arendt 1958), and many arguments of this article later entered the last chapter of *On Revolution*. Arendt's main point about this revolution is that it was spontaneous and thus free and that it generated councils as a form of rule. But the Hungarian Revolution of 1956 was important also for direct political reasons. The Union of Soviet Socialist Republics (USSR) considered it to have been organized by the US Central Intelligence Agency (wrongly, as it now appears). In truth, the United States was caught by surprise by the events, quickly pulled back its support, and allowed the USSR to regain control in Hungary. But prior to the revolution, there had been an obvious campaign by the United States to make the Eastern European countries secede. The United States instigated the Hungarians to revolt, through Radio Free Europe and the creation of émigré pressure groups, although the United States then did not follow up on the promise of support.[2] The situation does, in a way, mirror the 2014 crisis in Ukraine: there again, the United States is blamed for organizing the revolution for no obvious reason, but one can always evoke the existence of its political and moral support as a pivotal factor.

If we go back to Lenin and Luxemburg, we need first to remember that both of them were part of a revolutionary international. Their interest in the issue of spontaneity was, perhaps unconsciously, central not just for their perspectives on revolution but for their very survival as an international movement: sheer spontaneity risked leading to the national isolation of struggles (as Luxemburg [2004b: 282–83] notes in her critique of Karl Kautsky's nationalism), while the denial of mass spontaneity as such would turn party members into obvious foreign agents and conspirators. Luxemburg insisted on the importance of democratic spontaneity, but, precisely for this reason, she was bitterly opposed to the Bolsheviks' support for national self-determination. The spontaneity could be fruitful only on the condition of the universal nature of the platform. Lenin, who criticized "elemental spontaneity" in favor of organization but recognized its importance as a prerequisite of party struggle, could afford his strategic support of nationalism up to secession, because he felt secure about the universality of the movement's goals and could thus *select* which spontaneous movements to rely on. Luxemburg defended the democratic process as a way to reinvigorate the masses, only on the condition of the international nature of revolution. It appears that the relationship of party and masses was subject to a bitter aporia between the local and the international nature of revolution, which could have been resolved only through a continuous international expansion of the movement.

When Lenin returned to Russia from Germany in 1917 on a train with German permission, he was accused by the provisional government of being a German spy. But as we know, this did not prevent him from being a successful revolutionary leader. Why? Because the international involvement was not an issue: everyone knew Lenin's attitude to the world war, to the German government, and to German Social Democrats. If Lenin had been a local Russian "pro-European" politician like those of today, his standing would have been much more compromised.

Lenin, when he was defending the role of intellectuals and criticizing spontaneity, relied on an active movement that was already there. Luxemburg, based on her German and Polish experiences, was more concerned with energizing an apathetic population. So, although both were members of an international party, their conditions were different, and that made it hard to elaborate a unitary agenda for the global party: this proved to be possible only on the condition of building a hierarchical structure of the Comintern.

Contemporary Revolutionary Movements and the Problem of Spontaneity

We recently witnessed an impressive tide of antiauthoritarian revolutions / revolutionary movements throughout the world, which notably touched both the periphery countries with openly authoritarian regimes and the liberal democracies of the global "core," in Tunisia, Egypt, Bahrain, Libya, Syria, Spain, Greece, the United States, Italy, Russia, Turkey, Hong Kong, and, finally, Ukraine. The *enthusiasm* that this wave (as once the French Revolution) generated has dissolved in the face of several significant victories of the Right, and it is increasingly clear that these movements and revolutions *failed* to fulfill their apparent promise but, at the same time, changed the world in another, much more sinister way that had hardly been anticipated by enthusiastic observers: take, for example, the Middle East and the Russo-Ukraine border area.

One very important feature of the self-perception of these revolutions is their spontaneous and elemental character. Even their names refer to irresistible natural phenomena: the Arab Spring and the third wave of democratization, for example. The uprisings usually start from small or routine occurrences (the self-immolation of Mohamed Bouazizi, a regular antipolice demonstration in Tahrir Square, fake elections in Russia, the rejection of the Ukraine–European Union Associate Agreement) and *unpredictably* attract a large turnout and attention. The existence of small groups of organizers who act through social media does not contradict the supposed spontaneity but rather proves it, and in fact the social networks themselves, with their complex rhizomatic structure, seem to incorporate the spontaneity qua unpredictable coincidence of uncountable motions. The resulting movements are perceived as a miracle of freedom and then reflected by the participants as an enjoyment of encounter with those previously invisible people who are like themselves: "de-virtualization" in which materiality appears as a complex result rather than a raw starting point. There is a special significance of urban space, notably *squares* and *parks*, in the recent protests, some of which are even named after these *squares*, which are at the same time *events* (Tahir, Maidan, Gezi Park). The immediacy of passage to action correlates with the immediacy of its material content: these movements start not from big ideas but from occupying the immediate material surroundings and pointing at the collective corporeal existence: "We are here." The very presence of a crowd in the center of a city is then interpreted as a challenge to authorities, literally a *demonstration* of themselves. Judith Butler (2011) wrote on the occasion:

> After all, in Cairo, it was not just that people amassed in the square: they were there; they slept there; they dispensed medicine and food, they assembled and sang, and they spoke. . . . The bodies acted in concert, but they also slept in public, and in both these modalities, they were both vulnerable and demanding, giving political and spatial organization to elementary bodily needs. In this way, they formed themselves into images to be projected to all of who watched, petitioning us to receive and respond, and so to enlist media coverage that would refuse to let the event be covered over or to slip away. Sleeping on that pavement was not only a way to lay claim to the public, to contest the legitimacy of the state, but also quite clearly, a way to put the body on the line in its insistence, obduracy and precarity, overcoming the distinction between public and private for the time of revolution.

The issue of recapturing the public space and turning it into a genuine *public sphere*, an open space where anyone can act and become visible, is a starting point on which the political and economic slogans are subsequently grafted. A collective action and an event are a form that precedes its content. A revolution or occupation as such is what is important; its very possibility constitutes a statement against a conservative political routine.

Observers of the Occupy movement, such as David Graeber (2013), Todd Gitlin (2014), and Jeffrey Goldfarb (2012), emphasize the lively spontaneity that characterized it, in contrast to more traditional union and party movements. Sidney Tarrow (2011), in his immediate reaction to Occupy, rightly calls it a "We are here" movement. He seems to refer primarily to the fact that the participants of the protest called public attention to their mere presence in the society as representatives of a new identity: the presence of an urban-educated group with anticapitalist, socialist leanings, which is not represented in the mainstream electoral politics. But there is yet another connotation in his formula: one of spatial immediacy. It was important to be physically here, together, in a square of their own city. The same dynamic is characteristic of other crowds in the 2011–13 wave, particularly in Russia (Magun 2014; Yerpylova and Magun 2014).

The repertoire of square occupation is not new. Urban squares have served as sites for social protests and revolutions during the democratic age of the past two hundred years, even though the task of mobilization was more complex without Facebook and Twitter. The tactic of occupying and defensively protecting a strategic area was used not only in revolutions but also in military operations. What might be new is the reflexive turn through which the very *form of event* tends to dominate its content, so that the "spontaneity" is actually itself not spontaneous but reflexive and abstract.

Western Theory and Spontaneity

In the twentieth century, after an initial debate over spontaneity between Luxemburg and Lenin, and the apparent victory of consciousness over spontaneity in the Leninist USSR, we see the language of elemental spontaneity gradually returning in Western left-leaning theory. In the 1970s, the previously strict structuralist Marxist Louis Althusser introduced the "Epicurean" notion of "aleatory materialism," and Gilles Deleuze and Félix Guattari resurrected Bergson and created a social theory almost entirely based on elemental metaphors and notions. In the 2000s, Antonio Negri and Michael Hardt developed, based on Deleuze, an impressive political ontology in which the new revolutionary strata, the "multitude," is compared to "swarm" and presented as a source of vital agency (Hardt and Negri 2004: 93–95), even though Negri and Hardt carefully emphasized that the coming revolution of the multitude cannot and would not be "spontaneous" (220–27). Even Alain Badiou, who sharply opposes the anarchist tendencies of Deleuzianism, built his philosophy around the notion of revolutionary *event*, a concept with obvious anarchic, situationist, and spontaneist roots.

Now, if we look into empirical social science, which tended, since the 1970s, to emphasize the rational strategic elements of social movements, in recent decades it also increasingly looks at the *accidental* explanation of the revolutionary waves. Provided the general condition of a rising middle class in a backward country, revolution should and can happen anywhere: it all depends on a set of arbitrary constellations, such as contamination (Beissinger 2002) or an event in the sense of something accidental and contextually evolving (Sewell 1996; more recently, Della Porta 2013).

The reasons *why* spontaneity has become so popular again today, one hundred years after the Russian Revolution, are plural. First, after the discrediting of Marxism, there is a crisis of the general ideological framework that would help to premeditate and organize a large movement. Second, the existing society is increasingly characterized by social and political apathy. This is seen as a danger both by mainstream politicians who are concerned about vibrant "civil society" and by radicals, who have a hard time recruiting activists and mobilizing movements. Spontaneity is a superior political virtue in this case; it is a source of or synonym for *energy* that is leaking away in the contemporary bourgeois society. But also, an occasional impulsive activity is often the most that activists can count on from the masses. Third, spontaneity is a major source of *legitimacy* for social movements. In some countries, such as the United States, it is even a kind of *ideology*. Organized representative politics is viewed by citizens as both corrupt and too abstract. On the other hand, the establishment is not interested in major systematic movements: the "Tocquevillean" expectation is that civil society consists of interest groups or regional political clubs that would help maintain vibrancy and feedback but would not challenge authorities or the system in its entirety. Francesca Polletta (2006) and Nina Eliasoph (2011) both show how US activists systematically avoid macropolitical discourse and focus on "empowerment talk." Polletta even named her book *It Was Like a Fever* after a phrase of one of her subjects: "It [civic action] comes like a fever."

As she writes, "the word spontaneous means voluntary and instinctual (involuntary). Contradictory meanings are contained in the same word. In the sit-in narratives, in this reading, spontaneity functioned as a kind of narrative ellipsis in which the movement's beginning occurred. 'BOOM—It Happened,' as one account put it, and the non-narratable shift from observer to participant took place" (Polletta 2006: 45). It is more or less clear that the spontaneist tendency is at least in part responsible for the defeat of the recent movements, both in the core countries, where they were unable to institutionalize, and in the periphery countries, where the ideological vacuum was filled by anti-Enlightenment religious creeds. There is a growing awareness that movements like Occupy would have gained from some political representation and organization (see, e.g., Dean 2016).

The International Dimension

But the problem with spontaneism lies deeper. After all, a spontaneous movement can gradually obtain leadership and structure, and the Occupy movement did involve a great deal of thoughtful coordination and organization. It was an effort of both spontaneity and organization.

The original Leninist critique of spontaneity in *What Is to Be Done?* (Lenin [1902] 1961) just says that spontaneous uprisings do not rise above immediate economic claims to the political, universal level: the intellectuals must help there. This is not really a problem today: the revolutions go almost immediately to the political level, and even sometimes, on the contrary, they miss the economic agenda (as in Russia and Ukraine, for instance).

The key problem is elsewhere—at the level of international, not political/national, universality. In fact, the most striking feature of the recent tide of revolutions is that there was relatively little coordination among the numerous movements in different countries. Of course, there was emulation of *examples*, the borrowing of the tactic, and there were activists traveling from one revolution to another. But has there emerged an international movement with a unitary agenda? Surprisingly, that has not even now happened in Europe, where the conditions and issues across countries are similar (with the notable exception of Syriza and Podemos, which are both officially institutionalized, and that is probably the reason they cooperate). The only place where an international movement did emerge is the Middle East, and this on the basis of a religious movement—the Muslim Brotherhood.

Why were these movements unable to unite? I can only speculate—but this should be further empirically researched—that the movements remain disunited for the following reasons:

- They were built on a spontaneous situational solidarity and face-to-face contact as opposed to a clear ideology or a concrete purpose.
- They consisted of the educated strata, many of whom work with and through the national language and whose issues and slogans were more culturally grounded and context-specific than they would have been for a less sophisticated group. This is paradoxical, given the globalized way of life of the contemporary "cognitariat"; however, even the discourse of the English-speaking US Occupy movement, with its economist rhetoric, is hardly transferrable into the more politicized and ideologized protest milieus of the countries outside the United States and the United Kingdom.
- In many cases, they depended in their agenda on national politics. A major constraint on the movements is the national nature of the ruling "democracy," which, being relatively hospitable to public demonstrations, artificially keeps them within the national context, since the "power of the people" is supposed to exist only on the national level.

- They happened in structurally different groups of countries, such as the United States and Europe, with their concern for neoliberal capitalism; Russia, Ukraine, and Turkey, with their concern about authoritarianism, the demand for democracy, and a Westernized constituency; and the Middle East, where the demand for democracy combined with a revolt against poverty, a religious plea, and an anti-Western attitude.

Interestingly, the situation was different with the global justice movement of the 1990s and 2000s: there was plenty of international coordination, but there were few genuine movements. It was almost as though the head and the legs missed each other in time.

Anyway, let me return to the argument: What were the results of this national disjuncture of the movements, and what is the problem with them?

The answer to the first question is straightforward and stems from the *fact* of "spontaneity": a lack of international organization made each movement less sustainable and too dependent on the energy of the masses that tended to expire.

But there is another central problem that is not so obvious—that of *legitimacy*. Spontaneity, which as we saw is not only an appeal to popular energy but also a potent legitimating factor of revolutions and movements, is *from another perspective* a high *danger* to the legitimacy of revolutionary movements today.

Here the recent Russian experience is highly symptomatic.

The Russian government has long taken an explicit counterrevolutionary position. The main claim is that color "revolutions" in the former USSR are organized by the West in order to undermine Russian sovereignty or Russian influence in the countries of the former USSR. Thus, for example, Russian TV showed how the leader of the Russian opposition met with Georgian politicians and how Putin angrily repeated that Western politicians distributed "cookies" to the participants of the rallies of 2011–12. This claim became even stronger after the Maidan events in Ukraine in 2013–14: Russian TV convincingly persuaded its audience that the events were deliberately organized by the US State Department, offering as evidence that Victoria Nuland (assistant secretary of state) actually gave out cookies at Maidan or that recipes from cookbooks like that of Gene Sharp (1973) were perhaps followed by the protesters. This perception is at least used to legitimize the ongoing war: the revolution in Ukraine is presented in the Russian official media as a geopolitical move, not an organic expression of the people's will (in fact, the majority voted for the incumbent). The Izborsky Club, a Russian ultraconservative think tank, published in 2013 a detailed analytical report by Konstantin Cheremnykh and Marine Voskanyan in which it tries to prove the organized nature of the 2011–13 protests and particularly of the Russian case. Here is an example of this paranoid thinking:

> In 2010 Terry Winograd becomes codirector of the Liberation Technologies program at Stanford University, where the managers of "revolutions 2.0" are trained. Another codirector, Larry Diamond, led a project on Iranian democracy. . . .
>
> Thus the systematically circulated idea that "technologies 2.0" are "accidental inventions of young geniuses" is a triple bluff: first, they are not accidental; second, their elaboration follows the logic not of the free market but of a targeted selection from above; and, third, they serve the purpose of control rather than communication. . . .
>
> The enterprise of "revolution 2.0" emerges in the New America Foundation. In 2006 this foundation, together with the Berkman Center for Internet and Society at HLS [Harvard Law School] and two private persons, Rebecca MacKinnon and Ethan Zuckerman, creates the blog network Global Voices, whose first investor is the Rockefeller Foundation, later joined by the Omidyar Network, the Ford Foundation, the MacArthur Foundation, the Open Society Institute (now the Open Society Foundation), the Sunlight Foundation (instituted with support from the Rockefellers), and some other private individuals, such as Mitch Kapor, a sponsor of Facebook. (Cheremnykh and Voskanyan 2013; my translation)

The problem is that, even though these accusations are not really correct, it is hard to argue against them: against the anecdotal nature of evidence, US politicians and political scientists can only insist on the spontaneity of civic protest movements in general and to deride "conspiracy theories," but these arguments are as weak as the conspiracy theories themselves. How can one prove "spontaneity"? There is no evidence of planned US involvement in Ukraine, but there were at least some activists who received training from US institutions on democracy promotion, and the United States did give money to some Ukrainian nongovernmental organizations that supported Maidan—even though that could probably not have triggered the events. Also, although the United States did not organize the protests, it certainly voiced its support of them, which was not a minor help. This taken together created an international "window of opportunity" for them (see Foran 2005). The accidental spontaneity of revolution is rather a presumption of liberal intellectuals than an actual fact; therefore, it is easily beaten by a paranoid suspicion of deliberate agency. Moreover, if we look at the content of the claims by protesters, we see that in the Ukrainian case it was explicitly geopolitical (the original slogan was support for the association with the European Union), and it had been implicitly so in Libya, Syria, and even Russia. Spontaneity, as well as deliberateness, is in the eye of the beholder, while a real interpretation or plan of the protest wave starting in 2011 was, to an extent, *missing* for both the participants and the authorities.[3]

To topple its counterrevolutionary "big game," the Kremlin in 2014 did a twist and organized its own "revolution" in Crimea and Donbass, trying to use exactly the same tactic and language as the Maidan supporters in Kiev and other similar revolutionaries. This kind of cynical move mimics and counters the Western "wave of democracy" as it perceives it, by organizing a splinter movement within a revolutionary country and defending its "human rights" against a "punitive operation" by the authorities.

The result is, paradoxically, that precisely when an uprising is intranational and "spontaneous," it is vulnerable to the accusation that it has foreign instigators. This is true particularly for the present situation, when those who protest are not proletarians but rather, depending on the perspective, mass intellectuals, cognitive workers, or "angry urbanities." This group may be influential in a society, but it can neither constitute nor lead a majority! Therefore, members of this group are weak within their own countries and would be much stronger politically if they knew how to build an international and how to rise to universality. The elemental spontaneity that is here a reality, a credo, and a (weak) self-defense prevents them from doing so.

Concluding Remarks

A solution to the dilemma of spontaneity/consciousness has existed for a while, and it has to do precisely with the *internationalization* of emancipatory movements. Spontaneity in the sense of immediacy is vulnerable for the very reasons that it is impossible to demonstrate and that a nonspontaneous vision of events as a "conspiracy" can also be argued for. Therefore, we need a dialectical synthesis in which immediate spontaneity as "elementality" connects with Kantian spontaneity as a universal and principled act. Lenin ([1902] 1961: 374) already speaks of *stikhiynost'* dialectically in saying—I repeat the aforementioned quotation—that "the 'spontaneous element,' in essence, represents nothing more nor less than consciousness in an *embryonic form*." But, following G. W. F. Hegel rather than Gottfried Leibniz, we must add that the development of this "embryo" can only happen via a break: many of the local and national values would need to be sacrificed for the sake of the larger universal movement (what Kautsky and company were unable to do in 1914), while the central structures of this movement should sacrifice full control and delegate initiative to those who would need to maneuver locally on the condition of their fidelity to the cause. Ideas at the top, subjects at the bottom. Jodi Dean (2016: 183–90) gives a persuasive program of a dialectical synthesis between the party and the spontaneous masses with their "beautiful moments," through what she calls a relation of "transference." However, it appears to me that dialectics should be pushed further, and the party itself, to be universal, would need to incorporate the negative elements of "spontaneity":

- It would need to hide itself, to contain a system of secrecy. Secrecy is a dialectical transposition of spontaneity onto consciousness.
- It would need to "massify" itself, to alternate the motion of centralization with that of decentralization and blind "commissarial" delegation, while using forced rotation of members across organizations. Delegation is another dialectical transposition of spontaneity onto consciousness.

Today only an internationalization of the existing movements and their federalization can get rid of the deadlock of false spontaneity: an inevitable contamination of local protests by international support (be it from peers or from other governments) is a delegitimizing factor in the face of required spontaneity and the "democratic" organicity of a movement.

This internationalization, however, cannot be immediate and formal: there are reasons why it has not happened. Even if one were to overcome the localist limitations of the urban protests, there remains the substantive question. US and European Occupy movements were, in their content (but not in their form), essentially a continuation of the "alterglobalist" global justice movement. It was a protest against neoliberalism, inequality, and, more broadly speaking, capitalism. Protests in the countries in the periphery of Europe, such as Turkey and Russia, were antiauthoritarian, anticorruption (which does not at all equal anticapitalist in this context), and, most importantly, pro-Western, arguing for a rapprochement with Western liberal democracies. The Arab Spring carried the antiauthoritarian and equality-seeking slogans too, but they were contested between a secular liberal and an anti-Western religious interpretation. The Ukrainian Maidan was antiauthoritarian, pro-Western, and mostly nationalist. Can there indeed be an immediate alliance among these groups, which were so influenced by one another's repertoire? There would need to be some "hegemonic" magic of combining the incompatible, in the style of Ernesto Laclau and Chantal Mouffe.

Kojin Karatani (2014: 295), in the recent book *The Structure of World History*, makes a pessimistic but convincing point:

The notion of a simultaneous world revolution still persists today. But it is never clearly analyzed, which is precisely why it functions as a myth. If we want to avoid repeating the failures of the past, we need to subject the notion to a detailed analysis. . . . Simultaneous world revolution is sought by movements that seek to abolish the state from within. But the movements in different countries are characterized by large disparities in terms of their interests and goals. In particular, the deep fissure between global North and South lingers—now taking on the guise of a religious conflict. A transnational movement will always fall prey to internal splits arising due to conflicts between states, no matter how closely its members band together. The emergence of a socialist government in one or more countries may make it possible to avoid this kind of schism, but would only lead to a different kind of schism—that between movements that hold state power and those that don't. For this reason, any attempt to build a global union of countermovements that arise within separate countries is destined to end in failure.

For instance, says Karatani, the October Revolution of 1917 in Russia did not weaken but reinforced other European states, which were now much more mobilized against their own Left. He then makes a reasonable conclusion that one can only rely on the objective of building a world state, but then he has a rather strange mechanism for how to reach it (through states abandoning their sovereignty to the United Nations).

However, in spite of Karatani's justified skepticism, there may not be a simultaneous world revolution but there may be a *global revolutionary movement*, with exactly the goal of establishing the world republic that he speaks about. It cannot reconcile all the diverse claims of protesting movements. But it can agree on the *subject*: those who practice "immaterial labor" or the proletarianized intellectual/creative class and find themselves in a contradictory situation of virtual leadership and factual subalternity. And it can creatively integrate the disjunct and at times opposite values in the regional movements. Thus an internationalist Left, with all its justified criticism of colonialism, would need to address the value of the West as a historically progressive region, because this is a perspective of many antiauthoritarian revolutionaries outside Europe and the United States. And, symmetrically, in spite of their alliance with liberals and support from international charity funds, these revolutionaries would need to seriously search for a workable alternative to the neoliberal "spontaneous order." Such intellectual work is indispensable for eventually building an international progressive movement that would be responsive to the problematic and unforgettable challenge set forth by the Russian Revolution of 1917.

Notes

1   For a well-argued and nuanced defense of spontaneity, see Kolonitsky 2001.

2   For a detailed analysis of the Hungarian Revolution, see Gati 2006.

3   As Slavoj Žižek (2012: 128) rightly wrote, "[e]vents like OWS protests, the Arab Spring, the demonstrations in Greece and Spain, and so on, have to be read as . . . signs from the future. [W]e should bring in the perspective of the future, taking the [radical emancipatory outbursts] as limited, distorted (sometimes even perverted) fragments of a utopian future that lies dormant in the present as its hidden potential. . . [W]hile we must learn to watch for such signs, we should also be aware that what we are doing now will only become readable once the future is here."

References

Arendt, Hannah. 1958. "Totalitarian Imperialism: Reflections on the Hungarian Revolution." *Journal of Politics* 20, no. 1: 5–43.

Arendt, Hannah. [1963] 1990. *On Revolution*. New York: Penguin Books.

Beissinger, Mark. 2002. *Nationalist Mobilization and the Collapse of the Soviet State*. Cambridge: Cambridge University Press.

Butler, Judith. 2011. "Bodies in Alliance and the Politics of the Street." *Transversal*, no. 10. www.eipcp.net/transversal/1011/butler/en.

Cheremnykh, Konstantin, and Marine Voskanyan. 2013. "Anonimnaya voina" ("An Anonymous War"). Izborsky Club, July 23. www.dynacon.ru/content/articles/1468.

Clark, Katerina. 2000. *The Soviet Novel: History as Ritual*. Bloomington: Indiana University Press.

Dean, Jodi. 2016. *Crowds and Party*. New York: Verso.

Della Porta, Donatella. 2013. *Can Democracy Be Saved? Participation, Deliberation, and Social Movements*. Cambridge, UK: Polity.

Eliasoph, Nina. 2011. *Making Volunteers: Civic Life after Welfare's End*. Princeton, NJ: Princeton University Press.

Foran, John. 2005. *Taking Power: On the Origins of Third World Revolutions*. Cambridge: Cambridge University Press.

Gati, Charles. 2006. *Failed Illusions: Moscow, Washington, Budapest, and the 1956 Hungarian Revolt*. Stanford, CA: Stanford University Press.

Gitlin, Todd. 2014. *Occupy Nation: The Roots, the Spirit, and the Promise of Occupy Wall Street*. New York: It Books.

Goldfarb, Jeffrey. 2012. "OWS and the Arab Spring: The New 'New Social Movements.'" *Deliberately Considered* (blog), May 18. www.deliberatelyconsidered.com/2012/05/ows-and-the-arab-spring-the-new-%E2%80%9Cnew-social-movements%E2%80%9D.

Graeber, David. 2013. *The Democracy Project: A History, a Crisis, a Movement*. New York: Spiegel and Grau.

Hardt, Michael, and Antonio Negri. 2004. *Multitude: War and Democracy in the Age of Empire*. New York: Penguin.

Karatani, Kojin. 2014. *The Structure of World History: From Modes of Production to Modes of Exchange*. Translated by Michael K. Bourdaghs. Durham, NC: Duke University Press.

Kolonitsky, Boris. 2001. *Simvoly vlasti i bor'ba za vlast': K izucheniyu politicheskoi kul'tury rossijskoi revoliutsiya 1917 goda* (*Symbols of Power and Power Struggle: To a Knowledge of the Political Culture of the 1917 Russian Revolution*). Saint Petersburg: Dmitri Bulanin.

Krylova, Anna. 2003. "Beyond the Spontaneity-Consciousness Paradigm: 'Class Instinct' as a Promising Category of Historical Analysis." *Slavic Review* 62, no. 1: 1–23.

Lenin, Vladimir. [1902] 1961. *What Is to Be Done? Burning Questions of Our Movement.* In *Collected Works*, 5: 347–530. Moscow: Foreign Languages Publishing House.

Lenin, Vladimir. [1917] 1964. "The Russian Revolution and Civil War." In Lenin, *Collected Works*, 26:28–43.

Lih, Lars. 2005. *Lenin Rediscovered: "What Is to Be Done?" in Context.* Leiden: Brill.

Luxemburg, Rosa. 2004a. "Organizational Questions of Russian Social Democracy." In *The Rosa Luxemburg Reader*, edited by Peter Hudis and Kevin B. Anderson, 248–65. New York: Monthly Review Press.

Luxemburg, Rosa. 2004b. "The Russian Revolution." In Hudis and Anderson, *Rosa Luxemburg Reader*, 281–310.

Magun, Artemy. 2014. "The Russian Protest Movement of 2011–2012: A New Middle-Class Populism." *Stasis* 2, no. 1: 160–91.

Melancon, Michael. 2000. *Rethinking Russia's February Revolution: Anonymous Spontaneity or Socialist Agency?* Carl Beck Papers in Russian and East European Studies, no. 1408. Pittsburgh: University of Pittsburgh Center for Russian and East European Studies.

Polletta, Francesca. 2006. *It Was like a Fever: Storytelling in Protest and Politics.* Chicago: University of Chicago Press.

Ross, Lee. 1977. "The Intuitive Psychologist and His Shortcomings: Distortions in the Attribution Process." In *Advances in Experimental Social Psychology*, edited by Leonard Berkowitz, 10:173–220. New York: Academic Press.

Sewell, William. 1996. "Historical Events as Transformations of Structures: Inventing Revolution at the Bastille." *Theory and Society* 25, no. 6: 841–81.

Sharp, Gene. 1973. *The Politics of Nonviolent Action.* 3 vols. Boston: Porter Sargent.

Sorel, Georges. 1999. *Reflections on Violence.* Edited by Jeremy Jennings. Cambridge: Cambridge University Press.

Tarrow, Sidney. 2011. "Why Occupy Wall Street Is Not the Tea Party of the Left." *Foreign Affairs*, October 10. www.foreignaffairs.com/articles/north-america/2011-10-10/why-occupy-wall -street-not-tea-party-left.

Trotsky, Leon. 1959. *The Russian Revolution: The Overthrow of Tzarism and the Triumph of the Soviets.* Edited by F. W. Dupee. Translated by Max Eastman. Garden City, NY: Doubleday.

Yerpylova, Svetlana, and Artemy Magun, eds. 2014. *Politika politichnykh* (*Politics of the Apolitical*). Moscow: NLO.

Žižek, Slavoj. 2012. *The Year of Dreaming Dangerously.* New York: Verso.

Antonio Negri

Soviet: Within and beyond the "Short Century"

Anyone interested in the question of democracy in Marxist terms and seeking a constituent power that befits the working class must confront the issue of the historical relationship between the objective structure of the economic process and the subjective dynamics of decision making. The latter is not understood, along the lines of classical political science, as a punctual, dramatic, and *evenemential* aspect of institutional innovation; instead, it is meant as a process of destitution of old power that also expresses the *constituency* of a revolutionary subject. If we wish to understand how this process does not resolve itself into a mere "instant" and how it is an "excess" rather than an "exception," we can assume a genealogical standpoint, à la Michel Foucault, or a "working-class standpoint." This is the name workerists assigned to their description, preparation, and construction of a revolutionary process geared to actualize a tendency led by working-class struggle and interpreted by a subject that put its organization into practice. This is after all the method of Machiavelli's *The Prince*, but here the topic of our inquiry is different: our subject is the Russian working class when, in the development of the soviets (workers' councils), it organized itself into a party

The South Atlantic Quarterly 116:4, October 2017
DOI 10.1215/00382876-4235038 © 2017 Duke University Press

and carried out its struggles, between 1905 and 1917, before dissolving its original institutions in favor of a socialist management of capital during the short century.

Class Composition

Let us start with the most generic notion: class composition. By composition, we mean two things: first, the "technical" composition of the working class, that is, the material and technical quality of the relationship between the mass of workers and the system of production in which they are employed. In this, we point to the figure of "labor power" in relation to "fixed capital" (machines, raw materials, etc.) and trace the shape that the mode of production gives to the collective body of workers engaged in production and, in turn, how the collective body of workers influences the approach and machinic functioning of command in the enterprise. Obviously, class composition keeps changing following the transformations of the mode of production and vice versa. In Marx's *Capital*, at least two "modes of production" are given: one is established when "manufacturing," brought about by the primitive accumulation of capital, gets imposed after the "dispossession" of archaic and common conditions of production; in this, workers become associated without a preset work schedule, take on the formal structures of cooperation from capital, and produce "absolute surplus value." Another mode, "large-scale industry," becomes prominent when "relative surplus value" is extracted and turned into "surplus value," all of which is determined by technological development and extracted by the heightened productive capabilities of the cooperation of workers firmly organized within the factory. At the end of the nineteenth century, in *The Development of Capitalism in Russia*, Lenin discussed the composition of the Russian working class: applying Marx's definition of technical composition, he identified the situation of Russian development with the shift from "manufacture" to "large-scale industry."

And thus we arrive at the second element, complementary to the first: the "political" composition of the working class, which refers to the forms of "political consciousness" of the proletariat, the "reflexive" conditions connected to its comportments, and how they relate to its organizational practices. Keep in mind that each stage of development (primitive accumulation, manufacture, large-scale industry) is characterized by a proletariat displaying deeply different political comportments, be they active or passive. We have already hinted at how passive they can be when mentioning how the proletariat was included in the capitalist mode of production by means of primitive accumulation. The form of exploitation then was extractive and thus relatively indifferent to the life of the worker: it cruelly invested it but was not changed by it. The relation became totalizing, relational, and disciplinary with the advent of manufacture, and, eventually, biopolitical elements were introduced into the organization of large-scale industry as the social and cultural conditions of productivity began to play a central role in the determination of productivity rates. But this variety becomes even more pertinent when looking at the political composition of the proletariat from the standpoint of its activity. Here it is important to grasp the tonalities of the production of subjectivity that breathed life into this movement when expressed as forms of resistance and rebellion against exploitation. I obviously do not wish to recall the revolt of the Florentine Ciompi or the rebellions of the cities of the Reformation in the Upper Rhenish Circle, nor do I wish to go back to the French peasants' revolts of the sixteenth and seventeenth centuries amply documented by Marxist historians. I will merely refer to Marx's description of the revolts that occurred in the most recent phase of capitalist accumulation, which he divides into three types.

First came the revolts of, let's say, the *undifferentiated worker*, the unskilled laborer, during the early phases of the expansion of industry, as the latter became hegemonic in Western metropolises between 1848 and 1870. This type of revolt was of the crowd, manifestly displaying the characters of a collision, organized in assemblies whose order was determined by representation—the organization of uprisings needs leadership. The Paris Commune represented the highest peak of this type of revolt. Between 1870 and 1917, a new model emerged based on different forms of organization of the labor force. As manufacture was turning into large-scale industry and labor power was no longer generic and undifferentiated but skilled, the *professional worker* imbued the mass of workers, as a collective body, with an element of direction, an understanding of industrial development, a critique of exploitation, but, above all, an organization of the struggle. Suffice it to mention here, as an illustration, the examples of highly organized labor in struggle witnessed in the German *Räte* and the Russian *soviets*. There, forms of organization extorted industrial knowledge from the entrepreneur and brought it to the organized consciousness of the *skilled* workers in struggle. And here we come to the starting point of our analysis of the *soviet* in the short century.

But we also wish to discuss the relevance of the soviet ideal after and beyond the short century, and, to this purpose, two figures of the technical composition of the labor force that came to prominence after the revolution and had an influence on politics deserve to be mentioned. Between 1917 and 1968, the *mass worker* of the large-scale Taylorist industry represented the living side of total capital and operated in a disciplined relation with fixed capital, embodying the "technical" composition of the working class. The "political" composition that emerged from it, discernible in the relation between union and party and the dynamic of representation and leadership, turned the economic claims of the masses into a demand for power. The party, in the guise attributed to it by the Socialist Second and Communist Third Internationals, became the political form of the mass worker. After 1968, however, we were confronted with a new figure and a new epoch, that of the *socialized, multinational, cognitive worker.* We will later return to the definition of this type of worker and the political figures it expresses itself through.

Here let us draw attention to a problem. While defining the relation between "technical" and "political" composition, we have operated in a determinist fashion, so to speak. We have posited a necessary relation (though only as a tendency), a model of work organization and a model of political organization. However, all images of necessity applied to this relation must be corrected: its reality and truth are purely tendential; the process of composition can be interrupted, causally, at any point—that is, it can be willfully broken. Moreover, when speaking of specific organizational forms (the "council" or the party), we must remember that, on the one hand, they are determined—tendentially and thus dynamically and not definitively—by the mode of production, but, on the other hand, they are deeply influenced by social and cultural structures and general but historical conditions that are vital to them and specific to each single figure of the proletariat. *The ontological relation between the technical and the political composition of the working class is not static*—in no way can it be interpreted deterministically. Rather, it is defined by the different ways that the productive subject brings capital and dead labor into being. The international temporal and spatial analogy among these forms of organization increases in parallel with the deepening of the integration of the world market and the establishment of global cycles of struggle.

But let us return to the singular determinations of the movements. Antonio Gramsci proposed the slogan "Pessimism of the intellect, optimism of the will" as a model for communist thought during the resistance against fascism. This entails a strong intelligence of the negative and a contradictory injunction to militancy developed within a "passive revolution," when one resists and struggles to subvert a powerful negativity. In a period of insurrections, however, the slogan can be turned into "Optimism of the intellect, pessimism of the will," where the power of the tendency is felt as being prior to the difficulties of its concrete actualization. This happened during the insurrectionary period that opened the short century, when the soviets were tasked not only with the accomplishment of a revolution but also with the goal of "electrifying Russia." In other words, this *skilled* workers' organization was expected to industrialize and build the foundations of the entire development of large-scale industry in the whole of Russia. The revolution organized this optimism of the intellect and trusted this workers' organization of the council with the task—which it knew to be difficult and almost superhuman—of leading with tactical care and political caution in the establishment of a new society. Beforehand, though, it had to form the will to organize this leap forward. But with an optimism of the intellect and the huge effort of its will, how could it be possible to build from the soviets, from the base, and achieve this goal? To help in the task came another tool: the party.

> One single man may have two eyes
> But the Party has a thousand.
> One single man may see a town
> But the Party sees six countries.
> One single man can spare a moment
> The Party has many moments.
> One single man can be annihilated
> But the Party can't be annihilated
> For its techniques are those of its philosophers
> Which are derived from awareness of reality
> And are destined soon to transform it
> As soon as the masses make them their own.
> (Brecht 2012: 83, "Praise of the Party")

The Soviet as an Organizational Form

And with Bertolt Brecht's apology of the eminence of the party, we enter the history of the short century. A vast literature tells us how the soviets were born in Russia. They were invented by the working class struggling during the revolution of 1905. Suffice it to mention, in the global cycle of struggles, around the same period, similar forms of workers' organization emerged all over the industrialized world, from the United States to Germany to Russia, and from 1905 onward the birth of the soviets animated a formidable debate involving Lenin, Rosa Luxemburg, Eduard Bernstein, Karl Kautsky, and others. But we must remember that during the first wave of Russian industrialization in the 1870s, the first important forms of workers' resistance "councils" for the organization of workers' spontaneity in struggle had already been set up. The first sign of a workers' council dates back to 1885 in Ivanovo-Voznesensk, the center of the textile manufacturing industry, near Moscow (Anweiler 1958). From that moment until 1917 and beyond, workers' insurrection became characterized by the organization of soviets. The soviets were the original example of workers' democracy, as they presented themselves, immediately, as the expression of the economic emancipation and the political liberation of workers in struggle. They were carriers of a bottom-up democracy capable of spreading to the whole structure of Russian industry. During the revolutionary process in Russia, the figure and mission of the soviets underwent several transformations. First, they spread as a generic and basic instrument of democracy from the factories to the soldiers, the peasants, and the artists. Then, they became at once the expression of political counterpower and the indication of a specific constitutional direction: that of a federalism of the base and the organization of a democracy founded on workers' councils that were well organized and common throughout production. Mind you, this organization was also adopted by the Paris Commune when the central committee tried to organize the various workers' councils with the citizens of the metropolis in revolt. But that structure was defeated: Marx criticized the failure of the Communards to move to a model of efficient organization, and so did Lenin to the soviets. Lenin criticized the soviet as a simple democratic organization of the base and deemed its promise to constitute a democratic government from the bottom up illusory. However, he did believe their claim to be organs of the economic emancipation and social liberation of workers to be true and put them forward as the institutional figure in charge of development management.

This is what would eventually happen. Lenin, the "Westerner," succeeded in weaving the constituent power of the masses, of the soviets, into the fabric of the party's organization of insurrection and the state organization of production. The aporia of the relation between the technical and the political composition of the working class of this period was accentuated by the unevenness of a working class that was still largely "Eastern" in relation to the "Western" model of socialism building imposed on it. This aporia became multiplied on the screen of world politics and projected between a process of the active constitution of socialism and its institutional establishment, between the productivity of living labor and the organization of the enterprise. Lenin entrusted the Bolshevik party and its skill for enlightened centralization and technocratic vanguard with this task, and thus we came to the "Soviet compromise," a compromise between living labor and economic enterprise, between the constituent power of the working class and the regulation of industry. This time, there was no technological determinism in the "political" constitution of the working class; on the contrary, the decision to build a new "technical" composition was wholly political. Economic emancipation would be a consequence of political liberation, and the soviets straddled the two. For Lenin, constituent power was not merely the ability to legitimize the appropriation of the means of production of those who had been expropriated, but its *mise en forme* in industry. *The democratic spontaneity of the soviets had to be organized into the instrumental rationality of the enterprise.* It is possible to discern a Promethean aspect in this operation: while subverting it, it simulated the capitalist path of the constitution of the social, of its subsumption under capital, while, against it, it imposed the reappropriation of capital not only as an institution but as an activity. At the same time, a new concept of constituent power, the highest realization of the power and modernity of the soviets, was the radical nature of an act of creation of the social that was as economic as it was political. The soviet became the fundamental aspect of the revolutionary constitution. Having been rejected by Lenin as an instrument of spontaneity deemed inadequate to organize the whole of society, the soviet became the force assumed capable of guaranteeing this totalitarian operation: here, in the revolutionary design, the totality is not oppressive or alienating, but creative and liberating.

The horrible failure of this project is well known. However, the short century would be characterized by the *constant reemergence* of the "soviet instance," in every subsequent revolutionary experience, starting from the Chinese, then during the anticolonial wars, and throughout the numerous experiences of workers' resistance to fascism. The soviets kept coming back and organizing: think of the German revolution in the early postwar period; the many experiments with councils in Italy, in 1919, 1945; the Hungarian experience at the end of the First World War and in 1956; the various phases of the Chinese Revolution, and so on. Soviets kept resurfacing as the first instance of revolution. Too many Western anticommunist commentators have delighted in the thought that the soviets were an anti-Bolshevik experience. Some soviets were, but Bolshevism was also the only state experience that attempted a radical compromise with the soviets.

Why did they fail? Max Weber (1995) claimed that the conditions required by the model were not present in Russia. There was a revolt of the masses, and an insufficient capitalist development to overcome its obstacles, but there was no chance of social mediation, no social class capable of doing it, and thus no premises for democracy. The Leninist party was a miserable substitute for this lack; in any case, to govern, it would have needed a civil society with which to move forward in a fervid exchange. The only conclusion Weber predicted was "state socialism." In Lenin's solution, the absence of a civil society worthy of the name would soon turn the democratic dictatorship of the proletariat into a bureaucratic dictatorship of the party. The poverty conditions of the soviet experiment would determine its miserable end. One cannot deny that there is an element of truth in Weber's critique, despite its ideological violence. In fact, those material conditions influenced the democratic development of the Soviet revolution and prevented a democratic exercise of power. To add to that came the international isolation of the revolution, the capitalist bankrolling of counterrevolutionary armies that tried to subvert the new regime, and other problems such as the question of peace, the redrawing of borders, the recognition of nationalisms, the difficult agrarian question, and so forth, all of which were not mere obstacles to overcome, but often insuperable limits to the constituent process.

Can one conclude that these problems determined a change in the nature of the constituent soviet subject? Despite their seriousness, these were not decisive to its destiny. What was decisive was the fact that the party, *that party*, had taken power. That is the position of Luxemburg (2004: chap. 12), according to whom the conditions of an authentic development of communist constituent power were, in fact, present. The communist constituent power, for her, was made up of four elements: first, the initiative of the masses, their democratic organization, the soviet movement; second, an unbroken temporal progression of the revolutionary initiative, that is, the ability to develop the transformation and establish the limitlessness of its project; third, the economic rootedness of constituent power, or the power to impose democratic innovation not only on the political but also, and above all, on the industrial terrain, as democracy can be pushed as far as collectivization can go; and, fourth, the spatial dimension, that is, a dialectics between international centralization and national self-determination that makes it possible for the power of the international unity of workers to confront and win over the disaggregation and separation of the proletarian force determined by the enemy. *Only a mass, revolutionary, internationalist, Soviet democracy is capable of efficiently organizing the whole asset of the revolutionary components of constituent power.* Luxemburg has no doubts about the compatibility of proletarian dictatorship and universal suffrage: "Dictatorship of the class, that means in the broadest public form on the basis of the most active, unlimited participation of the mass of the people. . . . Dictatorship consists in the *manner of applying democracy*, not in its *elimination*." (308). In other words, according to Luxemburg there were no objective elements to prevent the realization of the Soviet constituent principle. What determined the short-circuiting of the Leninist compromise was rather the subjective aspect of the process, because democratic participation was not synchronized with other elements of revolutionary subversion. Luxemburg insisted on this: only thanks to the radical nature of the democratic project could communism conjoin the liberation of the proletariat with a project of productive reconstitution of social wealth. Instead, the soviets lost their power when they became institutionalized as organs for controlling the participation of the proletariat in the organization of production, as an instrument of planning. The soviets then took on the form of an institution subordinated to the needs of the organization of labor and at the service of the aims of accumulation, which then simply amounted to the reproduction of total capital. At this point, a sort of monstrous capitalist reflection came to be mirrored in the Soviet compromise.

The Creative Afterlives of Soviets

We are still in the "short century," and here we need to register the fact that, whatever the outcome in Russia, the contradictory relation between *soviet* and enterprise, between constituent power and the rule of the enterprise, can no longer be separated from a reflection on the constitution. In the development of the constitutional organization of labor power, in the West, the soviet ended up taking on a central role on the political stage and becoming a sign of market equilibrium in the project of capitalist reformism. *The horizon had turned upside down*. In the West and East alike, what was vital to the proletarian imagination was not the form of the Soviet compromise but the power of the soviet, yet the opposite was the case. A blind economism had blocked the constituent process in the Union of Soviet Socialist Republics and was now paradoxically becoming something worthy of analysis, a form that could not be excluded from political considerations every time a project of constitutional recomposition of labor power seemed possible. Immediately after 1917, far from being limited to the socialist state, the Soviet constituent experience became a problem of the capitalist state. In fact, starting from the blockage of the revolutionary experience of the soviet in Russia and its recuperation within the strictures of rigid planning, the reformist practice of capital came to confront the soviet. Capital drew precious lessons from the institutionalized form of the soviet. The first warnings and indications were fragmentary but could be discerned in the theory of the business enterprise of the 1920s, above all in the open and socializing forms of the institutes that regulated the socialized labor force found in the constitutionalism of Weimar. The dream was to reduce the mass of living labor typical of large industrial manufacture—thus far from any experience of craft or skill—into a figure of "democratic commodity." Some bourgeois ideologues, Hans Kelsen among them, effectively regarded the soviet as a model of widened parliamentarism whereby labor was included in the definition of citizenship.

However, the soviet model reappeared in a less ideological form in a second phase in the capitalist world: after the crisis of 1929 during the policies of state planning inspired by Keynesianism (Negri 1994). Here the participation of the working class was understood to play an active role in the distribution of social wealth. The capitalist planning state thus yielded to the need to face up to the magnitude of the force of class relations (in the "short century" with the constant looming presence of the Soviet Union in international relations), so as to stabilize, immobilize, and rigidify these relations, mold them onto its own exploitative objectives. Fascism and Nazism did not think in such different terms. The fact was, life had become *other*: it had become biopolitical, because production was carried out through society and implied not only workers' competences exploited within predetermined times and spaces but also the exploitation of the life of citizens, the circulation of languages and knowledges. This was to be the new fabric of production, and it soon caused the crisis of the Fordist and Taylorist form of control of the working class.

When Eric Hobsbawm (1994) called the twentieth century the "short century," bounded by 1917 and 1989 (the period of the Russian experiment), he undoubtedly grasped a crucial point of periodization. But the reflection of the Russian Revolution spanned beyond the "short century" and historically took on new figures. Of particular note is how *after the epoch of the soviet, any attempt to reduce the working class to pure labor power became futile*; every time this was tried, in politics, it was made inoperative by new aspects of the relations of exploitation. Today living labor, that is, the ability to produce, always presents itself paradoxically as if it had gone through the experience of the soviet, creates value only on the basis of cooperation, and seeks to liberate itself from command.

In the period of the hegemony of cognitive labor, the highest productivity derives from cooperating languages and knowledges that have no need to be ruled even though they reside within the capitalist structure of valorization. One might say that after trying to achieve this outcome through revolution, living labor has extended that experience to the inner workings of the mode of production in the following century. *Seen from this standpoint, the "short century" becomes very long.* Our time is one when a harsh reaction rules, one that does not seem to be willing to forget what happened in the era of the *soviet*, during that "short century." This is because of how deeply interwoven cooperation and the power of cognitive labor are in the mechanism of production—a seed that revolutionary *soviet* deposited—a real serpent's egg that will affect the future of capitalism and the class struggle to come. In neoliberalism, dead labor expects full control over living labor, but living labor, today, is a rebellious animal; since production has become biopolitical, productive activity has invaded society and forced the mode of production into the realm of social reproduction. The resistance and rupture that this transformation of the figure of the worker has determined can be seen on the squares where new experiences of struggles unfold today.

Can we call them soviets? The dictatorship of Russian bureaucrats ended in 1989. Ten years passed between then and the moment when countries began to emerge from the blackmail imposed by "cold war"—a false choice between opposite models of civilization that were really a single dictatorship of capital. In Seattle and the whole Western world, the first large movements against capitalist globalization began to develop. A decade later, starting in 2011, squares were filled again, with a multitude expressing desire for freedom, demanding institutions of the common, and opposed to the new forms of financial exploitation. From New York to Istanbul, Madrid, Cairo, and many more cities, the new knowledge workers expressed, in their squares, the same will to subversion that the workers of the *Räte* and the *soviet* had expressed. Each new cycle of struggles repeats the nostalgia for the soviet in the different forms that the mode of production and the form of exploitation have changed into. Surely, *the party is missing.* But how can it be reinvented without traversing those squares, without seeing them as a constituent process, soviets of a new mode of production that is social and cognitive? As was the case for Lenin and everyone who ever thought about the soviet—the party must be reinvented and confronted with the new conditions of work. Where is the vanguard today? In the factory or in the square? This is the point where the productive forces cross, in exploitation, the capitalist relations of production, in order to break the link. Today capitalist relations run throughout society and are in the square, so it is *in there* that one needs to tie together, again, the refusal of exploitation and the struggle of the soviet against power. The party is no longer rooted *outside* in a vanguard that rules the multitude and gives order to reality. It can only be rooted in the revolting multitude, that multitude that, alone, can demand power. *The party is a materialist immanence in struggles.*

The Proximity of the Virtual and the Potential

Let us come to the present. What has the working class become? It is essentially made up of workers who move within a socialized mode of production where all sorts of workers operate on different time schedules and contracts, precarious or full-time, using work tools that are material and immaterial or cognitive, and so on. On the working class today falls the greatest variety of working practices and hierarchies of command. The automation of the factory drastically shrank the size of the classical working class. Society was computerized; it has become digital; and production is carried out through information networks and organized in social hierarchies that span from the most refined cognitive work to manual labor and the harshest physical tasks. Between these extremes, it is no longer possible to sensibly relate work to the "law of value" (in its classical formulation); all theories of "democratic enterprise" that introduce a model of "social democracy" become redundant. The socialization of production is the backbone of the cycles of capitalist accumulation: within these cycles, crises operate as instruments of the governance of development. The relation between technical and political composition has been flattened such that the Leninist model of the transformation of the soviet from the technical structuration of factory work to the political project of proletarian domination is impracticable. *Political centralization cannot be given as an* outside *because social production knows no outside; it is only* inside. Surplus value and excess cannot but come from within, from the innermost point of socialized labor. At this point, one might raise the objection that if things have come to this, any independent association that lies between the production of commodities and the production of political subjectivity (especially of a soviet) is no longer possible. It seems, in fact, that the relation between constant capital and labor power, between the boss and variable capital, is impossible to identify and impossible to negotiate; command appears to be so wide reaching that any point of rupture, any critical or polemical intersection of one of these powers over the other would be impossible to find. This would be true, if it weren't that, right there, inside the crucible of production, life and commodities, work and machines, everything is dialectically interwoven. *Inside* is hell. And thus, in there, the labor force, living labor, the only power that determines and creates value, confronts capital neither disarmed nor solitary, but always in cooperation, expressive of a common force against total capital. Insofar as it is cooperative and cognitive, labor power is today more powerful than it has ever been in relation to capital, and it can embark on an aggressive relation with machines, transforming the times and the spaces of the productive process, initiating a project of the *appropriation of fixed capital* and the *production of subjectivity.*

This means that, first and foremost, when production becomes essentially biopolitical, socialized and intellectualized, the power of cooperation is directly expressed in the organization of work. Second, through cooperation and the direct incidence of cognitive labor we are witnessing a reconfiguration of the various forces and elements that make up fixed capital. The spaces occupied by machines become networks, logistical and algorithmic platforms; the time consumed by machines becomes fluid and continuous; and the mobility and flexibility allowed by these spaces and times of cooperative work become *machinic.* "Fixed capital" is thus mobilized, penetrated, and reproduced in a machinic way by living labor. The production of subjectivity is capable of traversing and taking over, within and against, the elements of fixed capital still controlled by the boss. This is a general condition determined by the social dimension of production. When cooperation becomes central to this process, the life of workers, in their multiple expressions, intelligence, affectivity, material and immaterial powers of labor, determines the quality of the product. Cooperation is given in biopolitical forms; life is produced and reproduced in desire and consumption, producing cooperatively and seeking wealth, well-being, security in cooperation. This is how the relation between the technical and the political composition of the new labor power and the new biopolitical powers of production is determined— in the new soviet.

But there might be another objection. All of this is not yet political; it does not express power. It is still subjected to the command of total capital in its financial guise. It is still dominated by systems of command that are perfected and multiplying and that chase after the flexibility and mobility of productive networks until they determine productions of subjectivity that are wholly adequate to capitalist development and its command. What sort of fantasies are these, then, that see the virtuality of a power in action when its chances are nil, crushed under capitalist biopower? Of course, the figure of the soviet that resurfaced in different forms throughout history is not here today. Pretending it is would be hypocritical and stupid. But, listen: *class struggle is built on the relation between virtuality (ontology, tendency) and potentiality (form and power of struggle, event).* When the party functioned in a revolutionary way, it did so by bringing the virtual to the potential. A realistic question, then, would be: *Today, how close is the virtual to the potential?*

Looking around, it is bizarre to see how, for example, the most sophisticated theoretical expressions of international law, like the most advanced theories of civil and commercial law, are more and more attentive to the spontaneous emergence of instances of domination and resistance and regard them as autonomous powers of juridical construction. These theories distinguish and conjugate each concept in two: powers and counterpowers emerge and define constituent demands and rights that are sometimes contradictory but always autonomous. It is strange to find how contemporary political science points to the consistency of elements that dissolve sovereignty and spread its powers along lines of governance of different levels of effectiveness. The old nineteenth-century institutionalism is back in fashion. Jurists and politicians struggle to define new instituent trajectories, always trying to recompose, on the side of capitalism, contradictions and antagonisms. But these antagonisms keep resurfacing, drawing an overall picture that is definitively broken. Instituent dynamics no longer converge to create institutions. The *Aufhebung* of the "master-slave" dialectic is no longer accomplished as a synthesis, but spreads out as a problem. *The virtual and the potential seem to lie side by side, leaving any resolution seemingly impossible.*

Whether a revolutionary shift is close or far off, it is there as an alternative. Therefore, one must choose and be militant on one side or the other. For us, the task is militancy within the 99 percent: an immersion both in the current condition of labor power, the misery of its precariousness, unemployment, insecurity, and its physical and psychic effort to produce and in the productive and ethical power of brain workers, in order to draw, with them, a plan that breaks with the conditions of their subjugation, the anxiety of competition and efficiency, and the automated prescription of cognitive goals, opening up spaces of freedom and unity among all workers. Here lies the soviet.

Centenary

One hundred years is a long time. When I was young, "one hundred years" ago was 1848, the year of national bourgeois revolutions in Europe. I saw it as so distant that its protagonists were dressed in a funny way, its wars were fought on horses and used ancient cannons, its constitutions were still *octroyées* (granted) by a monarch subjected to the command of the bourgeoisie. That temporal distance was accentuated by the experience of subsequent wars, the First and the Second World Wars, and by horrid events such as Auschwitz and Hiroshima . . . .

In contrast, the *Russian event-revolution* today, after one hundred years, still feels *present*. In fact, as Gramsci wrote, since then, since that October of 1917, we have inhabited an "interregnum": the victorious revolution caused powerful reactions and the counterrevolution has become generalized, but the interregnum survives as confusion, chaos, and instability until that rupture comes open again, until the soviet reemerges from the past. Now, after the struggles of 2011, we can welcome it back: not only as a mere instrument of struggle against the bourgeoisie but also as an institution and as the organizational force of a democratic power. Because only in communism is democracy possible, as the Marxist theory of the dictatorship of the proletariat prescribed. It is not possible to have democracy without the abolition of social inequality, the organization of the production of wealth must be entrusted to workers' cooperation, and their cooperation must be liberated from external command. Today the soviet appears as an assembly of intellectual, material, and immaterial workers, who already eminently produce value and who seek, inside this construction of value and wealth, the path to the seizure of power.

When at the beginning of the revolution Lenin proclaims that communism = soviets + electrification, he could not have imagined that today, a century later, we would be returning to this formula that combines the power of the political organization of the multitude (the soviet–the square) with a plan of economic development centered on the autonomous production of cognitive labor power. Lenin prescribed that we link revolutionary political organization and a social project of transformation. And the party? We say: it's in there, born out of the soviet.

—Translation by Arianna Bove

References

Anweiler, Oskar. 1958. *Die Rätebewegung in Russland, 1905-1921*. Leiden: Brill.

Brecht, Bertolt. 2012. *The Decision*. In *Brecht Collected Plays*, vol. 3, edited by John Willett, 61–89. New York: Bloomsbury Methuen Drama.

Hobsbawm, Eric. 1994. *Age of Extremes: The Short Twentieth Century, 1914–1991*. New York: Penguin.

Luxemburg, Rosa. 2004. *The Rosa Luxemburg Reader*. Edited by Peter Hudis and Kevin B. Anderson. New York: Monthly Review Press.

Negri, Antonio. 1994. "Keynes and the Capitalist Theory of the State." In *Labor of Dionysus: A Critique of the State-Form*, by Michael Hardt and Antonio Negri, 23–52. Minneapolis: University of Minnesota Press.

Weber, Max. 1995. *The Russian Revolutions*. Translated and edited by Gordon C. Wells and Peter Baehr. Ithaca, NY: Cornell University Press.

No More Deaths:
Direct Aid in the US-Mexico Border Zone

Sophie Smith, Editor

These essays were written just before the onset of the Trump administration. Since the time of writing, many of the direct aid projects described here have become more imperiled. Over the past several months, for example, the longest standing desert medical clinic run by No More Deaths has come under attack by the US Border Patrol with the cooperation of the US Attorney's offices. Aid workers are also now being denied access to multiple public lands jurisdictions, enduring escalating levels surveillance and intimidation by numerous federal and state agencies. In this context, it is becoming increasingly clear that the powers that be are working to disrupt the provision of basic necessities to those facing state violence and death in the Southwest desert. At the same time, white supremacy is on the rise in the borderlands. Right-wing paramilitary groups conducting armed vigilante patrols are becoming more organized and emboldened. From multiple sides, the humanitarian efforts of nongovernmental organizations are facing new threats. With criminalization and federal prosecutions on the rise, the border struggle is now taking place in a political landscape of heightened tensions.

We thus find ourselves writing in a moment of danger—for those in the border region, as well as for migrant peoples and communities across North America and around the world. For those of us living and working on the border, one thing is clear: the protection of migrants, refugees, families, and community members in the borderlands will not be guaranteed by the politicians and lawmakers. Rather, to disrupt the atrocities on the ground we must continue innovating and defending the work of direct aid.

Sophie Smith
Arivaca, Arizona
August 2017

Sophie Smith

Introduction: No More Deaths

Podrán cortar todas las flores, pero no podrán detener la primavera.
They can cut all the flowers, but they can never stop the coming of the spring.
(My translation.)
—Pablo Neruda

Over the past twenty years, the wilderness of the southwest United States has been transformed into a deadly arena for those attempting to enter the United States without documentation. The clandestine crossing is now governed by a militarized homeland security establishment and a widening set of exploitation industries that bank on the deepening of human tragedy. In the mix, volunteers with the humanitarian organization No More Deaths have been working to offer a critical measure of care and protection to migrants and refugees who find themselves stranded in the backcountry.[1] Every day in the arid deserts of southern Arizona, border activists and rural residents undertake concrete efforts to provide food, water, and medical care to those caught out in the struggle for survival. While the name "No More Deaths" expresses a political aspiration, aid work in the border region is in truth a highly pragmatic undertaking, as small humanitarian organizations cannot ultimately guarantee the protection of all those who enter the vast geographic expanse of the border territory. Nonetheless, providing on-the-ground assistance has developed into a powerful practice, ethos, and, arguably, a politics in the region—one that prioritizes direct antiracist intervention as a means of contesting the daily harms dealt by the border security regime.

The essays presented in this installment of Against the Day are authored by activist-scholars who have substantial experience working with

The South Atlantic Quarterly 116:4, October 2017
DOI 10.1215/00382876-4235062 © 2017 Duke University Press

No More Deaths to provide disaster relief on the ground in the Sonoran Desert of southern Arizona. Amid growing concern over the Trump administration's designs for wall building and deportation, we offer a picture of the deadly play of immigration and enforcement already taking place on the border. Our writing goals are ultimately transformative: to provide a closer view of the contemporary border struggle and to protest the massive loss of life being wrought by US immigration enforcement.

Walking in the Wilderness

The border is a broken strand of barbed wire lying on the dirt floor of a tranquil desert canyon. Gray-green mesquite trees reach up from the baking ground. Hawks, ravens, and vultures glide in a transnational network through the long blue sky. Nearby, a dry riverbed betrays dozens of footprints of those who have recently crossed through. Empty water bottles, tuna fish cans, and plastic granola wrappers left over from a nearby humanitarian aid supply drop toss about in the hot wind. Otherwise, all is quiet.

To the east, twenty-five-foot metallic poles propped in vertical succession slice a hilly city in two. On the north side sits Nogales, Arizona, dotted with fast food restaurants, gas stations, and taxi stands. To the south, the metropolis of Nogales, Sonora, rises. Colorful adobe homes, churches, and apartment buildings range across the sloping landscape. Downtown, near the colossal eggshell awning of the international port of entry, community members gather on both sides of the border wall to hold hands through the steel beams in the location where a sixteen-year-old was killed by a US Border Patrol agent.[2] Graffiti reading *SOMOS UN PUEBLO SIN FRONTERAS* (WE ARE A PEOPLE WITHOUT BORDERS) defiantly adorns its base. In such binational border cities where the wall has been built, it stands as an imposing architectural feat. Outside of urban areas, the construction dwindles into shorter slats, triangular vehicle barriers, and eventually diminishes to thin wire cattle fencing, or nothing at all. Foot traffic flows into the open desert.

At present, the specter of wall building on the Southwest border looms large. The protest anthem "no ban, no wall" rings out across the globe as a challenge to the nationalist rhetoric of the Trump administration. For those of us working on the ground in the US-Mexico borderlands, however, the demand for "no wall" is just as perplexing as it is encouraging: this cry to transnational solidarity seems to deny the existence of more than six hundred fifty miles of reinforced barriers already carving up the Southwest landscape. Moreover, what is missing from the national conversation is how walls already function as a powerful policing tactic on the southern border—one that is not only offensive and expensive but also, and most critically, deadly.

This history of walling reaches back more than twenty years to the 1990s—a decade that revolutionized US-Mexico border control. The year 1994 is often remembered as a moment of radical economic liberalization on the continent with the signing of the North American Free Trade Agreement (NAFTA). However, beyond economic expansion, 1994 was also a year of radical transformation for US border-enforcement policy. It was then, in anticipation of a new surge of unauthorized labor-driven migration, that the Border Patrol met with Department of Defense tacticians versed in low-intensity conflict doctrine to discuss militarizing the southern border. At the time, officials asserted that sealing off the entire two thousand miles of binational territory and achieving a 100 percent apprehension rate of unauthorized border crossers would be "an unreasonable goal" (US Border Patrol 1994: 6). Instead, the Border Patrol adopted an enforcement strategy called "prevention through deterrence," which would regulate undocumented migration by making the crossing increasingly dangerous (6).

The concept was a geographical one: historically, most undocumented border crossings cycled through urban areas where, at the time, it was relatively easy to enter the United States without inspection. In 1994, the Border Patrol decided to shift the flow of unauthorized immigration away from border cities and into remote wilderness areas just inside of the US interior. The agency resolved that it would build walls and concentrate personnel and surveillance technology in and around urban ports of entry as a means of deflecting unauthorized migration out into the open desert. In effect, to enter the United States, people without papers would be "forced over more hostile terrain," where they would have to endure multiday treks on foot through a treacherous landscape (12). The Border Patrol predicted that many would "find themselves in mortal danger," being cut off from civilization, resources, and rescue in the backcountry (2). By transforming the migration trail into a potentially deadly ordeal, the agency reasoned that others would be dissuaded from attempting the journey. In sum, the Border Patrol speculated that tactically enhancing the dangers facing border crossers would diminish the overall rate of unauthorized migration into the United States, amounting to a policing program of relative prevention through aggressive deterrence.

Over the last two decades, reinforced walls have gone up in and around border cities, and vehicle barriers have been scattered around the desert to force migration to flow on foot through the most rugged regions of the southwest borderlands. It is now in isolated deserts, treacherous uplands, and humid subtropical brushland corridors within the US interior that the infraction of unauthorized entry is now subjected to a plurality of on-the-ground punishments through tactical games of risk.

Banking on the Border

The border-policing approach of heightening danger for migrants and refugees has produced sizable profits for a diversity of nonstate actors. A growing set of markets now bank on the perpetuation of human crisis. First, war industry outfits have gained lucrative government contracts to provide the weaponry and manpower to militarize the home front. Outfitting the border with walls, towers, helicopters, drones, scopes, sensors, SUVs, rifles, and more has become a multibillion-dollar global industry, constantly expanding what some now term the "border-security industrial complex" (Miller 2014: 53).[3] In this military approach to border security, the traditionally "repressive" tools of the state are increasingly put to work to open and expand new markets, which has led Peter Andreas (2000: 141) to comment, "a liberalizing state is not necessarily a less interventionist state."

Second, border security has also meant big business for black-market actors. By routing migration through a vast, rugged, and unfamiliar landscape, it is now next to impossible to cross through the border zone without hiring a guide. Consequently, the contemporary border security approach has birthed a human smuggling industry—one which has quickly become monopolized by Mexican cartel organizations. Regional monopolies have allowed traffickers to charge three to five thousand dollars a head for covert escort through the wilderness. Many migrants pay part or all of this fee in advance; in effect, cartels often make a significant profit whether or not they successfully deliver their human cargo to their desired destination within the United States. Simply walking across the line to be apprehended by Border Patrol agents is now a value-adding enterprise. In this positive feedback loop of mutual enrichment among border defense contractors and organized crime, profits are ensured by the US deportation regime when those expelled from their homes in the US interior inevitably attempt to cross back again. This new peril-based transnational economy amounts to what Scott Warren terms in his contribution to this issue a "coupled smuggling interdiction industry." The US border security apparatus facilitates a cycle of violence and exploitation that uses the vulnerabilities of the undocumented as its currency.

The strategic aim of placing those crossing the US-Mexico border in harm's way has amassed untold casualties in the borderlands. Since the 1990s, the remains of more than six thousand people have been recovered from the US Southwest, the majority of whom died from dehydration and exposure. Such environmental afflictions are treatable when they occur within proximity to care, but they become life threatening when access to water, food, and rescue has been tactically severed. Official casualty counts represent only a fraction of those who have perished in the US Southwest.[4] Thousands more are never discovered; their remains are forever lost in the folds of the wilderness to disintegrate under the hot sun. In effect, over the last twenty years of risk-based policing, the borderlands have transformed into a gauntlet of survival and a vast graveyard of the missing.

While the threat of becoming lost to the desert haunts the migrant trail, in this deadly arena, nothing is certain. The program of state violence on the border largely takes the erratic and indirect form of possible abandonment to the elements. While many have lost their lives in the backcountry, people without papers also make it into the United States every day. By 2006, at least six million people were estimated to have successfully crossed into the United States between ports of entry (Pew Research Center 2006). At present, the undocumented population within the United States has ballooned to nearly thirteen million people (Passel 2016).[5] In the end, the military approach on the border and its opulent walling projects have not closed the border but only succeeded in contorting the experience in the backcountry into ever more risky permutations. In this perilous political theater, the pursuit of safety and stability among the undocumented does not find quick signature in the momentary act of border crossing. Rather, the protracted process of survival in the remote wilderness now sets the scene of social struggle, and the land itself offers up the main tactics.

Water Is Life

For more than twenty years, the movement of people without papers has embossed the Sonoran Desert with thousands of foot trails. In southern Arizona, paths follow vast canyons, dipping in and out of the soft surfaces of dry river beds, climbing up through rugged mountain passes around craggy peaks in measured switchbacks, opening into the rare shaded rest area, crawling along hillsides, through cactus forests, and perpetually splintering into new ways and other corridors. Migration traffic batters some paths with such frequency that trails widen to the size of small roads. Other ways are only barely perceivable, gently denting the brush. The busiest human highways of last summer might be largely silent places today, playing host only to deteriorating water bottles and abandoned clothing. Routes are in constant and increasing flux. Busy stretches are quickly identifiable for their footprints and freshly discarded items with food bits lingering in opened cans waiting to be scavenged by animals in the night. As masses travel the arid geography of the Southwest desert, humanitarian aid groups supply hundreds of footpaths with water, food, socks, and blankets. Migration trails provide a quiet point of access for this work, where gallons of water can be left at the confluence of several paths to be tapped by travelers on their own terms in the coming hours, days, or weeks. As border enforcement policy aims to increase the risk of harm and loss of life, aid workers labor deep in the backcountry to enhance the odds of survival.

Volunteers explore and map the complex web of migration trails moving through the Sonoran Desert to design effective supply drops. Aid workers walk the far reaches of the desert with water, food, and medical provisions in tow, providing emergency care to the sick and injured who are encountered in the remote wilderness. As part of the daily labor of resupplying water and hiking trails, volunteers develop a keen knowledge of the vast and tangled backcountry terrain. In partnership with other migrant justice groups, No More Deaths coordinates community search and rescue efforts, sending teams out on foot to scour the desert when someone without citizenship status is reported missing or left behind.[6] The organization maintains mobile and fixed desert aid stations where volunteers camp out and the sick and injured receive care. All told, the provision of direct aid represents a small yet consequential resource-based approach to mitigating human suffering on the border. Volunteers aim to strengthen the capacity for survival in the deadly games of risk and chance that now govern the clandestine crossing into the US interior.

The Humanitarian

In the postwar period, human rights discourse and the cause of humanitarianism have offered a means by which outsiders may intervene in campaigns of state violence. Large relief organizations like Médicins sans Frontières

(MSF; Doctors without Borders), Oxfam, the International Committee of the Red Cross, among others, largely based in Western liberal democracies, have worked to provide basic resources and services in global conflict zones. International aid efforts generally descend from the outside and vacate when the job is done or if the context on the ground becomes too perilous.[7] Through the emphasis on simply preserving human life, international humanitarian relief is now recognized as a legitimate form of intervention against atrocity when political processes fail. To this end, Didier Fassin (2007: 149) observes that, since the 1980s, "humanitarian workers have become legitimate actors on the world stage."

The convention of such global humanitarian efforts is to remain politically neutral so that they are able to gain access to target populations in times of war. In the words of former MSF president Rony Brauman (Brauman, Feher, and Mangeot 2007: 132) global humanitarian groups generally pursue political neutrality as a means of "establish[ing] a purely pragmatic relationship with warring parties on the ground." Many have observed how the aspiration for such neutrality often amounts to a mere rhetorical pose, as more than once, aid workers have found themselves the unwilling pawns of oppressive regimes.[8] Within humanitarian groups, the attempt to depoliticize these direct modes of intervention is a matter of contention; accusations of unexamined, sanitized, and otherwise naive saviorism are routinely directed at nongovernmental aid operations around the world.[9] Nonetheless, most global aid organizations uphold at least the rhetorical separation of the humanitarian from the political.

The grassroots mobilization to provide life-preserving aid in the US-Mexico borderlands has taken up the mantle of "humanitarian." In truth, the work of disaster relief in the desert both strategically upholds and, at times, definitively departs from the new humanitarian tradition. Relative to most global nongovernmental organizations, the humanitarian groups working in the wilderness of the Southwest are tiny; they are entirely volunteer-run efforts that operate on shoestring budgets. The humanitarian mission has been an important means of leveraging legal protection for aid workers in the border zone. Promoting moral action in the face of political persecution, direct aid efforts in the desert bring together people from diverse backgrounds who share a conviction that no one should be punished with death for crossing the national boundary. In principle, border relief efforts are above ground, transparent, and insistent on the slogan, "Humanitarian aid is NEVER a crime." The principle of transparency to the power structure manifests concretely in the establishment of known desert aid stations in the backcountry that are clearly marked with large red crosses and by the practice of group members attending meetings to dialogue with US Border Patrol officials.

Yet aid workers on the border are often in a substantially altered relation to many of the conventions that govern international humanitarian relief. As mostly US residents working in US territory and bearing the legal privileges and the civil protections ostensibly afforded therein, aid workers on the US-Mexico border appear to have a greater measure of protection when it comes to intervening in the march of human tragedy. In particular, humanitarian groups do not generally face the same level of threat of being punitively removed from the zone of conflict when government entities disapprove of their beliefs or activities. This is not to say that humanitarians have not faced political stigma or legal challenge by the US Border Patrol and its collaborating agencies.[10] Indeed, the rise of the Trump administration has brought unprecedented levels of surveillance, harassment, and intimidation to border relief efforts. No More Deaths' medical aid station in Arivaca was recently raided, and aid workers have faced threats of lethal violence by Border Patrol agents and newly empowered right-wing paramilitary militia organizations operating in the region.[11] Historically, such disturbances, though troubling, have not threatened to end the existence of humanitarian work, full stop. At the present moment, however, the endurance of humanitarianism on the border is being tested anew.

Unlike many global efforts, humanitarian assistance on the border is not only the province of outside specialists. During the course of border militarization, the cultures of direct aid, care, and hospitality have become increasingly entrenched among rural border residents. As migratory traffic first began to flow through remote terrain, small border communities quickly became natural sources of assistance for those in distress. Long before official humanitarian groups entered the scene, rural border residents had been doing what they could to offer care and hospitality to those they encountered. In border towns like Arivaca, Ajo, and Douglas, Arizona, community-based humanitarian efforts are in force and locals host trainings to support one another in an effort to prevent death and suffering in the community.[12] While living under a veritable Border Patrol occupation replete with checkpoints, drone surveillance, and thousands of agents armed for war, rural US border residents routinely station gallons of water at their gates for those crossing. Importantly, such community-based efforts challenge the conception of the humanitarian as a necessarily transient outsider.

Whereas the vocabulary of humanitarianism conjures visions of conflict zones in impoverished countries on the other side of the world, No More

Deaths is conducting humanitarian operations on US soil. By way of mounting humanitarian response in the desert, No More Deaths contends that the global exporter of militarized liberal democracy cannot ensure the well-being of the stateless and persecuted within its own borders. To assert the necessity of nongovernmental relief inside the United States to protect human rights thus amounts to an incisive political claim. It follows that, as No More Deaths publicly asserts that its work is, by definition, a humanitarian presence in the backcountry, the organization does not shy away from identifying the culprit of mass death and disappearance in the border territory. Most recently, such indictments have been delivered in Part One of the *Disappeared* report series authored by the No More Deaths Abuse Documentation Team, which proclaims, "the known disappearance of thousands of people in the remote wilderness of the US-Mexico border zone marks one of the great historical crimes of our day" (La Coalición de Derechos Humanos and No More Deaths 2016: 23). At this historical moment, aid groups, border residents, and migrant justice organizations are together laboring to expose the US border security regime as the architect of human tragedy in the Southwest.

Against this fraught political reality, many of us living and working on the ground in the border zone carry on the daily attempt to restore a measure of freedom and safety to those in distress in what China Medel (this issue) considers "the abolitionist gesture of direct action." The following essays share some of the on-the-ground lessons learned from participating in this new history of border struggle.

Notes

1   In addition to No More Deaths, there are many direct humanitarian aid organizations working in the US-Mexico borderlands, including *Aguilas del Desierto*, Humane Borders, the Samaritans, South Texas Human Rights Center, and People Helping People in the Border Zone.

2   In October 2012, on-duty Border Patrol agent Lonnie Swartz aimed his sidearm south through the border wall to shoot sixteen-year-old Jose Antonio Elena Rodriguez ten times in the back. Jose Antonio is one of more than forty people who have been killed by Border Patrol gunfire over the last decade (Ortega and O'Dell 2013). Swartz faces second-degree murder charges and is slated to stand trial this year.

3   Boeing, Elbit Systems, General Atomics, and G4S are among the profiteers, along with mass incarceration giants GeoGroup and the Corrections Corporation of America (CCA), who run private detention centers that now house tens of thousands of immigration detainees and refugees awaiting asylum hearings.

4   Advocacy groups contend that the true number of border deaths is three to ten times the number of recovered human remains, raising the total estimation to between twenty thousand and sixty-five thousand migrant deaths in the US Southwest.

5   Heightening the dangers of crossing has resulted in more permanent undocumented
     settlement within the United States by Mexican laborers who previously crossed tem-
     porarily for seasonal work and then returned home; they can no longer risk multiple
     crossings and have, instead, elected to relocate their entire families to the United States
     (CrimethInc. 2011).

6   Coalición de Derechos Humanos in Tucson, Arizona, has been key in these efforts.
     Derechos Humanos volunteers who staff the Missing Migrant hotline have docu-
     mented dozens of cases in which law enforcement agencies refuse to mount searches
     for the undocumented in the desert. A joint report on these discriminatory practices
     around emergency response is forthcoming from the No More Deaths Abuse Docu-
     mentation Team.

7   In October of 2015, US war planes bombed an MSF hospital in Afghanistan, killing
     nineteen relief workers (Rubin 2015: 1).

8   The most notorious of which is perhaps the case of MSF during the famine in Ethiopia
     in 1985, when international relief stations were allowed to establish themselves because
     they were then used by the government to entrap and deport fleeing refugees. Another
     potent example can be found in the instance of the Congo war in 1996, when liaison
     officers accompanying humanitarians on the ground searching for refugees in distress
     would alert death squads as to their whereabouts. The killing squads would then exe-
     cute anyone who had been found (Brauman, Feher, and Mangeot 2007: 139).

9   French groups in particular point to the lessons of the Red Cross sending food parcels
     to concentration camp prisoners just before being led into the gas chamber. Such histo-
     ries haunt the limited focus of humanitarian assistance within politically driven land-
     scapes of state violence and genocide.

10   Aid workers have faced pushback from public lands management agencies, who have
     ticketed volunteers with littering citations for leaving out water on known migration
     trails. Humanitarian groups have fought and won most of these cases access to numer-
     ous public lands for the purpose of providing life-saving resources (Cooper: 1). No More
     Deaths volunteers are currently fighting for access to a number of land jurisdictions in
     the western deserts of Arizona, such as in the Growler Valley on the Cabeza Prieta Wil-
     derness Refuge, where aid workers have recovered dozens of human remains in the
     past six months alone. And, perhaps more seriously, two No More Deaths volunteers
     were brought up on felony smuggling and conspiracy charges in 2009 when they were
     stopped by Border Patrol agents while attempting to evacuate critically injured and ill
     migrants to emergency medical care. At the time, the No More Deaths legal team
     asserted that delivering someone to the hospital does not constitute criminal activity.
     The case was eventually thrown out in court.

11   For a detailed account of the recent raids on the No More Deaths aid station, see Bood-
     man 2017.

12   And proprietors in places like Brooks County, Texas, many of them politically conserva-
     tive, have also worked to establish water stations on their ranches in a moral effort to
     stop the plague of death on their lands (del Bosque, and the Guardian Interactive Team
     2014: 1). In southern Arizona, rural communities in the militarized border zone have
     formed political coalitions to call for the demilitarization of the region and the immedi-
     ate removal of Border Patrol agents and infrastructure from the land (Duara 2015: 1).

References

Andreas, Peter. 2000. *Border Games: Policing the U.S.-Mexico Divide*. Ithaca, NY: Cornell University Press.

Boodman, Eric. 2017. "After Trump's Immigration Crackdown, A Desert Clinic Tries to Save Lives without Breaking the Law." *Statnews*, July 6. www.statnews.com/2017/07/06/immigration-desert-clinic/.

Brauman, Rony, Michel Feher, and Philippe Mangeot. 2007. "Learning from Dilemmas." In *Nongovernmental* Politics, edited by Michel Feher, 131–47.

Cooper, Marc. 2006. "Dead in Their Tracks." *LA Weekly*, February 22. www.laweekly.com/content/printView/2142020.

CrimethInc. 2011. "Designed to Kill: Border Policy and How to Change It." *Crimethinc.com*, May 22. crimethinc.com/2011/05/22/designed-to-kill-border-policy-and-how-to-change-it.

del Bosque, Melissa, and the Guardian US Interactive Team. 2014. "Beyond the Border." *Guardian*, August 6. theguardian.com/world/ng-interactive/2014/aug/06/-sp-texas-border-deadliest-state-undocumented-migrants.

Duara, Nigel. "Arizona Border Town 'Like a War Zone All the Time,' Protesting Residents Say." *Los Angeles Times*, May 27. www.latimes.com/nation/nationnow/la-na-nn-ff-arizona-border-protests-20150527-story.html.

Fassin, Didier. 2007. "Humanitarianism: A Nongovernmental Government." In Feher, *Nongovernmental Politics*, 149–60. New York: Zone Books.

La Coalición de Derechos Humanos and No More Deaths. 2016. *Disappeared: How US Border-Enforcement Agencies Are Fueling a Missing-Persons Crisis*. thedisappearedreport.org.

Miller, Todd. 2014. *Border Patrol Nation: Dispatches from the Front Lines of Homeland Security*. San Francisco: City Lights.

Ortega, Bob, and Rob O'Dell. 2013. "Deadly Border Agent Incidents Cloaked in Silence." *Arizona Republic/Azcentral.com*, December 16. archive.azcentral.com/news/politics/articles/20131212arizona-border-patrol-deadly-force-investigation.html.

Passel, Jeffrey S. 2016. "Measuring Illegal Immigration: How Pew Research Center Counts Unauthorized Immigrants in the U.S." *Pewresearchcenter.org*, September 20. www.pewresearch.org/fact-tank/2016/09/20/measuring-illegal-immigration-how-pew-research-center-counts-unauthorized-immigrants-in-the-u-s/.

Pew Research Center. 2006. *Modes of Entry for the Unauthorized Migrant Population: Fact Sheet. Pew Research Center Hispanic Trends*. pewhispanic.org/2006/05/22/modes-of-entry-for-the-unauthorized-migrant-population/.

Rubin, Alissa. 2015. "Air Strike Hits Doctors without Borders Hospital in Afghanistan." *New York Times*, October 3. nytimes.com/2015/10/04/world/asia/afghanistan-bombing-hospital-doctors-without-borders-kunduz.html?_r=0.

US Border Patrol. 1994. "Border Patrol Strategic Plan 1994 and Beyond." cw.routledge.com/textbooks/9780415996945/gov-docs/1994.pdf.

Scott Warren

In Defense of Wilderness:
Policing Public Borderlands

The town in which I live, Ajo, is located about forty miles north of the Arizona-Mexico border. Another twenty miles north of Ajo, on the only paved highway heading in that direction, there is a Border Patrol drug and immigration checkpoint. This checkpoint, along with the dozen or so others like it in southern Arizona, creates a secondary border some distance inland from the international boundary with Mexico. This particular checkpoint, however, is so far inland that it creates a long enforcement cordon stretching some seventy miles north as the crow flies. The land within this so-called Ajo corridor is rugged, dry, and sparsely populated, making it one of the longest and most arduous crossings for undocumented migrants anywhere on the US-Mexico border. Because so many migrants die from exposure while making this crossing, groups like No More Deaths regularly go out on patrol in the Ajo corridor to provide humanitarian relief. I volunteer with No More Deaths and spend many weekends out on patrol, working to distribute water, food, and first aid to migrants who find themselves in distress.

With the exception of a few settlements and a few private parcels, the land within the Ajo corridor is managed entirely by federal agencies, including the National Park Service, the Fish and Wildlife Service, the United States Air Force, and the Bureau of Land Management (BLM). On the one hand, this mosaic of federal lands reflects the aridity, remoteness, and dryness of the larger region. These were the lands that defaulted into federal control because they could not be practicably farmed, ranched, or settled. As a result, their highest and best use was determined to be for wildlife habitats, conservation, recreation, and military training.

The South Atlantic Quarterly 116:4, October 2017
DOI 10.1215/00382876-4235073   © 2017 Duke University Press

On the other hand, this mosaic reflects what historian Patricia Limerick (1987) has called the "legacy of conquest." Most obviously, this refers to US settler colonialism in the nineteenth century, in which control of this land was wrested from Mexico and independent indigenous nations. Yet, various forms of colonial dispossession continued through the twentieth century as well. As the mosaic of federal lands took shape, the new rules and regulations that governed Organ Pipe Cactus National Monument (Organ Pipe), Cabeza Prieta National Wildlife Refuge (Cabeza Prieta), and the Barry M. Goldwater military training range (BMGR) restricted the long-standing local uses of ranchers, prospectors, and woodcutters. These rules and regulations affected the indigenous O'odham the most, perhaps, as their traditional settlements were circumscribed within conservation and wilderness boundaries, and their uses of the land and its resources restricted by new management plans implemented by federal agencies. At best, this twentieth-century dispossession reflected the shortsightedness of otherwise well-meaning land managers who were guided by a wilderness ethic in which all contemporary human imprints on the land were deemed unnatural. At worst, it reflected a pervasive paternalism in which federal agencies not only denied local access to these lands but worked to erase the recent histories of indigenous people and Mexican citizens from the landscape all together.

Nevertheless, by the latter part of the twentieth century, the Ajo corridor had taken on the mantle of undeveloped and unbroken conservation space. Edward Abbey wrote romantically about it, a greater area was proposed for a national park, and even the BMGR was reimagined as relatively undisturbed habitat for wildlife. In the 1990s, for example, the botanist Richard Felger (1997: 403) described a remote arroyo in Cabeza Prieta as "a treasure house of information and experiences" because there were virtually no human impacts to the land in that area.

By the early 2000s, however, a new use for the land emerged. Planners from the US Border Patrol (1994: 6) and the former Immigration and Naturalization Service debuted a strategy called "prevention through deterrence," in which lands such as those in the Ajo corridor were imagined to be unpopulated and therefore better suited to carrying out enforcement activities than the cities and urban areas of the Border Patrol. As double-layer walls went up in places like San Diego and El Paso, the Ajo corridor increasingly felt the impacts of undocumented migration, smuggling, and an ever greater Border Patrol footprint entering public lands. For example, in 1996, there were twenty-seven hundred apprehensions of undocumented border crossers in the Ajo corridor, and in 1999 there were twenty-one thousand (OPCNM

2000). From the late 1980s to the early 2010s, the contingent of Border Patrol agents at the Ajo station grew from ten to five hundred. And whereas Cabeza Prieta had been imagined as free from human impact in the mid-1990s, Naturalist Bill Broyles (Broyles and Berman 2006: 197) chafed at the damage being wrought by smuggling and undocumented migration in the mid-2000s: "plants are trampled, cactus smashed, bird nests robbed, waterholes drained and fouled, [and] the biological soil crust churned into moon dust."

Many metaphors are used to understand the border, with perhaps the border-as-war-zone being the most common. But the best metaphor to use in understanding the transformation of the Ajo corridor at the turn of the twenty-first century is that of the border as the setting for a coupled smuggling-interdiction industry. The expansion of this industry is reflected in the physical infrastructure of roads, walls, forward operating bases, surveillance towers, and checkpoints, as well as an equal magnitude of expansion in the tools, techniques, and resources used by smuggling organizations to evade this detection infrastructure. Both sides of the industry have become interdependent, and as the size and scope of interdiction efforts has increased, so too has the size and scope of human- and drug-smuggling efforts. And while locales on both sides of the border may have experienced an economic boom as a result of this expanding economy, these same locales bear the overwhelming burden of militarization, violence, fear, and environmental damage. The smuggling-interdiction industry has further proven to be extractive in nature, as the profits of smuggling and the federal expenditures for interdiction are now enjoyed by people and corporations largely outside of the border region.

The environmental footprint of this extractive industry on border public lands is big, and land managers have expressed frustration with its expansion. Organ Pipe officials, for instance, have publicly recognized that migrants were being funneled into the desert by border enforcement policies, and because of this, on one high-profile occasion even denied the Border Patrol's request for increased access to wilderness areas (GAO 2010: 30). A certain amount of distrust, therefore, exists between federal agencies such as the US Border Patrol and the National Park Service, particularly as the goals of conservation and border policing continue to come into conflict.

Officially, however, all federal agencies—Border Patrol, Park Service, Fish and Wildlife—work together to achieve shared goals. Each of these public lands management agencies, after all, has a law enforcement arm with a mission to police not only the particular regulations of their land unit but also the laws of the United States in general. Seen through this lens, the Park

Service helps the Border Patrol with its goals of immigration control and drug interdiction, while the Border Patrol helps the Park Service with its goals related to conservation and recreation. Various department-level memoranda-of-understanding guide the two agencies in matters related to border policing and conservation, such that the Border Patrol can describe the Park Service as a willing partner in its drug interdiction and immigration control efforts, and the Park Service can describe the Border Patrol as an ally in conservation.[1]

The enduring legacies of conquest, however, become quite apparent when public land managers team up with the Border Patrol and even adopt the agency's paramilitary tactics in their own efforts to police undocumented border crossers.[2] Perhaps most troubling in all of this, however, is the ambivalence of the environmental community. Part of this is no doubt due to the lack of legal recourse available, as many environmental and cultural protection laws have been waived by Congress or circumscribed by the government to allow Border Patrol unfettered access to conservation lands (Ring 2014). However, this ambivalence might reflect deeper tensions within the environmental community regarding the intersection of social justice and environmentalism. Abbey, for instance, was a formidable defender of Organ Pipe and Cabeza Prieta against extractive industries such as mining. Yet, when it came to immigration he was an unabashed advocate of border enforcement:

> Most of the border runs through flat, wide open, sparsely vegetated desert country. Except for the far-scattered towns and cities, most of the border could be easily patrolled and easily "sealed;" a force of twenty thousand . . . properly armed and equipped, would have no difficulty . . . in keeping out unwelcome intruders. In and near the few towns and cities a physical barrier is obviously needed. . . . People do not cut holes through fences when the fences are watched and guarded. (Abbey 2006)

Fearing unchecked population growth and, ironically, increasing pressures on wilderness, Abbey proposed the above plan to curtail undocumented immigration in the 1980s. It has eerily come to resemble the Border Patrol's prevention-through-deterrence strategy implemented in the 1990s.

No More Deaths and Public Lands

In the course of our work, humanitarian aid volunteers with No More Deaths frequently interface with land managers and law enforcement agencies. Adding to the handful of federal land managers are law enforcement agencies such as the US Border Patrol and sheriff's deputies, which, together, make for at least eight different law enforcement entities with which humanitarian aid volunteers in the Ajo corridor regularly interact. Some of these encounters between volunteers and law enforcement take place in formal meetings, but most occur informally in the desert while servicing water and food drops in remote areas.

Informal interactions with law enforcement representatives in the field are unpredictable, but they offer critical insight into the complexity, diversity, and conflicting interpretations of the border and the nature of the crisis on public lands. Contrast, for instance, the Border Patrol agent that I encountered while providing aid who admonished me for "helping the illegals" on the BMGR with the law enforcement ranger who once thanked me for being on patrol in Organ Pipe. And lest the reader think that this simply reflects different agency cultures, contrast, for example, the words of another Border Patrol agent who approved of the efforts of aid workers to give water to migrants because, "they sure do need it," with the words of a park ranger who disapproved of our efforts to give water to migrants because, "we don't want to make it too easy for them."

There are as many different individual dispositions as there are individual rangers, agents, deputies, officers, and guards. It is perhaps no surprise, therefore, that law enforcement personnel would have different interpretations of the work that No More Deaths volunteers do. Still, I have heard law enforcement personnel repeat narratives that appear designed to delegitimize humanitarian aid on public lands. For instance, Organ Pipe park rangers have described the water and food drops of No More Deaths as ineffective, with one park ranger telling me they are akin to "driving around the desert and throwing cans of beans out the window." Cabeza Prieta officers have described the volunteer humanitarian response to me as not only ineffective but also redundant, citing Border Patrol beacons—tall towers equipped with lights and an emergency button that summons law enforcement—as the more effective solution to preventing deaths in the desert. Organ Pipe rangers and BMGR security guards have even suggested to me that water and food drops cause more harm than good. Migrants, they say, will develop a false sense of security knowing there is water in the desert and may even get lulled farther into the wilderness where there is little chance of rescue.

These arguments—that humanitarian aid is ineffective, redundant, and harmful—seek not only to delegitimize volunteer groups such as No More Deaths but also to legitimize the role of law enforcement agencies and lay claim to the rhetorical high ground of humanitarianism. The Ajo corridor, after all, is a rugged desert where migrants are forced to travel on foot for many days. Detentions of migrants by Border Patrol agents are therefore often cast as rescues, not arrests. Unwitting migrants, the argument goes, are victimized by smugglers who lie, cheat, steal, rape, abuse, and leave their clients for dead in the desert. This role of rescuer and protector even extends to the land itself. These same smugglers trash environmentally sensitive conservation lands, the logic continues, so agencies such as the Border Patrol and the Park Service work toward shared conservation goals in their efforts to combat drug smuggling and illegal immigration. This paternalistic attitude toward migrants is dutifully maintained even despite the many migrants who describe "rescues" in which they are chased, scattered, injured, and abused (see La Coalición de Derechos Humanos and No More Deaths 2016). And the role of protector of the land is even maintained despite the thousands of miles of vehicle tracks laid down by Border Patrol agents driving in conservation and wilderness areas (Abhat 2011).

At other times, however, law enforcement officers are quick to shift the focus away from their roles as rescuers and protectors and put the focus on the people who, apparently, are not deserving of humanitarian aid. It is not uncommon, for instance, for law enforcement representatives to say that "95 percent" of the people crossing the border in the Ajo corridor are drug smugglers. One ranger even described the majority of border crossers to me as being people who "are not coming here looking for work." In one instance, I encountered a group of individuals who were already in Border Patrol detention in the backcountry of Organ Pipe. When I asked whether the group needed water, I was assured by the Border Patrol agent on the scene that these were "bad guys" and "not the kind of people you are trying to help." After assuring the agent that humanitarian aid is nondiscriminatory and given solely on the basis of need, he relented and ultimately allowed our volunteers to give water, food, socks, and first aid to the group.

Further underscoring the ambivalence inherent in these various narratives are the direct actions of law enforcement personnel in response to humanitarian aid. Border Patrol agents have been documented destroying humanitarian aid supplies, and it is not uncommon for volunteers to find water bottles that have been slashed and otherwise vandalized in the Ajo corridor (see Epstein 2012). On the other hand, law enforcement officially approves of efforts by other humanitarian aid groups to site large stationary water barrels on public lands. Additionally, one Organ Pipe law enforcement ranger even shared with me and other aid workers how, when they arrest migrants in the summer, they leave water behind at the site in case other members of the group in hiding return to the area.

Law enforcement personnel seemingly struggle to define "good" water or legitimate humanitarian aid on the one hand, and "bad" water or illegitimate humanitarian aid on the other. One officer described himself to me as a supporter of "true humanitarian aid," but he nevertheless protested the food and water "dumps" of No More Deaths and other groups. One Border Patrol agent described his personal evolution on the matter, admitting to me as having slashed water jugs in the past, but assuring me that though he continues to destroy supplies left for drug smugglers he no longer destroys humanitarian aid left for migrants.

Perhaps no other issue, however, has proved as complicated and vexing as the issue of litter. Land management agencies have largely staked their claim on the problem of litter in the context of their relationship with humanitarian aid groups like No More Deaths. What No More Deaths volunteers consider to be the provision of life-saving humanitarian aid—putting out water, food, socks, and blankets—federal land managers argue constitutes an act of littering. The issue has been litigated in court with a judicial decision that avoided making a crystal clear distinction between humanitarian aid and litter, but it nevertheless marked a victory for No More Deaths' ongoing "humanitarian aid is never a crime" campaign (see Lacey 2010). Since this decision, only a handful of additional littering citations have been written by law enforcement officials against No More Deaths volunteers, and none of these have reached a trial.

The focus on litter may be due to the fact that the biggest challenge facing public lands along the border, the expansion of the coupled smuggling-interdiction industry, results from issues that are essentially beyond the control of local managers. The Park Service, Fish and Wildlife, and other agencies, therefore, work to manage what they can, which is often limited to restoring the environmental impacts—such as trails, camps, and trash—left by undocumented migrants and circumscribing the efforts of local volunteers to provide humanitarian aid.

Perhaps a less obvious effect of these efforts to clean up "trash" however, is the continuation of a long legacy of dispossession and erasure of those deemed to be illegitimate "users" of public lands along the border. This dispossession is not unlike the dispossession of indigenous people and Mexican citizens in the nineteenth century, and this erasure is not unlike the erasure of the traces of human use and habitation in the twentieth century. Not only are the migrants who cross the vast distances of the Ajo corridor subjected to arrest and deportation, but even the signs of their presence are being removed from the landscape.

In working to reduce the death and suffering of migrants along the border, No More Deaths volunteers and other humanitarian aid organizations also inherently work to counter this dispossession and erasure. Importantly, this is not to say that humanitarian aid legitimizes the physical presence of smuggling organizations on public lands along the border. Rather, humanitarian aid drops of water, food, socks, and blankets serve to acknowledge the struggle of migrants and force land managers and the public to recognize the ongoing humanitarian crisis. Simply put, the very presence of humanitarian aid forces land managers to publicly acknowledge a problem that they may wish to push into the remotest and least touristed areas of the desert, keeping it invisible to everyone but law enforcement personnel.

Rather than simply being an issue about the ecological consequences of trash versus the humanitarian value of water drops, therefore, the rhetorical effort to cast humanitarian aid as litter also underscores an attempt by land managers to control, or perhaps even silence, narratives about what is happening on public lands along the border. Organ Pipe officials, for instance, have repeatedly expressed frustration to me and other volunteers that visiting tourists "don't know what to make" of water and food drops, and that tourists have recently "begun asking questions" about the significance of No More Deaths' supplies left for migrants in areas of the park also frequented by hikers and campers. Interestingly, Organ Pipe offers very little public interpretation about the humanitarian crisis or the history of the border. Instead, the focus of public interpretation in the park is almost entirely focused on ecological issues, ancient Native American history, and early twentieth-century histories of ranching and prospecting.

And yet, the struggles of undocumented migrants in crossing the desert, and the subsequent humanitarian crisis, may prove to be the most significant story playing out on public lands in the Ajo corridor and elsewhere along the border. In 2003, for instance, the superintendent of Organ Pipe estimated that the number of tourists that entered the park that year, about two hundred forty thousand, was likely the same as the number of undocumented border crossers that entered the park that year (Eckert 2004). Some Organ Pipe employees have even speculated that someday in the distant future, the park may become more of a historic monument, in recognition of the mass movement of people coming across the border in recent decades (Piekielek 2009).

Until then, the dual efforts of No More Deaths and other groups in responding to the humanitarian crisis and resisting the erasure of migrant presence on public lands will continue. These dual efforts by no means contradict conservation and environmental protection. Rather, they are commensurate to a better ethic of treating both land and life with respect in the border region. Abbey (1977: 223) once famously said that "The idea of wilderness needs no defense. It only needs more defenders." And yet, he inadvertently advocated for a more militarized border that, when it came into being in the 1990s, ironically besieged wilderness and introduced a new kind of extractive industry on public lands. This new industry has been most violent to the migrants forced into it and most destructive to the land on which it works. Perhaps Abbey's sentiment would be made more holistic and appropriate if it were expanded to include the ideas of humanitarianism and human rights as well.

Notes

1   This interagency cooperation is a highlight of public relations campaigns. Beginning in 2013, for example, the Ajo Border Patrol station began offering a six-week "Border Patrol Citizen's Academy" that taught local residents about the agency and its mission. In 2016 this Border Patrol Citizens Academy was recast as the "Multi Agency Citizen's Academy," with representation from the Park Service, Fish and Wildlife, tribal police, the county sheriff, the Arizona Fish and Game Department, and others. This rebranding of the Citizen's Academy, however, belies the power imbalance reflected in the size of agency budgets and personnel. Organ Pipe's contingent of law enforcement rangers, for instance, numbers about twenty-five, Pima County's force of deputies in Ajo is about the same, and Cabeza Prieta has only a handful of law enforcement officers. Meanwhile, the five hundred agents of the Ajo Border Patrol occupy a new twenty-five million dollar station that was built to eventually accommodate up to nine hundred agents.

2   Take, for instance, the BLM's operation Regain Our Arizona Monuments (ROAM). Operation ROAM combines drug interdiction, immigration control, and conservation. The hallmark of operation ROAM is a two-week "surge," where law enforcement rangers—along with allied deputies, officers, and agents—deploy in force to particular areas affected by smuggling and undocumented immigration. During one surge in November 2011, for instance, BLM law enforcement rangers swept into the Sawtooth and Silver Bell mountains. With support from Border Patrol, Immigration and Customs Enforcement, Homeland Security Investigators, and sheriff's deputies, a total of two hundred ten undocumented migrants were arrested and about six thousand pounds of marijuana were seized (USCBP 2011). Teams of civilian volunteers are deployed following surges such as these to pick up trash, rehabilitate illegal roads, and map sites and trails used by undocumented migrants. As part of the "Take Back Antelope Peak Project," for instance, volunteers and law enforcement rangers worked together to "take back, hold, and maintain" a wilderness area that had been impacted by smuggling activities (BLM 2012: 3).

References

Abbey, Edward. 2006. "New York Review of Books Letter to Editor." In *Postcards from Ed: Dispatches and Salvos from an American Iconoclast,* edited by David Petersen, 109–10. Minneapolis: Milkweed.

Abbey, Edward. 1977. *The Journey Home.* New York: Plume.

Abhat, Divya. 2011. "Fenced Out: Wildlife Impacts of the U.S.-Mexico Border Fence." *Wildlife Professional* 5, no. 4: 23–27.

BLM (Bureau of Land Management). 2012. *Southern Arizona Project to Mitigate Environmental Damages Resulting from Illegal Immigration Fiscal Year 2012 Report.* Phoenix: Bureau of Land Management. www.blm.gov/style/medialib/blm/az/pdfs/undoc_aliens.Par .98448.File.dat/FY-12.pdf (nonworking link; accessed December 2014).

Broyles, Bill, and Michael P. Berman. 2006. *Sunshot: Peril and Wonder in the Gran Desierto.* Tucson: University of Arizona Press.

Epstein, Brian. 2012. "Crossing the Line, Part 2." *Need to Know on PBS* video, 22:14, July 20. www.pbs.org/wnet/need-to-know/video/video-crossing-the-line/14291/.

Eckert, Lisa. 2004. "Is It Safe?" *Ranger: Journal of the Association of National Park Rangers* 20, no. 3: 6.

Felger, Richard S. 1997. "A Botanist's View of the Center of the Universe." *Journal of the Southwest* 39, nos. 3–4: 399–410.

GAO (Government Accountability Office). 2010. *Southwest Border: More Timely Border Patrol Access and Training Could Improve Security Operations and Natural Resource Protection on Federal Lands.* www.gao.gov/products/GAO-11-38.

Lacey, Marc. 2010. "Water Drops for Migrants: Kindness or Offense?" *New York Times,* September 26. www.nytimes.com/2010/09/27/us/27water.html.

La Coalición de Derechos Humanos and No More Deaths. 2016. "Deadly Apprehension Methods: The Consequences of Chase and Scatter in the Wildnerness." In *Disappeared: How US Border-Enforcement Agencies Are Fueling a Missing-Persons Crisis.* thedisappeared report.org.

Limerick, Patricia. 1987. *The Legacy of Conquest: The Unbroken History of the American West.* New York: W. W. Norton and Company.

OPCNM (Organ Pipe Cactus National Monument). 2000. "Undocumented Alien Impacts on Backcountry Resources." Report to Arizona Congressional Delegation. 976.3 15, Assorted Newsclips 1994–2002, Visitor Center Library, Organ Pipe Cactus National Monument.

Piekielek, Jessica. 2009. "Public Wildlands at the U.S.-Mexico Border: Where Conservation, Migration, and Border Enforcement Collide." PhD diss., University of Arizona.

Ring, Ray. 2014. "Border Out of Control: National Security Runs Roughshod Over the Arizona Wild." *High Country News,* June 16. www.hcn.org/issues/46.10/border-out-of-control.

US Border Patrol. 1994. "Border Patrol Strategic Plan, 1994 and Beyond." cw.routledge.com /textbooks/9780415996945/gov-docs/1994.pdf.

USCBP (United States Customs and Border Protection). 2011. "ACTT Partners Participate in 14-Day Silver Bell Operation." Press release, November 25. www.cbp.gov/newsroom/local -media-release/actt-partners-participate-14-day-silver-bell-operation.

China Medel

Abolitionist Care in the Militarized Borderlands

Since adopting the 1994 Border Patrol Strategic Plan, a strategy called "Prevention through Deterrence" (PTD) has governed the enforcement of the US-Mexico border. Relying on heavy physical enforcement like walls, surveillance, and concentrating personnel in urban crossing zones, Border Patrol has funneled migration into rural and remote crossing zones characterized by dangerous terrain and climate in which migrants face "mortal danger" (De Leon 2013: 32). This approach purported to use the desert as its own kind of enforcement tactic; the extreme heat, scarcity of water, rugged and uninhabited terrain, and inhospitable plant and wildlife would discourage unauthorized migration. After the walls began going up in border cities, migrant bodies began piling up in the Pima County coroner's office. Death by exposure, hyperthermia, dehydration, and related complications increased, and the mortality rate at the border more than doubled between 1995 and 2005 (US Government Accountability Office 2006). This new border policing approach has not prevented migration but has turned the desert into what Joseph Nevins (2010: 174) has called "a landscape of death." As Jason De Leon (2013: 35) concisely puts it, "rather than shooting people as they jumped the fence," PTD "set the stage for the desert to become the new 'victimizer' of border transgressors." The Border Patrol factored in the loss of life at the border, banked on the bodies piling up in the coroner's office, and rationally calculated the death and suffering in the Arizona borderlands as an essential ingredient in their enforcement strategy.

And so people mobilized.

In this section I focus on the organization with whom I seasonally volunteer, No More Deaths, based out of Tucson, Arizona.[1] Specifically, I

The South Atlantic Quarterly 116:4, October 2017
DOI 10.1215/00382876-4235084 © 2017 Duke University Press

situate the practices of care entailed in No More Deaths' work within the intellectual tradition and activist praxis of abolition that thinkers from the prison abolition collective Critical Resistance define as three converging aspects: dismantle, change, and build. That is, the effort to abolish the prison industrial complex and other systems of racialized violence like it must not only dismantle the institution of the prison but also build new social formations in its wake. In our practices of care, No More Deaths actively works against the neoliberal process of strategic abandonment, in which governing bodies carefully eschew responsibility for a minoritized social group deemed valueless by a logic of racialized criminalization. Sequestered in the Sonoran Desert, the camp wakes up each day committed to practices of taking care, not only of migrants in distress, but also of one another. In the practice of care, desert aid workers prefiguratively build a world in which hierarchies of human value are abolished, where migration is an expression of life making, and where food, shelter, medical, and emotional care are available to all, regardless of notions of deservedness. This care work becomes an abolitionist gesture of direct action that builds alternative forms of recognition and inclusion against the logic of criminalization and the production of valueless life functioning to "protect" the United States.

Practices and Ethics of Care in Direct Action

No More Deaths emerges from an ongoing tradition of migration justice, mutual aid, and direct action in Tucson. The organization grew out of the work by participants in the Sanctuary Movement of the 1980s. That work was founded by Quaker minister Jim Corbett's concept of civil initiative, which proposes that people have the capacity and the obligation to respond in situations where governing bodies cause or choose not to respond to situations of harm (No More Deaths 2017). One of the central facets of civil initiative that distinguishes it from other forms of nonviolent direct action is that it forgoes symbolic and expressive actions as its means of intervention and, instead, focuses on "action that is germane to [victims'] needs for protection" (No More Deaths 2017). The direct aid action of protection emphasizes providing water, sustenance, medicine, shelter, and support against a desert that state security forces count on to kill them; protecting migrants became about providing care. Care is a radical departure from state-sponsored modes of intervention, which entail capture by Border Patrol and subsequent imprisonment and punishment, causing yet more harm.

Humanitarian efforts provide relatively simple but crucial first aid to those moving through what activist Carlos García (2015) calls the "death trap" of the US-Mexico border. It primarily takes the shape of what we call "desert aid," in which volunteers hike migrant trails where the highest concentration of bodies is found, leaving caches of water, food, socks, and blankets. Volunteers hike with medical kits in order to assist migrants upon encounter; they bandage blistered and injured feet, provide treatment for dehydration and stomach infections due to drinking bad water, and attend to other medical issues. Like other direct-action practitioners, volunteers hiking the trails become an insurgent and mobile presence within the site of dispossession and social violence.

In addition to the water drops and desert aid patrols, the organization established its first desert aid camp near the town of Arivaca, approximately eleven miles from the border. Occupied by volunteers nearly three hundred sixty-five days of the year, the camp has become a beacon of aid for migrants in distress; it is a place to find water, food, shade, rest, and medical attention. The encampment has become the hub of the direct action of care that No More Deaths calls "hospitality," a practice and philosophy of revaluing and respecting migrant life through a gesture of sanctuary and free access to care and respite.

Caring amounts to much more than merely fostering survival. Caring entails a relational ethic of interdependency. At the camp, volunteers practice multiple modes of care that fulfill three primary actions laid out by sociologist Evelyn Nakano Glenn (2000: 86–87): (1) ethics of care, or to care about, is expounded by the use of care as a larger response to the devaluation of migrant lives; (2) the activity of care, or caring for, is articulated by hospitality and civil initiative; (3) the physical and emotional activities of care are lived out in the practices of care in the camp and on the trails. These practices and what I would like to call "positionalities" of care take place between not only migrants and volunteers but also short- and long-term volunteers in the camp. This latter dynamic generates another, excess layer of the action of care by No More Deaths' volunteers. In the overlap between these two dimensions of care, for migrants and among aid workers, the camp becomes a living space of an ongoing abolitionist gesture, one in which people innovate and practice ways of protecting disavowed life in the shadow of a state that has strategically abandoned them to die in the desert.

The Necessity of Abolitionist Care in the Borderlands

PTD is an apt tool and by-product of neoliberalism in the Americas, becoming an enforcement strategy that allows US authorities to kill by way of abandoning bodies to die in the desert in the name of border security while also absolving itself of responsibility through a rhetoric of personal choice and responsibility. Neoliberalism, as Grace Kyungwon Hong (2015: 27) theorizes, is structured as an epistemological project of disavowal, one in which it works to "erase its racial and colonial brutalities and thus legitimate its self-definition as defenders of freedom and protectors of life." Contemporary border enforcement aims to "protect" the United States by criminalizing migrants, abandoning them to the dangers of the desert, and disavowing their deaths. Of course, the US-Mexico border brokers what is ultimately a racialized distinction between a white United States and a brown global South. The production of disavowable death at the border takes place through a racialized logic of value, to borrow Lisa Marie Cacho's (2012) framework, in which some bodies, especially those determined criminal through racialization, are deemed to matter less than others. The border performs a critical task in this racialized economy of disavowable death: unauthorized border crossers, as many have pointed out, are always already deemed criminal by the very act of their presence in the United States (Escobar 2016; Inda 2006; Nevins 2010; Ngai 2014; Cacho 2012). Rendered criminals, unauthorized migrants are vulnerable to punishment and abandonment by the state because they have not lived up to the rights and responsibilities of neoliberal citizenship that positions citizens as entrepreneurial subjects constantly working to become better, more effective citizens deserving of protection (Inda 2006; Escobar 2016). Labeling and punishing unauthorized migrants as criminals allows US authorities to disavow responsibility for the death and torture of those crossing the border.

Stranded as valueless life in the desert, migrants become the targets of what I call "strategic abandonment," building on Ruth Wilson Gilmore's (2007: 41–52) concept of abandonments, the turn in statecraft away from social welfare.[2] Strategic abandonment is the rational calculus by which governing bodies decide they have no responsibility for the health, well-being, safety, or sheer existence of a minoritized body of people due to its criminalized racialization and subsequent valuelessness. PTD becomes the tactic by which strategic abandonment is carried out in the borderlands, literally aiming to police the border by abandoning irresponsible subjects and valueless life to perish in the desert. But strategic abandonment is not a passive activity, as analyses of border security or other anti-immigrant legislation make clear (De Leon 2013). Legislation from the Illegal Immigration Reform and Immigrant Responsibility Act of 1994, which barred immigrants from welfare and social services and increased deportable offenses, to the Trump administration's recent executive orders to expand the scope of deportable offenses, increase policing, and criminalize giving aid to migrants function to exclude migrants from social welfare and strategically abandon them in the name of protecting the United States. Strategic abandonment functions as a neoliberal strategy of social reproduction and control in racialized communities, a strategy whereby the means of social reproduction are withheld, social needs are ignored, bodies are essentially left to fend for themselves, and migrant life, as a legislative supporter of Arizona's notorious bill SB1070 put it, becomes "untenable" (McDowell and Fernández 2012).

Within the market logics and paradigms of neoliberalism, care is itself a commodity accessible only to those rendered valuable by fulfilling the demands of entrepreneurial citizenship. Care has long been a pivot point on which struggles for self-determination and decolonization have organized precisely because it counters a key strategy of abandonment by the state, one that is drawn along racialized lines of value. For example, inspired by the Black Panther Party, the Young Lords, a militant Puerto Rican self-determination and decolonial organization active in the 1960s and 1970s, operated an ambulance service and health clinic as part of their struggle against domestic warfare. The Young Lords succinctly named the racism fueling strategic abandonment in their newspaper: ". . . preventative medicine is not done on Puerto Ricans and Blacks because this capitalist system wants to make the rulers live longer and let the spics and niggers die off as quickly and quietly as possible" (Enck-Wanzer 2010: 192). Anticipating the logics of Border Patrol's policing strategy of strategic abandonment, the Young Lords name the racialized lines along which notions of human value are drawn and organized to provide for their own care through practices of mutual aid and community self-determination. Through their practices, they articulated alternative worlds in which the health and safety of their people was built from within, by and for the people, within and against logics of market or state assigned value.

Abolishing Value: The Direct Action of Care

As Corbett notes of humanitarian aid on the US-Mexico border, civil initiative is distinct from typical deployments of symbolic and expressive direct actions. Unlike other encampments, such as Occupy Wall Street or the annual teacher's encampment in Oaxaca, Mexico, the No More Deaths encampment does not aim to disrupt or impede the flow of traffic, capital, or business-as-usual in order to discursively interrupt the violence and injustice of the status quo. On the surface, direct aid is not so much theater as service. Yet, to do away with its relationship to traditions and motives of direct action would miss the imaginative dimensions of this work. In the nexus of No More Deaths' care work that is "germane" to the needs of those affected by strategic abandonment is a form of direct action that functions prefiguratively—performing service *that opens onto* alternatives to the world in which they work.

The Blackout Collective, direct action trainers and organizers working for Black liberation based in the Bay Area, refer to this form of direct intervention as "abolitionist actions."[3] Abolitionist actions are conceived of as *longue dureé* actions that take place at a site of social violence or dispossession and work to imagine new forms of social and political life.[4] The practitioners call these actions abolitionist, situating their particular form of intervention within the tradition of abolition that thinkers such as Angela Davis, Joy James, and Dylan Rodríguez have taken up and extended from the work of W. E. B. DuBois, who insisted that abolition's project must include not only the dismantling of slavery but also the invention of "new democratic institutions" (Davis 2005: 75). As thinkers from the Critical Resistance Collective note, abolition is defined as three converging actions: to dismantle, change, and build. Abolitionist actions, by asserting and building alternative worlds at the site of social dispossession and violence, interrupt and negate the violence of the status quo. But most importantly, they engage in the abolitionist project that Rodríguez (2015) defines as the "production of freedom and liberation practices from within collective rebellion, insurgency, and community."

The abolitionist dimensions of direct-action humanitarian aid on the border is most vivid when we specifically consider the practices of care that No More Deaths performs at its encampment. Between care for both migrants and one another, we can see micropractices that evoke abolitionist projects to dismantle the notions of racialized value on which the border and its enforcement are built. In these micropractices, volunteers dismantle, change, and build the world they want to see within a site of state disavowal, dispossession, and violence.

Care work for migrants largely revolves around practical medical and health care: bandaging blisters, administering electrolytes for dehydration, and treating stomach infections resulting from drinking contaminated water. Usually, these interactions support migrants in becoming well enough or equipping them with supplies so that they can, of their own volition, finish their journey. However, if a person is in acute distress, such that volunteers, who are often Wilderness First Responders, EMTs, paramedics, and, at times, nurses and doctors, cannot sufficiently aid them and they need to be hospitalized, volunteers will call 911, only with the patient's consent. Any emergency call also summons Border Patrol and facilitates their detention, criminal trial, deportation, and likely repeat attempt at crossing. No More Deaths also performs search and rescue operations and will search out a missing companion or someone their group left behind because they were sick or injured. Witnessing the indomitability of the human will to migrate in the face of such relentless violence, suffering, and death demands a form of recognition that acknowledges another's agency and tendency toward survival and life making, rather than the specter of abject, valueless life that criminalization attempts to produce. In these interactions, volunteers attend not only to physical care but also to the ethical stance in which caring about means respecting the agency and desire to cross borders. In caring for and caring *about*, as Nakano Glenn (2000: 86–87) puts it, volunteers both dismantle a spectrum of valuable life and change orientations toward migration and migrant desire and will.

Yet, a bandaged blister and other forms of practical care is not where the work ends. In addition to providing medical aid, volunteers often provide some forms of emotional and spiritual support to the patients in camp or on the trail. Especially at the camp, the politic of hospitality takes the shape of a kind of emotional labor. Offering rest and respite, cooking, listening to people's stories, witnessing the aftermath of sexual violence as you perform their intake, providing support and reassurance, interfacing with requests to make phone calls to family members, all make up hospitality.[5] In these interactions, it is common to hear people's stories and reasons for migrating, to get glimpses of both the dangerous journey itself and the roots of and reasons for that journey. These interactions ask us to reckon not only with PTD or Border Patrol but also with the systemic and racially distributed effects of neoliberal policy in the Americas that work to value and devalue different kinds of life. Providing care that transverses physical, emotional, and spiritual dimensions dismantles and changes the logics of value that render migrants disavowable targets of strategic abandonment. In its place, care builds moments of community and connection where enforcement demands disavowal. Rather than hierarchies of valuation, the abolitionist actions of care in No More Deaths' work builds alternative forms of recognition and inclusion that center migratory movement as a human energy, will, and life force rather than as a right extended only to those rendered valuable through their purchase on whiteness.[6] While many desert aid volunteers enjoy the privilege of whiteness that allows them to access the time and resources to perform this care work, their work ultimately becomes about dismantling access to the freedom of movement. This is not to say that volunteers' whiteness disappears in the act of care; rather, care work allows them to become not merely allies but also accomplices—those engaged in a mutual and collaborative struggle against the violence and dispossessions enacted through white supremacy (Indigenous Action Media 2015).

Yet, care work exists beyond the patient-caregiver relationship. Contributing to care work's abolitionist politics are the excess practices of care that emerge between aid workers and the camp itself, creating the resilience necessary for the *longue dureé* temporality of the action and the practices of community that structure it, daily rhythms at camp during the volunteer program season, which sees a constant turnover of volunteers. While in residence at the desert aid camp, all volunteers participate in the general maintenance of the camp: cooking, cleaning, maintaining the latrine, managing the solar panels, organizing supplies, and checking the vehicles. Every day as a volunteer, I have witnessed and performed idiosyncratic practices of care that include sharing sunscreen and tips for staying cool, reminding one another to stay hydrated, sharing cigarettes on top of the trailers, lending generous ears, taking refuge in perfect sunsets, and helping each other see the beauty of the land even as we confront the violence it is used to perpetrate. Together, volunteers process the things they have witnessed and experienced during patrols at the structured nightly debriefing. During these debriefings, volunteers engage in a kind of democratically distributed talk therapy, or a collective and mutual holding of the troubling, traumatic, and infuriating dimensions of Border Patrol's strategy of abandonment. While in residence at the desert aid camp, volunteers are not passive consumers of a service experience, not merely guests on the land, but also active interdependents engaged in the care, maintenance, and protection of the patients, of one another, and of the camp. Community interdependency and mutual aid become excess forms of sociality created in the process of doing desert aid. The practices of care that structure life in the camp open onto a kind of politics of friendship that, as Michel Foucault (1998: 137) wrote, "introduce[s] love where there was supposed to be only law, rule, or habit." Moving from this practice of friendship that centers the collective coproduction of care and dislodges the rules and laws of value and markets, the camp produces an abolitionist action that dismantles and changes hierarchies of value and builds alternative modes of recognition and inclusion through moments of community.

As stated in its mission statement, No More Deaths (2017) works fundamentally to end the loss of life and suffering on the US-Mexico border. Seeking an end to the suffering and death on the border is an abolitionist project, but one that I claim opens onto a larger and more visionary project of abolishing the racialized hierarchies of human value and regimes of criminalization enforced by the border by transforming perceptions of migration and migrant agency. Performing actions of care is not something that can be done simply by treating wounds or offering water; it requires that volunteers see and acknowledge the full humanity of their patient, inclusive of their will, desire, and investments in facing their journey. As Nakano Glenn (2000: 86–87) contends, care includes both practical activities of care and an ethical orientation. The ethical orientation in the borderlands refuses the hierarchies of valuable life and the logics of disavowal cultivated by neoliberal border enforcement strategies.

Direct-action humanitarian aid enacts abolition's three converging actions—dismantle, change, and build—in the micropractices of care that structure the work of aid givers. Centering these actions specifically on the ways in which border enforcement generates schemas of human value, care by humanitarian aid workers dismantles logics of criminality that otherwise bar some from inclusion and recognition. Direct aid work alters approaches to care, making it about providing both physical and emotional care. Moreover, in these micropractices of emotional care and the act of "caring about," No More Deaths changes the ways in which migration and migrants are recognized, seeing them not as abject criminals but as fighters, people striving and moving toward their lives. Finally, they build, in the practices of hospitality and care extended to migrants as well as each other, alternative instances and models of community, inclusion, and recognition. Through these direct actions of aid, No More Deaths generates positionalities of care, dismantling logics of value by making medical attention, hospitality, respite, and sanctuary available to all, regardless of citizenship status, criminal record, gender, sexuality, or race. In hiking these trails and establishing an encampment that takes up space in terrains of state violence and disavowal in the name of saying "no" to that violence, No More Deaths' practices of care for migrants connects points of intervention that insurgently erupts into the disavowing silence on migrant death and disposability. In the daily rhythms of hospitality and resilience, the collectivizing of aid, of spiritual and emotional sustenance, we can practice new modes of human value and community predicated on care.

Notes

I am deeply grateful to the trainers at the Combahee Alliance Direct Action Training in January 2016 for seeding the concept of abolitionist actions and helping me see my work with

No More Deaths in a different light. This paper could not have been written without the help of Meghan McDowell. Thank you for the conversation, books, and persistent orientation toward an abolitionist imaginary.

1   No More Deaths, along with other organizations like Aguilas del Desierto (Eagles of the Desert), The Samaritans, and Border Angels, have performed over ten years of direct-action humanitarian aid at the border, recruiting volunteers to provide water, food, medical aid, and other lifesaving resources to migrants crossing through the deserts.

2   For a further analysis of the concept of abandonment, see Povinelli 2011.

3   The Blackout Collective has not published these frameworks. I use this concept in my writing after having participated in a training led by them and the Indigenous People's Project from the Ruckus Society.

4   The Blackout Collective draws upon the histories of maroon communities and the *kilombos* of Brazil to historicize abolitionist actions as sites where communities came together in rejection of an existing racist power structure, building up infrastructures of resistance and alternative social forms that provided for their own need.

5   In response to patients in the aid camp hoping to phone home and let their families know that they have not disappeared in the desert, No More Deaths has partnered with the International Committee of the Red Cross to offer a free family reunification phone service that allows migrants to contact their loved ones.

6   For a discussion of freedom of movement as a definition of human freedom, see de Genova 2010.

References

Cacho, Lisa Marie. 2012. *Social Death: Racialized Rightslessness, and the Criminalization of the Unprotected*. New York: New York University Press.

Davis, Angela. 2005. *Abolition Democracy: Beyond Empire, Prisons, and Torture*. New York: Seven Stories.

De Genova, Nicholas. 2010. "The Deportation Regime: Sovereignty, Space, and the Freedom of Movement." In *The Deportation Regime: Sovereignty Space and the Freedom of Movement*, edited by Nicholas De Genova and Nathalie Peutz, 33–65. Durham, NC: Duke University Press.

De Leon, Jason. 2013. *The Land of Open Graves: Living and Dying on the Migrant Trail*. Berkeley: University of California Press.

Escobar, Martha. 2016. *Captivity beyond Prisons: Criminalization Experiences of Latina (Im) Migrants*. Austin: University of Texas Press.

Enck-Wanzer, Darrel, ed. 2010. *The Young Lords: A Reader*. New York: New York University Press.

Foucault, Michel. 1998. "Friendship as a Way of Life." In *Ethics: Subjectivity and Truth*, edited by Paul Rabinow, 135–40. New York: New Press.

García, Carlos. 2015. "Nine Phrases the Migrant Rights Movement Needs to Leave in 2015." *Latino Rebels*, December 31. www.latinorebels.com/2015/12/31/ninephrases/.

Gilmore, Ruth Wilson. 2007. "In the Shadow of the Shadow State." In *The Revolution Will Not Be Funded: Beyond the Non Profit Industrial Complex*, edited by INCITE! Cambridge: South End.

Hong, Grace Kyungwon. 2015. *Death beyond Disavowal: The Impossible Politics of Difference.* Minneapolis: University of Minnesota Press.

Inda, Jonathan Xavier. 2006. *Targeting Immigrants: Government, Technology, Ethics.* Malden, MA: Blackwell.

Indigenous Action Media. 2015. "Accomplices Not Allies: Abolishing the Ally Industrial Complex." In *Taking Sides: Revolutionary Solidarity and the Poverty of Liberalism,* edited by Cindy Milstein, 85–96. Oakland, CA: AK Press.

McDowell, Meghan G., and Luis A. Fernández. 2012. "Sobre la Vida Insostenible in el Estado de Arizona: Inmigración y Limpieza Etnica" ("On Untenable Life in the State of Arizona: Immigration and Ethnic Cleansing"). *Revista Juridica Argentina* 3, no. 2: 211.

No More Deaths. 2017. "Civil Initiative." forms.nomoredeaths.org/about-no-more-deaths /civil-initiative/ (accessed February 28).

Nakano Glenn, Evelyn. 2000. "Creating a Caring Society." *Contemporary Sociology* 29, no. 1: 84–94.

Nevins, Joseph. 2010. *Operation Gatekeeper and Beyond: The War on Illegals and the Remaking of the U.S.-Mexico Boundary.* London: Routledge.

Ngai, Mai M. 2014. *Impossible Subjects: Illegal Aliens and the Making of Modern America.* 2nd ed. Princeton, NJ: Princeton University Press.

Povinelli, Elizabeth. 2011. *Economies of Abandonment: Social Belonging and Endurance in Late Liberalism.* Durham, NC: Duke University Press.

Rodríguez, Dylan. 2015. "The Production of Freedom and Liberation from within Collective Rebellion, Insurgency, and Community: Dylan Rodríguez on Abolition." *Abolition Blog,* July 15. abolitionjournal.org/dylan-rodriguez-abolition-statement/.

US Government Accountability Office. 2006. "Illegal Immigration: Border-Crossing Deaths Have Doubled Since 1995; Border Patrol's Efforts to Reduce Deaths Have Not Been Fully Evaluated." Report to the Honorable Bill Frist, Majority Leader, US Senate. www.gao.gov/new.items/d06770.pdf.

Sophie Smith

Crisis Time, Constant Border:
On Direct Aid and the Tactics of the Temporary

The world outside the walls
has had its turbulent say
and history like a long
snake has crawled on its way
and is crawling onward still.
—Adrienne Rich

Everything is temporary.
—Adi Ophir

The makeshift desert clinic wears out on repeat. Under the constant sun, the tent's heavy-duty vinyl turns to fragile crepe paper. Whipping winds pull at the seams, tearing a wide gap along the shelter's base. During the summer monsoons, water floods in. The provisional floor, made of pallets and plywood, turns to rot. The PVC skeleton that holds the large structure aloft begins to strain and warp: bolts pop out, linkages detach, and all, slowly and steadily, falls down. The metal cafeteria cabinets that have been repurposed to store medical supplies are quickly shuffled to another temporary location. Aid workers plan a workday to rebuild the failing structure. In the meantime, someone donates another massive backcountry-ready shelter—this time a geodesic dome—and the medical cabinets are moved again. The makeshift clinic quickly settles into this next provisional iteration. Patients seeking respite from the treachery of the migrant trail immediately fill its keep.

The South Atlantic Quarterly 116:4, October 2017
DOI 10.1215/00382876-4235095 © 2017 Duke University Press

The medical tent is not the only structure in the constant flux of ruin and repair at No More Deaths humanitarian aid stations in the Arizona desert. Sleeping trailers are in perpetual deterioration—their windows pop out, insulation crumbles, roofs leak, and they collapse into heaps on the ground, overtaken by rats' nests, left in place to live on as the installation art of border disaster relief. But, as so many things fall apart at the desert refuge, new infrastructure constantly digs in. Replacement campers are dragged onto the property and nestle into the burgeoning settlement. A solar panel trailer arrives, bringing lights and refrigeration: new luxuries. A phone line awakens. Antennae go up. A well is installed. A faucet. A shower. A garden. The daily labor of placing water on migrant trails is now joined by the ritual work of rebuilding aging infrastructure. Over time, the provisional camp mutates into an indefinite shelter; the border crisis perpetually births the tactics of the temporary.

The transformation of the US Southwest into an arena of death and survival seems to have occurred in a flash. The quick buildup of walls, agents, and infrastructure in border cities have pushed migrants and refugees out into the open desert. In effect, the transnational crossing now takes shape as a life-threatening ordeal. Myriad possible dangers threaten the survival of those traveling for days on foot through the remote wilderness. After being chased by the Border Patrol or falling behind their group due to injury, many find themselves stranded without access to water, food, or rescue. An empty water bottle, a wrong turn, a twisted ankle, a dead cell phone battery, the loss of life-preserving medication, among other contingencies, form the variable forces of human destruction. For nearly two decades now, thousands of migrants and refugees have lost their lives in the borderlands due to dehydration, exposure, and other preventable maladies. Untold numbers have simply vanished, their remains swiftly disappeared by the quick heat, winds, and wildlife of the Sonoran Desert.

As the new age of border security began to sow death across the land, the rapid onset of mortal punishments on the border was taken by many to constitute a temporary state of affairs. The conversion of the desert into a vast graveyard of the undocumented appeared so egregious in its harms that border activists presumed this governing error would soon be corrected once the tragedy had been made public. In what was expected to be an interim period between public outcry and policy change, rural border residents and outside humanitarians began delivering emergency relief to the many migrants newly wandering the far reaches of the desert. The disaster in the borderlands has multiplied in scale and duration over the years. With it, official efforts to provide water, food, medical care, and shelter began to take clearer shape, all the while delivered in the ephemerae of pop-up tents, mobile trailers, and a constantly rotating cast of volunteers.

In the desert of the Southwest, we are confronted with a political scenario that is routinely deemed a crisis both by the powers that be and those providing disaster relief on the ground. This essay interrogates how these temporal terms shape the tactics and strategies afoot in the border struggle, exploring what a sense of urgency empowers and what political approaches the declaration of crisis might elide or disavow.

Crisis Time

An aura of crisis has come to cloak the border environment. Taken all at once, the production of mass death and disappearance wrought by the contemporary border-security strategy constitutes a staggering and ongoing catastrophe. At ground level in the US-Mexico border zone, crisis manifests in the infinity of daily harms in an always volatile survival scenario. For those attempting the perilous journey into the US interior, the erratic play of risk, luck, and contingency in the deadly game of crossing makes for perplexing gambles over timing: Is it best to wait for the cold of winter—for the light of the full moon? Is it best to go before the heat kicks up, before the vote is cast, before the mafia returns to the door? When could conditions let up? When will they have become too dire to wait any longer? So many temporal contingencies make the calculations around personal safety unruly. In the Southwest border zone, the thin line between life and death is so often a temporal one: a quickly closing window of intervention in which help may come to a sick or injured person stranded in the backcountry in the nick of time. In other cases, the time of action stalls out; human remains wait in the desert for months or years, turning skeletal and disintegrating before anyone happens upon them.

The desert buzzes with a nagging sense of urgency, tragedy, and possibility around which all actors are all challenged to orient themselves. Decisions over which road to drive, which trail to walk, when to do a trash run, and when to leave on patrol are forever terrorized by so many microcrises ruled by the ambivalent serendipity of timing. The effect of humanitarian aid efforts is thus both painfully partial and seriously consequential. By circulating daily in the terrain of struggle, those on the ground in the border zone at times respond to unexpected encounters with migrants in severe distress by providing resources, care, and often a critical measure of protection.

Yet the temporal mechanism of this potent mode of direct life-preserving intervention is based largely in the unforeseeable play of coincidence—a material truth that belies the powerful force of contingency to shape the course of events on the ground.

If crisis constitutes time on the border, then with it has come dynamic and creative modes of direct life-preserving action. A declaration of crisis generally invites immediate intervention, authorizing improvisatory modes of action that may elide preestablished norms, models, protocols, and institutions. When it comes to political struggle, the timeframe of crisis propels its activity with great speed: representing the border as a humanitarian crisis, for instance, has been an effective means of fostering public challenge to the brutal practices of the security regime. It has been a hook for new volunteers to join the relief effort. In the contemporary movement, urgency, event, and singularity have distinct political traction. Crisis responses are quick and on the ground. They are employed in scenarios wherein the urgency of mitigating immediate suffering cannot adhere to the slowed tempo of the official political process and all its bureaucracy, particularly when there is no promise of official redress to be found therein. Yet, despite the best relief efforts, most of the lost, sick, injured, and ill go undiscovered, perishing in the remote wilderness. The erratic, indirect, and geographically expansive design of border violence ensures that the tragedy will never find full resolution in direct aid. Such is the logic and ethos of direct aid in the US-Mexico border zone—its limited action lies in the time of the present.

The claim to crisis has political utility both among those working to topple its reign and those working to undo its grip. On the side of government, the declaration of crisis on the border slackens the regulatory hold of law and eases the troubles of measure and accountability. Emergency border enforcement tactics have been delivered in the ephemera of pop-up checkpoints, hiring surges, and mobile surveillance units. In effect, the political freedoms unleashed by the time of crisis have also come to work on behalf of the powers that be. The claim to crisis is a means of quickly authorizing violence and militarism: the innovation of the new border security strategy was originally posed as a reactive measure in a historic moment of temporarily increased migration caused by the passage of the North American Free Trade Agreement. Its later enhancement with checkpoints, sensors, and thousands of agents on the ground was posed as a stop-gap security response to the sudden events of September 11, 2001. And now the power of crisis is being played again in the Trump administration's orders for the quick hiring of at least five thousand new Border Patrol agents and the reconstruction of the border wall. In effect, the implementation of militarized border operations proceeds by way of the discursive elision of permanence. The contemporary border security approach evinces a temporal formation of political power that functions by denying its own perpetuity. This declaration of emergency is an amnesiac political force. Its fever pitch tempo relentlessly dissolves the recent history of militarized border policing of death and disappearance, sowing political disorientation. The provisional and erratic organization of aggressive "security measures" perpetually displaces programmatic government and its proceduralist violence.

Constant Border?

If crisis time emits the tactics of the temporary, then this temporariness is based on the implication of a coming end of catastrophe, which holds the eternal possibility of sudden reversal or radical transformation in view. The proclamation of emergency entails the hope of relief: a phoenix rising from the ashes. As it happens on the border, however, this potent yet always latent "we'll see" in the present leans into oblivion. As the years pass, new questions draw near: If the lethal policing of the border is indeed a political crisis, then what is its duration? A week? A month? A year? A decade? A generation? What happens when a crisis does not end? When does the event of crisis turn into a historical process? When does rupture become structure?

While the effects the Border Patrol's strategy of prevention through deterrence ignited in a sudden surge, the march of militarization and mass death has now stretched across two decades. Time drags on the border scene. Looking around at the weathered work of a dozen years of ad hoc direct aid on the desert floor, the speculative end to the disaster appears to be increasingly remote at present. The political vernacular of temporariness has pitched time on the border toward the endless, the siege state, and the stalemate. For those of us on the ground, the new calls for emergency wall-building signal not an entirely new crisis but the extension and intensification of an all too familiar social terror. We now find ourselves mired in what Adi Ophir (2004: 48) calls "the squall of the temporary." It appears that the endurance of the border crisis over historical time has shifted the interventionist life of the temporary into the comatose politics of the indefinite.

To be sure, some elements have changed in the design of enforcement across the decades of militarized border control. In Arizona, unauthorized migration is now moving west into the most remote regions of the desert. South Texas rises as a second principal theater of immigration policing.

Brand new eighty-foot surveillance towers leer over the Sonoran Desert. The Border Patrol has more than quintupled in size and, we are told, will soon balloon further.[1] And humanitarian aid work is being subjected to new legal pressures under the Trump administration. In May 2017, the Border Patrol obtained its first federal search warrant to raid and arrest migrants receiving care at one of the No More Deaths aid stations. All told, these recent shifts are certainly consequential on the ground. However, in the general strategy of using the threat of death in the desert to police migration, the border security game continues to curve about its original plan. Far from approaching a point of reversal, the struggle in the backcountry, in the detention centers, on the trains, and in the shelters seems to be only deepening. New populations are being brought into the dangerous migration system designed for others a generation ago. Refugees from cartel violence in El Salvador now join deported Mexican nationals who, a decade past, crossed the same desert in search of work and now attempt the trek again in search of family unification. Displaced Haitians fleeing the disastrous impacts of climate change wait en masse at the Nogales, Sonora/Arizona, port of entry seeking asylum. Deported DREAMers who cannot remember their early childhood crossings now walk out into the wilderness once more. In the border zone, crisis no longer forms a cut between before and after but seems to only move in a circle.

Those of us living and working in the rural Southwest now gaze at the same ocean of tragedy we first confronted years ago and begin the work of telling its history—not from an external future place looking back on the rubble of the past, but from within its indefinite arena. With time and witness, the border struggle has emerged not as a singular event but as an ongoing social process: "history like a long snake has crawled on its way, and is crawling onward still" (Rich 1993). Through the vector of protracted time, what once seemed to be a de facto production of human crisis on the border can now only be taken for de jure policy.

Looking closer, one cannot help but begin to notice the quiet signs of permanency that were somehow there all along: the gargantuan feat of erecting eighty-foot Border Patrol surveillance towers in the Southwest desert is not a provisional undertaking. The walls in border cities, which have been built, remade, layered, and fortified, are not architecturally temporary. The second freezer installed at the Pima County Office of the Medical Examiner to house the unidentified remains recovered from the far reaches of the border zone looks to be a permanent infrastructural investment. The myriad Border Patrol substations and opulent headquarters scattered across the Southwest are not designed as makeshift compounds. A strong set of industries now bank on the indefinite stability of the forces producing human destruction in the region. On the side of enforcement, the rhetoric of temporariness gives way to practical, if not planned, permanence.

If the policing approach on the Southwest border is not an exceptional or momentary state of affairs but a vested political reality, then can its violence be called a crisis any longer? If we face a lasting border struggle, then have we been left with the tactics of the temporary in a playing field of the permanent? What is to be gained by retaining the concept of crisis over the indictment of the terminal? How do crisis and permanency inflect our sense of what can be altered and what will remain? These are some of the questions of time that now face all those circulating in the border arena.

As participants, one thing is certain: we may no longer operate under the assumption that the end of suffering and disappearance in the Southwest borderlands draws near. And this apparent longevity of the deadly border security regime offers a moment to take pause. For at least several years to come, the border crisis promises to stay. And perhaps it was intended to make dominion of the Southwest desert from the outset, as the border massacre has always been a bipartisan invention.[2] If time is a rubber band, then it seems that crisis is a temporal force that not only contracts but also expands: "the state of emergency is not limited in time and space . . . it, too, enters onto an indefinite future" (Butler 2004: 64).

On the side of strategy, perhaps this long view offers a period of planning—an occasion to pitch the tempo and planning of crisis intervention forward much farther into the future than it has ever been allowed to travel. As relief workers, we begin to catalogue the ambivalent promises of permanency on the ground: the growing imposition of institutional structures on grassroots, shoestring, volunteer-run, donations-driven, ad hoc, and direct action modes of political intervention. The possible mutation of disaster relief into social service, of stopgap actions into institutions, of DIY into NGO. After more than ten years of organized aid work, these transformations are perhaps already creeping in, bringing with them the dream of permanent infrastructure and long-term paid staff, among other institutional stabilities.

Yet, even if our tactics dig in for the long haul, it is clear that we cannot fully turn away from the special powers of crisis as a political vernacular: the claim to crisis continues to communicate the need for immediate action. While political authorities wield the power of crisis discourse to cause sudden hiring surges and construction projects, among aid workers, the same discourse is a matter of political savvy that acts as an effective means of galvanizing direct on-the-ground responses. And beyond the matter of rhetoric, the struggle over survival in the US Southwest continues to issue new daily disasters at a frenetic pace—an on the ground formation of social terror which seems to resist all powers of normalization.

But the commitment to ad hoc tactics may be haunted by a deeper political hesitation: Would forgoing the proclaimed temporariness of the border crisis for the declaration of policing conditions on the ground as a functionally "permanent" system amount to an admission that the violent program of Southwest border control is so thoroughly entrenched that it has become unchangeable? If those opposed to the border disaster admit that the conditions sustaining its growth are ubiquitous and thoroughly entrenched, would this mean that no power can be exercised to alter the political world in which we find ourselves? A loss of agency, a loss of scale, and a loss of historical time all seem to flow rapidly from this suggestion.

Yet the answer is clearly no: the border crisis will indeed end one day, as all things change, transform, shift, and move into other patterns, alignments, styles, and forms, growing up and dying off. We may never see the end of tension between the ruled and the rulers or the end of hardship and the human systems that make and mediate our world, as long as we are here. But just as we have seen the end of other formations of political rule, other horrific scenes of state-sponsored violence, so will we see the passing of the rigged game of risk and abandonment catching the lives of so many in the net of border terror. The vision of the coming end of the catastrophe, even if it is cast generations in the future, begs the question of remembrance: How will others look back on the events at the border? Will the system of family detention centers be recounted as the internment camps of our day? Will the borderlands themselves be mourned as former killing fields? Will the hospitality, safe haven, and means of survival provided by those on the ground be celebrated as the Underground Railroad of our time? "Whatever we do, we are in the posture/ of one who is about to depart/ Like a person pausing and lingering/ for a moment on the last hill" (Rilke 1992).

Be it a year from now or three hundred, the forces acting to give the crossing its catastrophic shape will move along. The tents can be packed up, the trailers dragged away, the towers dismantled, the sensors unearthed, the drones grounded, the agents laid off, and the walls torn down, for "every epoch bears its own ending within itself" (Forché 1994). There is no guarantee that the end of the border struggle will be catalyzed by the forces of resistance already in motion any more than they will be catalyzed by the forces of domination, the force of nature, or the game of chance, with great speed or at a terrible crawl. The political embrace of the present crisis as no longer a momentary event but as an ongoing social process that we call border security, therefore, requires no implicit surrender of the historicity of the situation—no loss of the possibility of transformation endemic to the march of time. For, whereas the temporary is never without the indefinite following close behind, the permanent is forever terrorized by the powerful force of the conditional.

Notes

1   In 1992, there were approximately four thousand Border Patrol agents. Today, there are more than twenty-one thousand. The Trump administration plans to hire five to ten thousand more.

2   Prevention through deterrence was adopted in 1994 under the Clinton administration. The system of death and disappearance on the border was enhanced with the passage of the 2006 Secure Fence Act under President George W. Bush. The Border Patrol expanded further under the Obama administration, which became known for its "deportation regime," removing a record 2.7 million people without papers from the US interior and vastly expanding the private immigration detention system.

References

Butler, Judith. 2004. *Precarious Life: The Powers of Mourning and Violence.* New York: Verso.

Forché, Carolyn. 1994. *The Angel of History.* New York: HarperCollins.

Ophir, Adi. 2004. "A Time of Occupation." In *The Other Israel: Voices of Refusal and Dissent,* edited by Roane Carey and Jonathan Shainin, 48–56. New York: New Press.

Rich, Adrienne. 1993. "At the Jewish New Year." In *Early Collected Poems: 1950–1970.* New York: W. W. Norton.

Rilke, Rainer Maria. 1992. *Duino Elegies.* New York: W. W. Norton.

Notes on Contributors

Giso Amendola teaches sociology of law in the Department of Political, Social, and Media Sciences at the University of Salerno, Italy. He is the author of four books and many articles and reviews focusing on the crisis of modern sovereignty, political and legal globalization, social movements, and constituent processes. He also participates in the Euronomade network.

Martín Bergel is an assistant professor in the School of Humanities at the University of San Martín, Buenos Aires, Argentina. He is also a researcher at the National Scientific and Technical Research Council (CONICET) and at the Center for Intellectual History at the University of Quilmes. He is the author of *El Oriente desplazado: Los intelectuales y los orígenes del tercermundismo en Argentina* (2015) and numerous essays on Latin American and global intellectual history. Bergel has edited a forthcoming anthology of texts by Mariátegui.

Kathy E. Ferguson teaches political science and women's studies at the University of Hawai'i at Mānoa. Her research focuses on nineteenth- and twentieth-century anarchism. She is writing a book on women in the anarchist movement from the Paris Commune to the Spanish Revolution; this work expands on her book *Emma Goldman: Political Thinking in the Streets* (2011). She is also writing a book on the role of the letterpress printers in anarchism.

Michael Hardt teaches in the Literature Program at Duke University. His most recent book, coauthored with Antonio Negri, is *Assembly* (2017). He serves as editor of the *South Atlantic Quarterly*.

John MacKay is a professor of Film and Media Studies and Chair and Professor of Slavic Languages and Literatures at Yale University. The first volume of his three-volume study of filmmaker Dziga Vertov is forthcoming.

Artemy Magun is a professor at the European University at Saint Petersburg. He also teaches at Saint Petersburg State University (Smolny College), Russia. He is the author of *Negative Revolution* (2013) and a number of articles on political theory and philosophy and editor of *Politics of the One* (2013). He is the editor of the journal *Stasis*.

China Medel is an assistant professor in the Department of Communication at the University of North Carolina, Chapel Hill. Her work focuses on visual media, performance, and activism on the US-Mexico border and for immigrant justice. Medel is also a member-leader organizer with Southerners on New Ground (SONG), working on immigrant justice issues and anti-deportation projects with LGBTQ communities. She has articles forthcoming in *Camera Obscura* and *Third Text*.

Sandro Mezzadra teaches political theory at the University of Bologna, Italy, and is currently a visiting professor in the Department of Politics at the New School for Social Research, New York. He is author, with Brett Neilson, of *Border as Method, or, the Multiplication of Labor* (2017).

Antonio Negri is coauthor, with Michael Hardt, of the Empire trilogy (*Empire* [2000], *Multitude* [2004], and *Commonwealth* [2011]) as well as *Assembly* (2017). His most recent books in English include *Marx and Foucault: Essays* (2017) and *Factory of Strategy: Thirty-Three Lessons on Lenin* (2016).

Sophie Smith is a writer residing in Arivaca, Arizona. She is a desert aid facilitator and search and rescue coordinator with No More Deaths. She is also a cofounder of the community organization People Helping People in the Border Zone. She received her PhD in literature from Duke University in 2016.

Enzo Traverso is Susan and Barton Winokur Professor in the Humanities at Cornell University. He taught political science for twenty years in France and was a visiting professor in many European and Latin American countries. His most recent books include *Fire and Blood: The European Civil War, 1914–1945* (2016); *The End of Jewish Modernity* (2016); and *Left-Wing Melancholia: Marxism, History, and Memory* (2016).

Wang Hui is a professor of literature and history and director of the Tsinghua Institute for Advanced Studies in Humanities and Social Sciences in Tsinghua University, Beijing, China. His main interests are Chinese intellectual history, literary history, and social and political theory. His publications, including the four-volume book *The Rise of Modern Chinese Thought*, are mainly available in Chinese, though several have been translated into other languages. Five of his titles are available in English: *China's New Order: Society, Politics, and Economy in Transition* (2003); *The End of the Revolution: China and the Limits of Modernity* (2009); *The Politics of Imagining Asia* (2011); *China from Empire to Nation-State* (2014); and *China's Twentieth Century: Revolution, Retreat, and the Road to Equality* (2016).

Scott Warren is a cultural geographer who lives in Ajo, Arizona. He is a lecturer in the School of Geographical Sciences and Urban Planning at Arizona State University, and as an academic he researches and teaches about the intersection of people and place at the US-Mexico border. He is also an activist, volunteering with groups such as No More Deaths, Ajo Samaritans, and others, working to advocate for human rights, demilitarization, and environmental protection in the border zone.

DOI 10.1215/00382876-3961783

Erratum for Juliet Hooker, "Black Protest / White Grievance: On the Problem of White Political Imaginations Not Shaped by Loss." *South Atlantic Quarterly* 116, no. 3 (July 2017): 483–504.

On page 494, the first sentence of the first complete paragraph should read "White grievance in the Obama era was thus not driven primarily by material losses."

This sentence has been corrected in the online version of the article.

DOI 10.1215/00382876-4297121

EXTENT AND NATURE OF CIRCULATION: Average number of copies of each issue published during the preceding twelve months; (A) total number of copies printed, 472; (B.1) paid/requested mail subscriptions, 104; (B.4) Paid distribution by other classes, 0 (C) total paid/requested circulation, 104.; (D.1) samples, complimentary, and other nonrequested copies, 78; (D.4) nonrequested copies distributed through outside the mail, 52; (E) total nonrequested distribution (sum of D.1 & D.4), 130; (F) total distribution (sum of C & E), 234; (G) copies not distributed (office use, leftover, unaccounted, spoiled after printing, returns from news agents), 239; (H) total (sum of F & G), 472.

Actual number of copies of a single issue published nearest to filing date: (A) total number of copies printed, 472; (B.1) paid/requested mail subscriptions, 133; (B.4) Paid distribution by other classes, 0(C) total paid/requested circulation, 133 (D.1) samples, complimentary, and other nonrequested copies, 55; (D.4) nonrequested copies distributed through outside the mail, 52; (E) total nonrequested distribution (sum of D.1 & D.4), 107; (F) total distribution (sum of C & E), 240; (G) copies not distributed (office use, leftover, unaccounted, spoiled after printing, returns from news agents),232 (H) total (sum of F & G), 472.

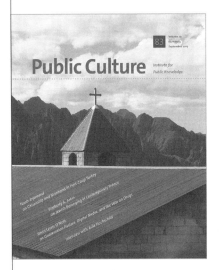